# FAVRE

# BRETT FAVRE

## WITH

# CHRIS HAVEL

# FAVRE

## For the Record

Main Street Books

**DOUBLEDAY**

NEW YORK  LONDON  TORONTO  SYDNEY  AUCKLAND

**MAIN STREET BOOKS**

A Main Street Book
PUBLISHED BY DOUBLEDAY
a division of Bantam Doubleday Dell Publishing Group, Inc.
1540 Broadway, New York, New York 10036

MAIN STREET BOOKS, DOUBLEDAY, and the portrayal of a building with a tree are
trademarks of Doubleday, a division of Bantam Doubleday Dell Publishing Group,
Inc.

*Text design by Stanley S. Drate/Folio Graphics Co. Inc.*

The Library of Congress has cataloged the Doubleday hardcover edition of this book
as follows:

Favre, Brett.
   Favre: for the record / by Brett Favre with Chris Havel.—1st
ed.
     p.  cm.
   1. Favre, Brett.  2. Football players—United States—Biography.
  3. Green Bay Packers (Football Team)  I. Havel, Chris.  II. Title.
  GV939.F29F28  1997
  796.332′092—dc21  97-23234
  [B]
  CIP

# ACKNOWLEDGMENTS

### BRETT FAVRE

To my wonderful wife, Deanna, who has always been there for me, and to Brittany, who will always be her daddy's little girl.

I'd also like to express my gratitude to my parents, Irvin and Bonita, my brothers, Scott and Jeff, and my sister, Brandi—you're the best family a guy could ever have. I'd also like to give special thanks to James "Bus" Cook, Steve Mariucci, Mark McHale, Jeff Bower, Bryant Medders, Chris Ryals, Billy Ray Dedeaux, Ron Wolf, Mike Holmgren, Mark Chmura, Frank Winters, Reggie White, my teammates, and everyone who has stood by me in good times and in bad.

### CHRIS HAVEL

To my parents, John and Carole, my sister, Teresa, and my darling daughter, Josie Rae. Thanks for believing in this project from the start.

The authors gratefully acknowledge the following for their contributions to the production of this book: Judy Johnson, Paula Martin, Deanna Favre, Irvin Favre, Bonita Favre, Scott Favre, Ron Wolf, Virgil McRyhew, Pete Dougherty, Olga Halaburda, Bill Nusbaum, Eric Goska, Patrick Ferron, James Biever, the Green Bay Packers, the *Green Bay Press-Gazette,* and the University of Southern Mississippi.

We wish to give special thanks to Paul Kennedy, a fine writer and friend, whose suggestions and written contribution proved invaluable to the project; Don Langenkamp for his time, talent, and perspective; Shawn Coyne for his patience, brilliant editing, and helpful advice throughout; and the Basil Kane Literary Agency.

# FOREWORD

I first approached Brett Favre with the idea of collaborating on a book in the summer of 1993. Three days into his second training camp with the Packers, I walked up to him and said, "Brett, I think you might have a book in you someday. How do you feel about getting together to write one when the time comes?" He had a mere fourteen National Football League starts under his belt, but in typical Favre fashion, he was game. He had one question, though: "Who are we going to write about?"

I laughed. Favre smiled. Then we shook hands and seldom spoke of it again.

Favre had games to win for the Green Bay Packers; I had columns to write for the *Green Bay Press-Gazette*. Our roles were clearly defined. When he played great, I praised him. When he screwed up, I was critical. Favre respects candor and hates kiss-ups. The entire conversation regarding this book couldn't have lasted more than two minutes.

In that short span, a deal was struck, one Favre didn't forget even when big-time authors came knocking at his door.

Loyalty is one of Favre's most endearing traits.

When famous player agents wined and dined him after his senior season at Southern Mississippi, he stayed true to a personal injury attorney from Hattiesburg named James "Bus" Cook. It wasn't because he had to; it was because he wanted to.

Favre explains, "So what if Bus never represented a player before? I'd never had an agent before, so I figured we were a pretty good match. I trusted him, I liked him, and I gave him my word. What else is there? It turned out to be a great decision on my part."

That is how Favre operates. He is instinctive, impulsive, and impetuous. If he likes something, he goes for it. If he doesn't, he moves on. Either way, spare him the details. He hates to waste time deliberating when he could be doing. In this book, you will discover that Favre's capricious nature routinely gets him into—and out of—trouble.

And you will discover that Favre is likable.

The strongest evidence of that is provided by his teammates and his friends, many of whom are both. Simply put, they would take a bullet for him, probably because they trust he would do the same for them.

Brutal honesty is another of Favre's characteristics.

In this book, Favre admits to a great many human frailties, chief among them an addiction to painkillers. He relates how he came to depend on dangerously high dosages of Vicodin to achieve a relaxed state of mind. He tells of his nightly pill-popping and the insomnia, dehydration, week-long constipation, and violent vomiting that transpired.

He tells of that fateful decision when he flushed the pills down the toilet and waved good-bye to a lifestyle of addiction and embraced the realization that he could lose everything he'd worked so hard for if he failed to face his sickness.

Quite simply, Favre found a reservoir of inner strength that goes far beyond engineering a scoring drive in the last two minutes of a game. Counseling sessions began to reveal to Favre the amount of pain he had caused others during the downward spiral of his drug addiction. By recognizing his sickness and declaring it to the world, Favre escaped a fate of certain human wreckage and emerged with a newfound maturity. His is a story of tragedy, perseverance, and triumph.

He entered the 1996 season newly married and drug-free. He was on a mission to prove his supporters right and his detractors wrong, then he delivered in grand fashion by leading the Packers to victory in Super Bowl XXXI. The indomitable quarterback with the youthful exuberance and cannon right arm was back, and so was the Pack.

That Favre ever arrived in Green Bay at all is a credit to Packers General Manager Ron Wolf, who in 1992 made the bold move to send a first-round pick to the Atlanta Falcons for their third-string quarterback. Wolf received hate mail for his trouble, but he stood by his man. He felt strongly that the key to an NFL team's success ultimately rests with its quarterback. He developed that philosophy during his years with the Raiders, even though owner Al Davis didn't subscribe to the theory.

"We got Daryle Lamonica and we were able to draft Ken Stabler and those were the things that kept it going with the Raiders," Wolf said. "Al Davis, to this day, doesn't believe it's the quarterback, but I certainly believe that."

Wolf has believed in Favre since day one. The reason, he said, is simple.

"When he runs onto the field, the field automatically tilts in your favor. He's highly competitive. There's still a fire burning in his belly. He wants to achieve. He wants to win. More importantly, he likes to play the game. That is such an important trait today. He likes to play the game."

Favre first caught Wolf's eye at a private workout in Hattiesburg and then again during a Falcons-Seahawks scrimmage in Portland, Oregon, in the summer of 1991. The general manager saw a certain something in the southern gunslinger that he liked.

Said Wolf, "It's exceptional when you see a rare player. It's exceptional when you have an opportunity to be around true greatness. Brett's on his way to that. He's as rare a player as there is in this league."

Favre is the third-rated passer in NFL history. He has thrown 147 touchdown passes in six seasons. By comparison, San Francisco's Steve Young has thrown for only 174 in twice that many seasons. At age twenty-seven, Favre is one of five players to win two MVP awards. The others: Jim Brown, Johnny Unitas, Joe Montana, and Young. Favre and Montana are the league's only back-to-back MVP award winners.

Wolf thinks Favre is just getting started.

"I don't think he's scratched the surface of his ability. I think he can take it further and achieve even more than he already has. I think he can become the consummate quarterback. Now, some things have to happen. He's got to go another seven years before he gets up there with the big shots. To do that, he has to take advantage of what the good Lord has given him and he's got to stay healthy. Those are two big ifs now, but if that happens, he'll achieve things that people never thought could be done in this game."

Miami's Dan Marino threw an NFL-record forty-eight touchdown passes in 1984. Asked if Favre could surpass that, Wolf said, "I don't think there's a record that's safe with him, but I don't know if it's about records. I think it's about accomplishments. I think he can accomplish whatever there is that needs to be accomplished. If his goal is to be in the Pro Football Hall of Fame—and that's his main focus—he's well on his way."

Wolf is keenly aware of Favre's wild side.

"I've been around some guys who are wild and they've been very, very, successful at that same position," he said. "Maybe that's part of playing quarterback."

Clearly, Favre likes to have fun.

Fans have wondered for years if all the stories about his late-night barhopping and brawls are true. In this book, he sets the record straight: Damn right they're true. He isn't the kind of guy to run from his past.

However, he is determined that those days are over.

Well, mostly, anyway.

He no longer tends bar after home games and he is light-years past the day he shook off a wicked hangover to come off the bench and win a game at Southern Mississippi. But in the tradition of an earlier hell-raiser of a quarterback, Bobby Layne, he will never shy away from the reputation he earned in the past. Instead, he wants to meet new challenges head-on while he takes a long, hard look at his life—in print.

That doesn't make him serious or boring. Far from it.

Next to country, Favre's favorite music is laughter, and the punch lines of his best jokes often sound like country lyrics. He gets a kick out of dirty, down-home humor and if it offends someone's highly sophisticated sensibilities, he's apt to break into a little David Allan Coe for their benefit, "If that ain't country, you can kiss my ass."

Favre's sense of humor leans toward the sophomoric, but like the man, it is very real and very genuine. One night while visiting his good friend and quarterbacks coach Steve Mariucci a few years back, he offered to put Mariucci's sons to bed. Steve accepted but soon questioned the wisdom of that decision. The boys' laughter—and that includes Favre's—grew so loud Steve couldn't resist poking his head into the bedroom to see what was up. Much to his chagrin, the Packers' starting quarterback was breaking wind and pulling the sheets over the heads of a giggling Tyler, Adam, and Stephen.

Clearly, Favre isn't one to put on airs, so to speak. Pretentious, he ain't.

He is proud of his little one-horse town called the Kiln and the childhood he spent there. He goes back to visit because it's where he belongs. The folks there love him and he loves them. He splits residences in Hattiesburg and Green Bay, but the Kiln is home.

However, Favre is something of an enigma.

He is easily amused and easily bored. It's what makes him both charming *and* confounding. His high energy suggests he is a doer, not a thinker, but that would be too narrow an assumption. His experience during the past five years has encompassed a sufficient range of highs and lows to balance the scale.

Favre was smart enough to master one of the NFL's most complicated offenses and wise enough to stop his drug-induced free fall before he crashed. The wild-eyed southern boy is slowly and steadily learning to coexist with the NFL's two-time MVP.

The possibilities are endless.

CHRIS HAVEL,
May 1997

# FAVRE

# 1

# THE ADDICTION

I know just about everything there is to know about painkillers. It's knowledge gained by trial and error. Percodan. Lortab. Vicodin. You name it, I've swallowed it.

I can tell you about recommended dosages, side effects, all that stuff. When it comes to getting Vikes, which is what my teammates and I call Vicodin, I can tell you who, what, where, when, and how. And I'm not talking Walgreen's, either.

You could say I'm a painkiller connoisseur, except there's nothing glamorous or sophisticated about my experience with it.

I was a drug addict.

I can say that now and it doesn't bother me. In a way, it's therapeutic to talk about it and for good reason. I don't ever want to forget what Vicodin did to me because I don't ever want it to sneak up on me again. I've learned that just when you think you're over an addiction, it can come back and bite you in the ass.

I'm not stupid enough to think it couldn't happen to me.

Sure, I'm the National Football League's two-time Most Valuable Player and starting quarterback for the defending Super Bowl champion Green Bay Packers. That's pretty good, but it doesn't make me invincible. I used to think I was bulletproof. Who doesn't when they're twenty-five and they think they've got the world by the ass? I don't think like that anymore. Not after the way Vicodin dominated my life for two years.

Hell, the Vicodin *was* my life.

At the height of my addiction in 1995, I'd do anything to get it. Lie. Beg. Borrow. You name it. In the back of my mind I knew it was a pretty screwed-up way to live but I didn't care because when I got my hands on those pills, it was awesome. They were my diamonds, my security, my escape, and my obsession. Whatever I was doing, the Vikes helped me enjoy doing it even more. I planned every weeknight around those damn pills.

They were the most important things in my life.

When I close my eyes, I can still see those big old horse pills. I can still taste them, too. They're bitter, grimy, and sandy, like dirt. I can't imagine taking Vicodin now, not that I'd want to. If I tried to swallow one, I guarantee I'd throw it right back up.

Then again, that's nothing new.

Throwing up was a regular part of my 9:00 P.M. pill-popping ritual in 1995. During that season I was taking as many as fifteen pills a night and it really tore up my stomach. It was like being on a nonstop roller-coaster ride. One minute I'd be watching late-night TV and the next minute I'd be sticking my head out the back door vomiting all over the sidewalk. Like I said, I know all about the side effects.

Sometimes my longtime girlfriend, Deanna Tynes, who

was living with me at the time, would wake up and hear me puking. She would come downstairs, step outside, and say, "What's wrong?" And I'd say, "I don't know. I just feel like shit tonight."

Other nights she wouldn't hear me.

The vomiting went on a pretty good bit because my stomach was a mess. I'd throw up everything. Blood. Acid. What little food was in me. I wasn't eating very much.

I wasn't sleeping much, either. Maybe two or three hours a night because the more pills I took, the less I felt like sleeping.

I was dehydrated like you wouldn't believe. I was so dry my lips and my face and my arms and my hands were chapped. I'd drink bottled water by the gallon, but I could hardly piss a drop. I'd go into the bathroom, stand there, and nothing would happen.

I couldn't do the other, either.

Sometimes I'd go ten days without taking a crap. I could've been the national poster boy for prunes, the way I was going.

Still, it was hard to say no to Vicodin because it made me feel good. It's a powerful, highly addictive narcotic analgesic that gives a sense of euphoria. It can last for several hours depending on how many you take. There's no hangover, no calories, and no sluggishness the next day. I thought, "This is better than beer."

It seemed pretty harmless.

At first I took them because they helped me get through the week after an especially brutal Sunday. Then I started taking them because I liked the buzz.

There is this myth that I took Vicodin so I could play with pain. That is so far from the truth it's unbelievable. If I swallowed three or four Vicodins and I tried to catch or throw a football, I couldn't do it. If I took that many pills before a game, I'd probably get killed out there. There is no way I could take Vicodin and play. I have to think clearly and be on my toes. I couldn't imagine trying to run our offense with a buzz.

Hell, it's difficult enough the way it is.

The fact is I've never taken Vicodin, or any narcotic, before or during a game. I've never taken it the day before a game, or even two days before a game. I guess I could let people think I needed to take the pills to play with pain. It makes it sound more acceptable, I suppose, except for one problem: It isn't true. I'm not going to try to blame my addiction on pro football. As an NFL quarterback I deal with pain constantly, but so does every other quarterback, and not all of them get hooked on painkillers. Who knows, though? Maybe if I was a high school teacher or a mechanic or a carpenter, I would've never been exposed to Vicodin.

Then again, a lot of people in all kinds of jobs get hooked on pain pills every day.

I happened to be one of those people.

My pill-popping was pretty much off and on until the 1995 season. That's when it really started to escalate. The way the Vicodin was consuming me, it's a wonder I ever won the MVP award that season because I was in pretty sad shape.

It got so bad I'd do things I can't imagine doing now. Ever try choking down fifteen pills in one sitting? Especially horse pills like Vikes? Take it from me, it ain't easy.

The problem isn't getting the pills down; it's keeping them down. I'd go into the upstairs bathroom at home, take a big slug of water, and try swallowing a handful of pills. Most of the time I'd just throw them right back up and they'd land on the floor. No big deal. I'd just pick the pills out of the vomit, rinse them off, and try again. It was just awful and it went on every night.

I'd take seven or eight pills and sit back and wait for the buzz to hit. When it kicked in, I'd feel relaxed and I was right with the world. Best of all, after I got those first few pills down, it made the rest easier to swallow.

It wasn't always this crazy.

My first contact with painkillers occurred during my sophomore year at Southern Mississippi. It was no big deal. I got a prescription for Vicodin or Percodan or Lortab, one of those three, after I had elbow surgery in the spring.

Jim Andrews, a doctor from Birmingham, Alabama—the same doctor who did Bo Jackson's hip surgery—removed some bone spurs from my right elbow. I remember taking a few pills for the pain, but I never thought twice about it. I just took them when it hurt, which is what I was supposed to do, and that was it. It was the same after my car accident the summer of my senior year. I lost thirty inches of intestine and I was really hurting, but I only popped a pain pill when I needed it.

In fact, I never saw anyone taking painkillers the whole time I was playing at USM. A few Schaefer Lights and a shot or two of tequila was about as crazy as it got.

It was the same when I was a rookie with Atlanta in 1991. I didn't know if anybody on the team was taking them, probably because it never occurred to me that they might be. Now it wouldn't surprise me, but back then I didn't know and I didn't care.

I was a beer drinker.

I'd hang out with Bill Fralic whenever he asked and he asked a lot. Fralic was this huge veteran offensive lineman, a real joker, just my kind of guy. I was always up for anything and I loved hearing his war stories. Some nights

I'd drink two beers and other nights I'd drink ten. It really didn't matter because I wasn't going to play.

I was the third-string quarterback behind Chris Miller and Billy Joe Tolliver. There was no way I was getting off the bench because Jerry Glanville, the Falcons' head coach at the time, didn't have much use for me unless you count holding a clipboard. I tried to be patient and make the best of a tough situation, but that didn't stop me from going out on the town whenever I felt like it. Painkillers weren't part of the deal, though. Hell, it never even occurred to me to take them. I was a rookie. What did I know?

That changed when I was traded to Green Bay in 1992.

Up until then I'd only thrown a total of five passes in the NFL, two of which were intercepted. The only beatings I took at quarterback were when I tried to tackle the defensive back or whoever it was that picked me off.

In Green Bay it was different. I burst onto the scene almost overnight.

My first year there Don Majkowski, the starting quarterback, tore some ligaments in his left ankle the third game of the season. I really didn't know what I was doing because I was so young in the offense, but I managed to lead us to a last-second victory over Cincinnati anyway. I'll never forget that game.

I hit Kitrick Taylor on a 35-yard touchdown with thirteen seconds to play. We won 24–23 and the fans in Lambeau Field went crazy. As I was walking off the field, I knew I'd have to be dead before I'd ever come out of the lineup again. I was feeling such a rush; I didn't even notice the pounding I'd taken from being sacked five times.

The soreness didn't set in until the next morning. Then it was way real.

Such is life for a NFL quarterback. Hero today, sore tomorrow.

The worst Monday morning of my career came after a November 15 game against Philadelphia at Milwaukee's County Stadium. We fought to a 27–24 victory but my good friend the Reverend Reggie White, who was playing with the Eagles then, beat the living hell out of me. I got hit on every play and was sacked three times. Reggie led the assault with Clyde Simmons hot on his heels. Reggie got me really good in the first quarter just as I released a swing pass to Harry Sydney. The Eagles' Andy Harmon wrapped up my legs and Reggie nailed me in the chest. He drove his 300-pound frame—and my left shoulder—straight into the turf.

God, that hurt somethin' awful.

My left shoulder was separated but I didn't want to come out of the game. When Coach Mike Holmgren asked if I was okay, I tried to be tough and said I'd be all right. I got an injection of Novocain at halftime and stayed in. The Novocain numbed my shoulder so I could get by, but it still hurt every time I threw a pass or handed off with my left hand.

Sore as I was, I managed to have a pretty damn good first half, which was followed by a really lousy second half, although I came through in the clutch.

My best throw was a 34-yard lob over Eagles cornerback James Booty in the fourth quarter to set up the tying field goal. After the game Ron Wolf, our general manager, told reporters, "Your quarterback has to be your leader. In time, this locker room will be Favre's locker room, and in time, this team will be his team."

Ron was right.

That game set the stage for my future and Green Bay's. It sold Reggie White on the belief that the Packers, with me at quarterback, could win a Super Bowl someday. When Reggie signed his free-agent contract with the Packers the next spring, he said my toughness that day was a big factor in his decision to come to Green Bay.

That game also showed my teammates I was willing to win at any cost. I had played with pain—which is a badge of courage in the NFL—and I had prevailed over a really talented Eagles team. It was a really important game, but there was a downside.

I took Vicodin after that game.

Thanks to Reggie and his pals, my shoulder was hurting something fierce, so I went to the training room and asked our team doctor for some painkillers. He knew I had a separated shoulder, so he didn't even question it. He prescribed Vicodin and it eased the pain, which is the whole point of painkillers. It made me feel 100 percent better.

I took Vicodin a couple more times after games that year but I wasn't hooked.

The best buzz I got during my first season came after a Sunday night game in Houston and it had nothing to do with Vicodin. It was December and we were on a four-game winning streak, but we needed to beat the Oilers to keep our play-off hopes alive.

Early in the game I hurt my left ankle and it swelled up right away. I had it retaped and I kept on playing. We won 16–14 when I hit Sterling Sharpe for a 6-yard touchdown late in the game, but I paid the price. My ankle was swollen so bad I asked Clarence Novotny, our team physician then, if I could get something for the pain.

He took one look at my ankle, which was purple and swollen, and he said sure. Then he pulled out a really long needle and gave me a shot of Demerol right in my butt. Man, I was out of it. I was in hog heaven on the plane ride back to Green Bay. It's a good thing I'm scared to death of needles because that Demerol was unbelievable. The flight home went by like a snap. I've never taken it since then, but the effect was great.

I still wasn't using Vicodin with any regularity in '93, but I had my moments.

We crushed the Rams in the opener at County Stadium and a few of us stayed in Milwaukee to celebrate. The next day we were hung over, so somebody pulled out a few Vikes during the two-hour drive to Green Bay. There we were, cruising north on Highway 43, popping pills along the way. I took a few and my headache was gone.

I felt like a new man.

Vicodin affects different people in different ways.

Some players take it and get sick to their stomach, so they don't do it again. Other players think it feels pretty good, but they'd never take it enough to get addicted. Then there are players like me, who take it and get hooked.

It's like I was on a fence and I fell over on the wrong side.

The pill-popping evolved slowly.

My first three seasons, I'd get hit and banged around during a game and afterward I'd ask one of the doctors for a couple of pain pills. They'd ask me where it hurt and I'd tell them and they'd write it down and give me two or three pills.

If I saw a teammate who was injured getting six pills, I'd stop him in the locker room and tell him I was really hurting and I wondered if I could borrow a couple.

He'd say, "No problem, man. Sorry you're hurting."

On the plane ride home after road games I'd have a beer and pop a pill and feel great. Then on Wednesday or Thursday night I might take a couple more just to pass the time. I wasn't taking very many and it wasn't every night,

especially in '92 and '93, so it was easy to build up a supply. I wasn't scrounging for them back then.

My first two years in Green Bay I would stop taking
Vicodin in the off-season. I would pack up for my home
in Diamondhead, a resort area near the Mississippi Gulf
Coast where I rented a house, and I wouldn't give painkillers a second thought. I was too busy working out and playing golf with my brothers and my buddies to worry about
it.

That started changing late in the 1994 season.

By then I was into the painkillers pretty deep. It was
no longer a matter of me wanting them. I had to have them
and it didn't matter to me one bit that the sleeplessness,
the vomiting, and the dehydration were taking a serious
toll.

The dehydration was particularly bad because it led to
acute constipation. It got to the point where sometimes I
couldn't take a shit for a week. It just kept building up and
building up inside me until it was as hard as a rock and
the size of a softball. I'd eat a little chicken or something—I didn't have much of an appetite—and I'd try to
go to the bathroom but I couldn't. Finally I'd be able to go
and it was like an explosion.

That went on for weeks and it led to an ugly episode
two days before our New Year's Eve home play-off game
against Detroit. I went to bed on that Friday night feeling
fine, but I woke up about three in the morning with severe
cramps. I thought it might be related to the stomach surgery following my car wreck in college.

Finally I couldn't take the pain anymore, so I called
John Gray, one of our team physicians, and told him about
being plugged up. My dad was in town for the game and
drove me to the hospital. The doctors ran some tests and

said, "My God, you've got this big ball of stool built up in your intestine."

Dr. Gray said, "Why is that?"

I said hell if I know.

They gave me an enema and it cleaned me out but I didn't get to sleep until nine in the morning. I missed practice and I didn't have a very good game Sunday. We beat the Lions 16–12 but it was the first time in nine games I didn't throw for a touchdown.

I shrugged it off. We won, so I figured it didn't matter. And sure as shit, I was back to taking the Vicodin after the game. I didn't want to have another enema, though, so I started drinking magnesium citrate every three or four days. Magnesium citrate tastes awful, just like gasoline, but it makes you go to the bathroom. I'd drink it and it would blow everything out. Talk about sick. But that wasn't enough to make me stop. In fact, my addiction only grew worse.

The next week we got hammered at Dallas 35–9 in the divisional play-offs and the season was over. I packed up my stuff in Green Bay and headed home to Mississippi. For the first time the Vicodin migrated south along with me. I brought a bottle of thirty pills from Green Bay and they didn't last very long. When you're taking six a night, they go quick. The only reason I had that many pills in the first place was that I'd stop taking them for three or four days to build up my supply. I hated doing it because I was miserable when I didn't have them. Then I'd hit 'em good for three or four days.

My supply would've dried up quick in Mississippi except I needed hernia surgery that off-season. The doctor put some plastic mesh in my side so the torn muscle would mend. It was pretty painful. It was so bad I couldn't play golf for three months.

The only good thing about the surgery, to my way of thinking then, was that it gave me a direct pipeline to Vicodin. This time I had a big supply and it was legitimate.

There was a point, maybe a month after surgery, where I didn't really need the pain pills anymore but I kept taking them anyway. I was still asking for them. I still had the prescription going. I would tell the doctor, "I tried to play golf a little quicker than I should've" or "God, it's painful when I work out," and he would write me a refill. It was like, "Okay. Here's your prescription." That spring is when I started hitting the Vicodin harder than ever. I went from six to eight to ten pills a night just like that.

By the time I returned to Green Bay for the start of the '95 season, I was in deep.

During the off-season, Deanna and I decided she and Brittany, our eight-year-old daughter, would come to live with me in Green Bay. We weren't married, but we'd been dating on and off for twelve years. We decided it was time to see if it was ever going to work out between us. I bought a four-bedroom home on the west side about five minutes from Lambeau Field and everything was great at first except for one thing.

Deanna had no idea I was addicted to Vicodin.

When I started messing with it in '92, I'd ask her if she wanted to take some pain pills with me. I told her we could enjoy the buzz together. It was the same with my brother Scott or whoever happened to be out with me.

I'd ask if they wanted a Vike and they'd say, "Hell no."

At first I'd be like, "Too bad."

But the next day I'd be really glad they didn't do it because I had two extra pills. Now I'm relieved I never dragged anyone else down with me. By the time Deanna moved to Green Bay, there was no chance of that happening because I was selfish. I didn't want anybody else to do pills with me because I didn't want to share.

I also knew that if I didn't ask anyone to do it, they'd be less likely to discover what I was up to, so it made my addiction easier to hide. Besides, I was very disciplined within my drug abuse. I never took Vicodin two days before a game. I'd only take it after a game and on Monday through Thursday, but never Friday or Saturday.

And I always took it at exactly nine o'clock at night. I'd take it then so I could be certain the buzz would last until I fell asleep, which was usually two or three in the morning.

On weekdays I would come home from practice, take a nap, get up, and start getting anxious for nine o'clock to come. I would sit around staring at the clock, saying to myself, "Shit, it's 8:55. It's getting close."

People wonder who gave me the Vicodin.

Hell, it was no particular person. It was whoever I could get them from. It would be hard to name names. I could give you a list of fifty names and none of the people on it would have a clue they were contributing to my problem. If you asked them now, they probably wouldn't even remember it.

I didn't rely on any one person. A drug abuser never does that. It's too risky. When it comes to keeping a steady supply, you always hedge your bet.

I'd go to some pretty great lengths to get Vicodin. If I had something to do that was pretty important, I would put it on hold because I had something else that was more important. I had to get more pills. If driving to see a doctor forty-five minutes away was what it took, I would do it and not think twice.

I told some serious lies to get more pills and anyone who knows me knows that's not me. I'm not a liar and I hate it when people lie to me. But that was another ugly side effect of Vicodin.

I'd do things like ask Deanna to call her dentist and tell him her tooth was sore. She'd say, "Why are you asking me to do this?"

I'd tell her my side was killing me and there was no other way to get pain pills. I'd ask Scott to do the same thing. I lied to my team doctors, my trainers, and my teammates. I would call players at night and tell them I was really hurting. I'd ask them if they had any Vikes and they'd say yeah, sure, if you're hurting that badly. I didn't care what time of night it was. If I needed them, I'd drive over to their place or they'd stop by mine. It could be anyone on the team, even guys I hardly knew. It didn't matter.

What mattered was getting more Vicodin.

I knew it was wrong to lie but at the time I didn't care. The next day I would tell myself how stupid it was to act like that, but a couple of hours later I'd start wanting the pills again and I'd say, "Well, here I go again."

I did whatever I needed to do to deceive people. I've heard of people injuring themselves or burning themselves to go to the emergency room so they could get more pills. It never got to that point with me because it was pretty easy to get them on my own. Almost too easy.

I work in a profession where guys get hurt all the time.

If a player had surgery, I would go to him a couple of days later and ask if he was hurting. Then I'd ask if he had any extra pills because I was hurting. I'd tell guys my shoulder hurt, my ankle hurt, my side hurt. I'd say anything to get pills.

Now when people ask who got me the pills, I tell them the truth.

I tell them it was me.

The whole deal was pretty tough on Deanna. God, she's

a saint for putting up with it. My personality, my behavior, my attitude, it all started to change as my addiction grew worse. Sometimes when I couldn't get pills, I'd be pretty pissed, but I tried not to take it out on anyone else, mostly because I didn't want anyone to know.

It would be four in the morning and Deanna would say, "Honey, come to bed."

I'd say, "Hell no."

We used to spend evenings talking about our day or our family or our goals. I stopped doing that when I was taking the pills. I'd have these horrible mood swings but I didn't want Deanna to know what was going on so I'd try to be nice, but sometimes I'd end up being bitchy or rude anyway. I never got physically abusive, but I was pretty ornery.

It was either that or I'd neglect her. She spent a lot of evenings reading in bed while I was downstairs playing Sega golf or messing around on the Internet or watching TV or whatever. It must've been a nightmare for her.

Deanna knew something was wrong. She just didn't know what.

I'm not much of a hider, which is probably a good thing. I'd move my pill supply to different spots around the house, but I never went to any great lengths to keep them out of sight. Sometimes I would keep a few bottles behind my T-shirts in the closet or I would hide them in the guest bedroom upstairs, which was hardly ever used.

After a couple months Deanna started finding pill bottles around the house. At first she didn't know what they were. Most of them weren't labeled, but eventually she found one that read "Vicodin" on it. Now she knew how I could stay up all night and why I was throwing up out in the backyard late at night.

Deanna tried to keep track of the bottles. When she'd

go back the next day, one of two things would happen. Either a lot of pills would be missing or the bottle would be gone. That's when she knew I was in serious trouble, so she started keeping a closer eye on me. All the while she felt helpless. She was fed up with the way I was acting and she had a right to be, but she also thought if she and Brittany left, I'd only get worse.

Besides, she still loved me.

Finally in November she came right out and asked if I was abusing painkillers. I told her no and said she was overreacting and I got really defensive. That's when I started to distance myself from her. I didn't want to admit I had a problem even though it was becoming more evident to me each day. By the end of the '95 season I was sleeping about an hour a night. I'd have this weird sleep where I'd drift in and out but I always woke up feeling really refreshed.

Deanna knew better. The problem for her was nobody else suspected.

Not my teammates, my friends, my coaches.

My parents didn't even know and we're about as close as it gets.

Mike Holmgren doesn't miss a trick and he never suspected what was going on. He was totally shocked when he found out in the spring of '96. He had no reason to suspect anything was wrong. The team was winning and I was playing pretty damn good.

My work ethic was amazing even though I wasn't sleeping, eating, or shitting. I showed up early in the morning and stayed until late at night. The only time I ever took a day off because I wasn't feeling good was after the enema episode in '94.

I'd go to bed at four in the morning, wake up a few hours later, and feel fine. I'd get up and drive Brittany to school and then I'd go to the stadium and work out hard. I'd be there at nine o'clock for the team meeting and everything seemed fine.

When lunchtime came, I'd try to eat a little bit. Then I'd go to practice, work hard, move around, and feel good. I'd do everything. After practice I'd go back up to the stadium, take a shower, and go to our afternoon meetings. That was the only time the lack of sleep caught up with me. I began dozing off during our quarterbacks meeting.

Steve Mariucci, my good friend and position coach at the time, figured I was just tired like a lot of other guys on the team. He would hit me and say, "Wake up." I would be out cold. That went on just about every day in 1995, but it didn't hurt my preparation, as crazy as that sounds, because I'd make up for it at night.

I'd go home and study after I took the pills. Hell, I'd study even harder, so I was preparing as much as usual, if not more. And then Sunday I would go out and play and play well. It was normal enough on the surface. When people saw me, I was either working out, practicing, or studying. I was doing what I was supposed to be doing.

We won six of our last seven games going into the playoffs. We throttled Atlanta 37–20 in the wild-card game at Green Bay. The next week we upset the 49ers 27–17 in San Francisco. That victory in the NFC divisional playoffs got everyone's attention.

People started talking Super Bowl, but first we had to knock off our old nemesis, the Dallas Cowboys. I played well enough to put us in position to win the game by throwing for 307 yards and three touchdowns.

But I also threw a costly fourth-quarter interception that killed us. We ended up losing 38–27. The Cowboys were the better team. I think everyone will agree on that. Besides, back then we were just glad to be there.

Even though we didn't go all the way to the Super Bowl, nobody had a whole lot to complain about. I led the NFL with 4,413 yards and thirty-eight touchdowns. I was on my way to a third Pro Bowl and the Packers had won their first NFC Central Division championship in twenty-three years. I had everyone fooled.

Everyone except Deanna.

Before the regular-season finale against Pittsburgh, she picked up my parents at Green Bay's Austin Straubel Airport. On the drive home, she told them she thought I had a problem with pain pills. My parents think the world of Deanna. They've known her since she was a kid, but they didn't want to believe I'd be involved in something like that. They said she might be overreacting—which she'd heard before—and they let it go.

In the back of their minds, though, they started to wonder if maybe Deanna was onto something. Dad remembered thinking it was strange that players who I wasn't close with were stopping over at the house at all hours of the night. Mom started to keep a closer eye on how I was acting and what I was doing. The trouble was they were only in Green Bay on weekends when we had a home game, and most of the time Mom stayed home to watch the game with Grandma Mee-Maw and Aunt Kay-Kay.

Eventually Steve started wondering if something was wrong because I kept falling asleep all the time. He went to Pepper Burruss, our head trainer, to see what kind of medication I was taking. Pepper didn't have a record of anything out of the ordinary because I wasn't getting pills from the training room. I was getting them from players.

I'd covered my tracks well.

Two weeks after the season was over, Deanna and I flew to Hawaii for the Pro Bowl. We had a lot of fun that week and it was just like old times. We talked a lot and we spent a lot of time together. Bus Cook, my agent and best friend, was there with his wife, Jeanine. Scott and his girlfriend, Morgan, were also there. Everyone had a blast.

The flight home was another story.

I didn't play much in the game, but I was really tired and worn-out afterward. I don't think I've ever been that tired after a game. I don't know why. Maybe it was a combination of the heat and a pretty hectic week. Maybe it was the Vicodin.

We had about four hours to kill before our flight home, so we sat around the pool and began partying. I had two beers and felt like I was ready to pass out, I was so exhausted. That's when I thought, "I know what I'll do." So I went up to the room and checked my pill supply. I had about fifteen pills left. There were some Lortabs. Vicodins. Percodans. Tylenol 3. A pretty good selection. I didn't like to mix them, but you take whatever you can get. So I took all those pills and went back down to the pool. It didn't take long before I was feeling good again.

When it was time to leave, I packed up and went to the airport.

By the time the plane took off, I was already flying.

It was a late-night flight and everyone was trying to sleep. Everyone except me. I pestered the heck out of this older woman next to me, the poor lady. She was trying to sleep and I'm grilling her for her life story. Where are you from? How many children do you have? Did you have fun in Hawaii?

She was from Kansas City. I'll never forget it. I went on and on like John Candy in the movie *Planes, Trains & Automobiles*. She'd get groggy so I would poke her in the side and say, "Hey, wake up." She must've thought I was crazy. Later, Bus told me he looked over at me and for the first time he thought to himself, "Wow. Brett must be on something."

After a while I gave up on the lady from Kansas City.

I got up and walked to the back of the plane to talk to the flight attendants. They said, "Oh, you're so nice. No one else ever does this." This went on for hours.

Eventually my stomach started hurting, so I went to the bathroom and threw up. I cleaned up, sat back down next to the woman from Kansas City, and started talking to her all over again.

It was daylight when we landed in Los Angeles. I'd been wired the whole trip. From there we got on a plane to Dallas. That's when I hit a wall. The next thing I knew it was eight o'clock on Monday night. I didn't even remember getting home.

A week later, Deanna and I flew out to New York to attend the ESPYs. ESPN had selected me pro football's Performer of the Year. If only they knew.

Deanna and I got all dressed up to attend the ceremony and I'm thinking, "This is going to be pretty fun." I was the first one to receive an award that night. Dennis Hopper presented me and everything went pretty smooth.

The whole time I'm up there giving my acceptance speech, I've got a bottle of Vicodin tucked in my pants pocket. It was like my own little secret. After I got the award, I went back to the table and watched the rest of the ceremony.

It started dragging and around ten o'clock—which would be nine o'clock back in Wisconsin—I started getting agitated. I told myself, "I've got to take these pills."

I told Deanna I had to go to the bathroom. I was gone for over an hour. It took me about twenty minutes to get the pills down. I had to be careful that no one saw me, but it's awfully hard to be discreet when you're throwing up.

So I'd peek over the stall to see if anyone was in the bathroom. When the coast was clear, I'd try to choke them down. I took about fifteen. When I left the bathroom, I went to pose for pictures with Hopper. All of a sudden the buzz hit in. I was back. I was walking around, talking everyone's ears off.

I was pretty smooth at this shit anyway, but now I felt like I was really good. Finally I went back to the table.

Deanna was pissed.

She said, "What took so long?"

I told her I had to have all these pictures taken, but she knew I was acting different. She said, "Did you take something?" I lied and said no. That night we went out to a party until four in the morning. I drank Coke the whole time.

Deanna figured I'd popped some pain pills. By now she was pretty fed up with me. She'd had enough. The next day I flew back to Diamondhead and she went to Green Bay. She was so upset and frustrated she was ready to pack up and leave. She had wanted to go to graduate school for so long, but she held off because of me. Now she was thinking, "Why am I in Green Bay? Brett doesn't care about me. He doesn't pay any attention to me. We've got totally separate lives." So she applied to the dietetics program at Southern Mississippi and was accepted.

That's when she told me she wasn't going to deal with my crap anymore. She said that if things didn't change, she was going to move to Hattiesburg and get on with her life.

I thought, "Yeah, right." I didn't believe she'd actually leave me. I just kept on taking the pills. I still had five prescriptions, which is 150 pills, when I got back to Mississippi after the ESPYs. That sounds like a lot of pills, but when you're taking fifteen a night, it goes by pretty quick.

Clark Henegan, a friend of mine since college, lived with Scott and me at the house in Diamondhead. He knew I was taking pain pills and he told me to stop. I suppose Scott knew about it, too, but we never talked about it. Every night I'd take the pills at nine o'clock and start buzzing. Clark and Scott would be falling asleep and I'd smack them and say, "Get up. Let's watch TV. Let's get a movie. Let's play Sega."

Clark said, "Man, you've got to stop with the pills. It's gone too far."

Slowly I was beginning to realize I had to quit.

Bus figured something was up because of the way I acted on the plane ride from Hawaii and he started asking questions. Then I heard from someone in the family that Dad called the Packers' doctors because he thought I might have a problem with pain pills. Everything was starting to close in on me. It was time to stop. It was a couple of days before Valentine's Day and I thought, "The best present I could give Deanna is to stop taking this stuff."

I had about fifteen pills left, so that night I decided to take them and quit the next day. When nine o'clock rolled around, I took them and enjoyed the buzz. The next day I got up, grabbed the bottle, and flushed it down the toilet. It was kind of sad to see them go. I just watched them and said, "See ya later."

I haven't taken a pain pill since.

When I tell people I quit cold turkey, they have a hard time believing it, but it's true. I think my strong personality and the fact that I didn't get into it as deep as I could've made it possible to stop the way I did. If this stuff had gone on for another year, there's no telling where it would've ended.

Besides, I was sick and tired of not sleeping, vomiting all the time, and having to drink gasoline to take a shit. Enough was enough.

Now, I'd be lying if I said quitting was easy. I was miserable for the first week. It wasn't like I was sweating or shaking or having real serious withdrawal. I was just depressed. I felt like I didn't want to do anything, which isn't me at all. I'd wake up in the morning and I didn't want to work out. It would be a beautiful day and Scott would say, "C'mon. Let's go play some golf." I wouldn't go.

I'd just lie around the house feeling sorry for myself.

I don't exactly know why but after a week I started to snap out of it. I got up and started moving around. I went and worked out. I played golf. From then on it just got better and better. My appetite returned.

Man, I'd forgotten how much I really love shrimp po' boys. And slowly I started to get my priorities straight again. Every day I would think about Deanna and Brittany and our future together. I would think about all that I wanted to accomplish in football.

The old Brett was starting to come back.

I didn't think it was going to be so easy. A few weeks later, I found out it wasn't.

# 2

# THE REHABILITATION

In late February of 1996, I flew up to Green Bay to have surgery on my left ankle. It wasn't going to be any big deal. Pat McKenzie, one of our team physicians, was going to remove a bone spur and some bone chips. He said it would stop the discomfort I'd been feeling during the season. Pretty routine stuff.

The Packers scheduled the operation February 27 so I could play in the Pro Bowl and still be healthy in time for our post-draft minicamp in late April. The day before my surgery, I drove over to Bellin Hospital with Deanna and Brittany to check in. The staff put me in a private room on the second floor.

Dr. Gray and Dr. McKenzie stopped by the night before to shoot the bull and answer any questions I might have about the operation. It was good to see those guys. I really like them and they do a great job of making you feel at ease, which is what good doctors are supposed to do. The next morning I got up early and had what I'd call routine surgery. The anesthesia made me vomit, but Doc McKen-zie said that was pretty common.

What happened next wasn't.

I was sitting up in bed and Brittany was stretched out next to me flipping through TV channels with the remote control. I was talking to Deanna, who was seated at the foot of the bed, when the nurse came in to check my IV.

I hate needles to begin with and, to make matters worse, the back of my hand was getting sore and swollen, so I wanted her to take a look at it. When the nurse started pulling the needle out, I looked at Deanna and rolled my eyes, which is my way of telling her, "God, I hate this shit." Then everything went black.

The only thing I know about the next twenty minutes is what Deanna told me later.

She said we were sitting there talking when all of a sud-den my eyes rolled into the back of my head. At first, she thought I was joking around like usual. Then she realized what was happening. I was having a seizure. My arms and legs started thrashing around and my head snapped back. Brittany got really scared and started crying.

I guess I started gnashing my teeth and Deanna screamed because she thought I couldn't breathe and I was going to choke to death. She yelled to the nurse, "Get his tongue! Don't let him swallow his tongue!" My whole body started to jerk and then I went stiff as a board. De-anna got Brittany out of the room, but not before Brittany turned to her and asked, "Is he going to die, Mommy?" Deanna didn't know what to say to her. She didn't know what to think. She'd seen people have seizures before, but this was different. This time it was me lying there.

When I opened my eyes, Doc Gray was standing over me.

He said, "You've just suffered a seizure, Brett. People can die from those."

Talk about a blow. I was crushed.

The first thing that shot through my mind was "The Vicodin caused it."

Now, I'd told Dr. Gray and Dr. McKenzie that I'd been taking painkillers, but I hadn't totally leveled with them. I had made it sound like a small problem that I'd already licked, which honestly, I figured I had. I thought I was through with the pills for good. It had been three weeks since I'd flushed that last bottle down the toilet and I didn't have any urge to start taking them again.

Now, because of the seizure, all sorts of crazy things were racing through my mind. Was I going to have these the rest of my life? Did I screw up my body with the Vicodin? I'd be lying if I said the seizure didn't scare me. It scared the hell out of me. Right then, I decided I better tell the doctors exactly what had been going on. Well, they listened and promised to do everything they could. I felt a lot better.

A few days later, Doc Gray called and said he'd arranged a meeting with some league-appointed doctors in Chicago the second week of March. He thought it was important to make sure we knew exactly what caused the seizure and to find out where to go from here. I totally agreed. I wanted to have peace of mind and I figured, "Why not talk to someone who's an expert on this? What can it hurt?" So off to Chicago I went.

The thing that neither my doctors nor I knew was how the counselors would react. Man, they were all over me. That's where this whole mess about me being in the NFL's substance-abuse program got started.

Doc Gray and I explained to them what had happened with the seizure and the painkillers. The first thing the doctors did was start asking about my experiences with alcohol. When did I start drinking beer? "At eighteen," I said, which was true. How much did I drink? I told them that was a vague question. It could be one beer. It could be ten beers. It just depends. When? During Mardi Gras? Lots. Out on the town with the guys?

Right away they got off the questions about the pain pills and they were only asking me about my drinking. This went on for about an hour. Finally one of the doctors said, "We know you're addicted to painkillers and we think you have a drinking problem, too. We think you should go to Topeka, Kansas. They have an excellent drug and alcohol rehabilitation center there called the Menninger Clinic."

Topeka? The Menninger Clinic? You've got to be kidding. I said, "Thanks, but no thanks."

I wasn't going to go to any rehab clinic because sure enough, I'm the NFL's Most Valuable Player and someone would find out and then it would be broadcast everywhere. On TV. On radio. In all the newspapers. The last thing I needed was that kind of hassle. The way I figured it, I'd already been through enough. Besides, I'd stopped taking the pills and I didn't drink all that much anymore. I told the doctors to forget it. They said, "Well, we recommend that you go."

I got up and walked out.

Three weeks later, the doctors contacted me again. They said I needed to meet with an independent doctor to get a second opinion. I thought what the heck, so I went.

We met in New Orleans and went over the whole thing again. I told the doctor I was over the pills. She said, "Well, you think you are, but you never really are." I said I understand that, but really I am. She said, "I think you need to go to Topeka, too." By now I was convinced all of these doctors were in cahoots. I left the doctor's office that day hoping that would be the end of it.

In the back of my mind I knew different, but I'm not one to worry myself to death, especially over the opinions of a bunch of doctors who really didn't know me or what I had gone through.

Shoot, I was doing okay. I was working out constantly. I was spending more time with Deanna and Brittany. And best of all, I didn't miss the pills one bit.

I'd gone to see two neurologists and they assured me that the Vicodin didn't cause the seizure. They said it could've been triggered by one of three things: the three concussions I'd had during the 1995 season; a bad reaction to the anesthesia; or the lack of sleep when I was still taking the pain pills. So really, there was no reason to be concerned. They said the odds of me having another seizure were almost nonexistent. That reassured me.

Besides, I was excited about my first annual charity golf tournament: the Brett Favre Celebrity Golf Tournament in beautiful Gulfport, Mississippi, on May 17 and 18.

It was only three weeks away and there was still plenty of work to do. I had to get a few additional sponsors, make sure everything was on schedule at the Windance Country Club, which hosted the event, and I had to confirm commitments from several of my teammates and players around the league.

Deanna and my parents worked on it every day with me, but it was still hectic.

The last thing I needed was the telephone call I got from one of the league's doctors two weeks before my tournament. He said I was "in the program" and that I needed to go to Topeka. I told myself, "In the program? What the hell is he talking about?" He explained that I was classified by the league as behavioral-referred, rather than self-referred, because the Packers' team doctors had contacted the league about my addiction to painkillers.

I explained to him that the Packers called to set up that first meeting in Chicago on my behalf. I told him the only reason they knew I had a problem with painkillers was that I stepped forward and told them.

I also said the seizure had nothing to do with the Vicodin, which I wasn't taking anymore anyway. He said it didn't matter. He said I had to report to the Menninger Clinic, and if I didn't, the league would fine me four weeks' pay, which was about $900,000. I said, "Screw that."

Well, Bus and I argued with the NFL's doctors for the next two weeks.

We fought back and forth, back and forth, back and forth. I didn't know what to think. I didn't know my rights. If I had to do it all over again, I would've explored it more instead of just going down to Chicago to meet with the doctors on a whim.

Finally the doctor called and said, "If you don't go in two days, you're going to be fined, so you better get everything situated."

I couldn't believe it. I didn't know if he was going to carry it out, but I didn't want to take the chance. A million bucks is a helluva lot of money.

Most of all, I didn't want to do anything that might get me suspended for the upcoming season. I knew we had a terrific shot at winning the Super Bowl and I didn't want to screw that up. I sat and thought about it all day. Finally I called Bus and asked him if there was anything I could do. He said, "Yeah. You can start packing."

I really wanted this all to just fall off the face of the earth.

Now, I knew there was no way that was going to happen. I told Bus, "All right. I'll go." Then I got on the telephone to Coach Holmgren. I told him there was something I needed to discuss with him in person right away. Mike sounded concerned, obviously, but he didn't ask me what was wrong. He said, "If that's what you need to do, that's fine. Just come on in and see me. I'll be here." I was on a flight to Green Bay the next day.

More than anytime in my career, I was glad Mike is so down-to-earth and easy to talk to. Bus and I walked into his office and we laid the cards on the table. We told him I had to report to drug rehab right away. All he could do was sit back in his chair and go, "Wow!"

The league's substance-abuse program is confidential, so even though our team doctors knew about the painkillers, they were obliged not to tell Mike or Ron Wolf, so this thing hit Mike totally out of the blue.

Naturally he wanted to know everything. How many pills was I taking? Where did I get them? Who was responsible for this? All the while, he's going, "I can't believe this," and he's writing like mad.

He said, "Who did you get them from?"

I wouldn't tell him, so he said, "You've got to tell me."

Well, I really didn't have to tell him. There's a confidentiality clause in the NFL's substance-abuse program that protects players' privacy. I could've just gone to Topeka and not explained anything but that's not my style. Besides, I trusted Mike enough to tell him everything.

When I was all done, Mike said, "Oh, boy. What are we going to do?"

He wasn't panicked or anything. Actually he stayed pretty cool, all things considered. It's not every day your MVP quarterback comes in and says, "I've got to go to drug rehab."

He thought the best thing to do was hold a press conference and get it out in the open, but first he talked to Ron Wolf and a couple of his assistant coaches. Going public was the consensus.

Mike said, "You don't have to do this press conference if you don't want to. If you just want to go to Topeka, we can do that. But I think this is the best thing."

I agreed with him. I was going to miss at least one mini-camp and probably two. Reporters would start asking questions, and sooner or later, the word would get out. It was just better to be up-front about it. Mike called the NFL and told them we were going to have a press conference to announce my entrance into drug rehab. They said we didn't have to hold a press conference. Mike told them he was going to go ahead with it.

Ron came down to Mike's office and he was really supportive.

Ron said, "If rehab is the best thing, then it's the best thing."

I told them I hadn't taken any painkillers since February and they said, "Then why do you have to go?" I told them this has been going on back and forth since the seizure in late February. Finally Ron said, "We'll try to help you out of this, but in the meantime you better go to Topeka."

First, we had to have the press conference.

I told Mike, "It's not going to be easy going in front of the media and telling them this." Mike said he would be there, as would Ron and Dr. Gray. He also said Deanna should be there, too. Once again, I agreed. We called a noon press conference at the Packers' media hall at Lambeau Field, which barely gave me time to get home, change into a suit, and hurry back.

When I returned, the Packers' public relations staff

helped me put together a prepared statement, which I memorized. We weren't going to answer any questions. I thought, "This won't be any big deal." When I stepped out onto the podium, everyone in the media was smiling at me. I guess they thought I was going to announce a lucrative contract extension. Typical me, I smiled back. Then I started talking and my leg started shaking something awful. I was nervous going on *The David Letterman Show,* but that was nothing compared to this. My leg was shaking so bad, if they had moved the lectern, the media would have said, "What in the hell is wrong with this guy?"

They'd have thought I was having a seizure on the spot or maybe withdrawals right there in front of them. I was shaking more than Elvis in *Jailhouse Rock.* I'd never had to do anything like this before. Hopefully I'll never have to do it again. I was so damn nervous. Here I am, with this goofy look on my face and everyone is thinking I'm going to tell them how pleased I am to get this new contract.

The next thing you know, I'm standing there telling them my life story. That was the hardest part of all. It was a pretty humbling experience, to say the least.

My statement was simple, but it was also straight from the heart.

Essentially I told them I had a serious problem that I needed to take care of. I said my main objective is to get better, first for myself and for my family, and to help this football team win.

Whew. I wasn't the smoothest, but I managed to get through it.

Then the questions started.

What kind of painkillers were you taking? How did you get them? How many did you take? Were you taking it to play in games? Did you do marijuana or cocaine? It was intense. Mike waved off most of the questions, but we did explain that I wasn't doing any illegal drugs off the street. I've never done cocaine. I did marijuana and I hated it. All it did was make me hungry and sleepy. I did it twice in college and wondered what the big deal was all about. I tried it in college because everyone else did it, kind of like President Clinton, and I don't know if I inhaled because it didn't work on me. I didn't get what everyone else was apparently getting. That is the extent of my drug use beyond painkillers. It was important to me that people knew that. And if they didn't believe my addiction was limited to painkillers, then that was their problem.

Afterward, I told Deanna I was nervous and she said, "I was shaking, too." Mike told me I did well. I said, "Were you nervous?" He said, "Hell yes." We all were.

Next stop, Topeka, Kansas.

Now, I have nothing against Topeka, but I sure didn't feel like going there, especially under the circumstances. I had never been there before and, if it wasn't for the rehab, I doubt I would've ever gone there at all. But here I was, off to see the wizard.

I started having these terrible dreams about the clinic. That it was going to be really awful, just like prison where they lock you in and you can't get out. To make things worse, the day between my press conference and my flight was another nightmare.

I was pissed because my golf tournament—my first annual—was going to start in two days without me. A lot of players backed out of the tournament because I wasn't going to be there. I don't blame them. If I was scheduled to go to one of their tournaments and the host wasn't going to be there, I'd figure, "Well, why should I bother?" The only disappointing thing is that it ends up hurting the charities.

It's funny how everything comes full circle. When I

first started being invited to charity golf outings by other NFL players, I'd always say, "Heck, yeah. I'll be there." And I really meant it when I said it. Then I may or may not go, depending on what else there was to do that weekend.

That probably sounds selfish, and it was, but I really didn't know better. Then I'd wonder why those players would be ticked at me the next time I saw them. Now I know why. They were counting on me to show up and help their charity and I let them down.

Hosting my own tournament gave me a whole new perspective. Fortunately the people who did come were very, very generous. The Brett Favre Fourward Foundation, of which Deanna is CEO, raised about $110,000 for the Boys and Girls Club and the American Cancer Society last year. It's why I had a second annual event. To raise money for charity and to stop my teammates from giving me shit, saying, "Yeah, yeah. I'll be at your tournament. The big question is 'Are you going to show up?' "

A friend offered to fly me to Topeka on his private jet. I was grateful. Traveling through airports has become a hassle. The autograph seekers are nonstop; the flights aren't. Deanna, Bus, Brittany, a baby-sitter, and I flew down together. I ordered pizza for the plane ride, but no one felt like eating. Everyone was pretty upset.

I hadn't packed much. I brought some T-shirts, flip-flops, and tennis shoes. I figured I was just going to be walking back and forth from meals anyway. I packed pictures of Deanna and Brittany to put up in my room.

My mom and my grandma sent some prayer books, with the kind of prayers that you say when you get up in the morning and go to bed at night. I thought it was a great thing to do, because as it turned out, I had plenty of time to sit around at night and pray. I thought a lot about what was good and bad in my life. And about what I could do to be a better person. It was the first time I ever actually sat back and thought about it.

When we got to the airport in Topeka, a man from the Menninger Clinic greeted us and drove us to the place. I was impressed the minute I saw it. All that worrying had been a waste of time. It was like a college campus. Huge. Pretty nice.

Too bad the rooms weren't as spacious as the grounds. They were about twelve by twelve with a small bed, a couch, a desk, and a jack to plug in the telephone, which you had to check out at the front desk. You could only use it fifteen minutes, and then you had to turn it back in. The bathroom and the shower were small.

It was home.

The days were pretty regimented. Every morning I would get up at seven, do fifty push-ups and one hundred sit-ups, go for a three-mile run, and hit the gym. I'd do lunges for twenty minutes, and then I'd play racquetball against this fifty-year-old named Roger who ran the work-out area. He worked me over for two weeks before I got into shape. Then I started to beat him. When I first got there, I could barely touch a ten-foot basketball rim. When I left, I was dunking a basketball. My vertical had increased by six inches.

I was really starting to shape up.

After my morning workout, I'd eat breakfast. The cafeteria was awesome. The food was all there for you. When I first walked in, I told myself, "This is a perfect opportunity to go on an unbelievable diet." So I did. I ate fresh fruit. Fish. Chicken breasts. Vegetables. Cereal with skim milk. Rarely, fried foods. I didn't drink anything but water the whole time I was there. No milk. No Coke. No Diet Coke. No tea. Just water.

My only vice in there was dip. Cherry Skoal. Long cut.

I'd be in a meeting and spit and they'd look at me. I'd say, "Don't worry. I won't hit the rug." I went through two or three rolls a week. Some people smoked in there. I dipped. That was my crutch.

Otherwise, everything else I did was healthy. Between the dieting and the working out, I lost six pounds and 10 percent body fat. The bloating and puffiness in my face was gone. I could see the slim-down taking place. I looked 100 percent better when I left than when I arrived.

We had group meetings every morning at nine o'clock. Every day it was a different topic. Safe sex. Dietetics. Addiction. You name it. Those lasted about an hour. After that, I'd go to individual psychotherapy. They recommended it, so I went. I didn't have anything better to do. Besides, the NFL was paying for it, and at $250 an hour, I couldn't pass that up.

I met with the same doctor for six weeks. He was pretty cool. He'd ask questions. I'd respond and elaborate. I enjoyed going. Fifty minutes would fly by. People ask me what I learned in psychotherapy. I don't know. I guess I learned that I could be a better person. The psychiatrist made me see that I wasn't treating Deanna like I should.

I realized that whenever I had some success, especially on the field, I'd sort of push her to the side and want to celebrate with my teammates. But when I was sick or down or whatever, I'd lean on her. I'm sure it wasn't much fun for her. It wasn't even fair. He also made me see that either I needed to marry her or give her a break and let her go. I had a lot of time to think in there.

What I thought was "Deanna and Brittany are the best things I've got going in my life." That's when I knew I wanted to marry her. Besides, I was tired of introducing her to everyone as "my girlfriend." It was getting ridiculous. After three years at the Quarterback Challenge, enough was enough. I could picture us still dating at thirty-five. That would be great. Or me wheeling her down the corridor at the nursing home, stopping and telling people, "This is my girlfriend, Deanna." I'd be like seventy-eight years old—if I make it that long, which I doubt—and all dried up like a prune. Hell, I didn't want that. She deserved better. Someone told me that if we did get married, I should get Deanna to sign a prenuptial agreement. Shit. Deanna deserves half of everything I've got for all she's been through.

When I finished my psychotherapy session, I'd go eat lunch. The first week we had to go to the cafeteria as a group and we had to leave as a group. If you built up enough marks for good behavior, you could go eat by yourself. I really didn't care either way. Lunch was from 11:00 to 12:30. Afterward, I'd hang out in my room or go for a walk until group meetings at two o'clock. That's when PIC—Professionals in Crisis—would meet. This was something different every day. One day we had to act angry or happy or sad. I'd just watch. Another day we had to write down the five things that had given us the most joy and the most pain in our lives. Then they'd sit there and talk about it.

Hell, I didn't want a bunch of total strangers knowing my problems. I figured if I said too much, some asshole would sell the story to the *Enquirer* and make a fortune. So I'd make up things. Or I'd write down generic stuff. It was easy.

Stuff like, The Five Most Painful Events in My Life:

1. The loss at Minnesota in '92.
2. The loss at Minnesota in '93.
3. The loss at Minnesota in '94.
4. The loss at Minnesota in '95.
5. The loss at Dallas in the '95 NFC Championship.

I'm sure some people thought I was just being a smart-ass, but I didn't want to put down anything too revealing or too bad. It turned out mine were like nothing compared to what other people were writing down.

For example, they'd be writing down stuff like, "I saw my mom blow her boyfriend's head off with a shotgun from three feet away." Then they'd start talking and crying and talking some more. I'd be like, "Holy shit. That's pretty awful." It was like being on *The Oprah Winfrey Show* every day. It made me realize I wasn't the Lone Ranger out there. Other people had some pretty screwed-up lives, too.

When I saw the statistics regarding the number of pain-killer addicts, I was shocked. In 1994, an estimated 3.9 million people used painkillers for nonmedical reasons, according to the government's National Household Survey on Drug Abuse. That's the same number as those who used cocaine.

When you matched those numbers with real people—and the tragedy they'd experienced because of painkiller abuse—it was a real eye-opener. There were lots of patients at the Menninger Clinic whose problems were a lot worse than mine were. Listening to addicts talk was unbelievable.

We had a couple of doctors in the group who were sex addicts. I thought, "Damn, that can't be too bad." And they said, "Oh, yes it is." They were doing things like screwing patients and getting caught and all sorts of wild shit.

There were crack cocaine addicts in there that said they smoked it just once and were hooked forever. They said they'd go a week without eating.

There was a guy in there—a real successful business-man—who got into painkillers with his ex-wife. It got to the point where they'd take turns burning their arms on the stove so they could go to the emergency room and get a new prescription. I'm thinking, "Ain't love grand."

At that point, neither one cared about the other person, only about what they could get from each other in the way of painkillers. This guy said he knew he had to stop when she asked him to crush her arm against the garage with their car.

I'd get chill bumps hearing that stuff.

At three o'clock, we'd have biofeedback sessions. They'd sit you in a chair and hook the tip of your finger to a temperature gauge. The counselor would tell you to think mellow, relaxed thoughts. The more you did, the warmer your finger got and the gauge would go up. Then the guy would yell and blood would rush to other parts of your body, away from your finger, and the temperature gauge would shoot down. It was pretty cool.

After that, I'd go to the gym to play basketball or work out some more. They also had what they called self-improvement classes. Wood shop. Gardening. Painting. I took piano lessons. The counselors were shocked. One said, "Damn, you're really changing." I just laughed and said, "What the hell else is there to do in here?" I learned to play "O de Joy" and one other tune. I haven't taken a piano lesson since.

At night, we'd eat dinner and then sit around the TV lounge shooting the bull.

At first, I was like, "God, I'm in here with a bunch of junkies." But as time went by I came to see it wasn't like that at all. These were just normal folks who had their own problems like me. Alcohol. Cocaine. Crack. You name it. That was when we'd all compare notes. It would be nine o'clock and I'd say, "This was the time I'd take my pain pills." Another guy would say, "I always took mine first thing in the morning." Or another, "I always took mine right when I got off work." It was strange how much I had in common with the other patients. Or maybe it wasn't.

When I first arrived, the counselors strictly told me there would be no autograph signing. I said, "Sure. Whatever." After a while, I made friends with the other patients and they'd be like, "Brett, can you sign this ball for my kid?" I was glad to do it until one of the nurses caught me. She got really upset and said, "You're not here because you're a big football star. You're here to get over this." Hell, I knew that. But what was I going to do? Tell this guy no? She said, "You're killing yourself." I shook my head and said, "Whatever." I think the other patients kind of liked me for not taking the stupid rule so seriously. Pretending I wasn't a football player wasn't going to help me cope with my addiction.

I never got as lonely as I thought I would. There were people my age who'd made a lot of money and we could relate in different ways. We talked about where we grew up, how we grew up, things like that. I missed my family and friends, but I would talk to them each night on the telephone, even if it was brief. They were more worried than I was. I'd tell Mom and Dad not to worry.

Then I'd turn in around eleven o'clock.

Most patients at the clinic participated in off-campus meetings at night, such as Alcoholics Anonymous or Narcotics Anonymous, but I never went to those because you had to deal with the general public. I didn't want any part of that. Too much of a hassle.

One night a few of us decided to drive into town to see the movie *Twister*. What a nightmare. I was walking through the ticket line and somebody recognized me. Before I knew it, I was standing in the middle of the lobby signing autographs. Finally I got in to see the movie. About halfway through, the whole theater started to shake and the power went out. A guy came on the loudspeaker and said, "A twister just hit the theater, but everything will be okay. Please remain in your seats." I was like, "Damn, what next?" Everyone was all teary-eyed and scared. I was just pissed I ever went to the movie in the first place. A few minutes later, the movie came on. Afterward, I went out the back door to avoid signing autographs.

That was my last trip to town to see a movie.

The weekends were pretty boring. At first, I thought it would be fun to sit around on a Saturday or a Sunday and watch TV, which is something I never do. Let me tell you, it sucks. About the only interesting thing on TV was the College World Series. It was fun watching Louisiana State kick some butt.

After two weeks, I built up enough good marks so the counselors let me play golf at a local course. The manager there was real nice. He loaned me some clubs and got me on the course. Frankie Winters came to visit me a couple of times and we played golf together. It was like being set free. Frankie spends his off-season in Kansas City, which is about fifty miles away, so it was pretty handy for him and great for me.

Deanna also came up to visit me a couple of times. It was always really good to see her. We'd go out to dinner and talk about everything that was going on with me in the clinic and with her back home. That's when I started asking her to marry me.

I could tell she thought it was just a phase. She didn't think I was serious. She'd just say, "We've got a lot of wrinkles to iron out."

I kept on asking her every time I'd see her and every

time we'd talk on the phone. I'd say, "Let's get married this summer before the season." Deanna never brought up the subject. She wanted to make sure it was what I wanted, probably so I'd never blame her if things didn't work out. This went on for weeks.

Mike also visited me, which was really nice of him. I didn't ask him to do that. He just came down on his own for a day. Pepper Burruss, our head trainer, tagged along.

It was funny. Everyone at the clinic was used to seeing me around, but when they heard Mike Holmgren was in the building, they got really excited. We'd be walking down the hallway and people would say, "Look. That's Mike Holmgren. He coaches the Packers."

It was great to see him. It meant a lot to me. Here he was, my head coach, making a totally nonfootball visit at a time when he could be off vacationing with his family or doing a million other things. I don't know how many head coaches would do that for a player.

It may have been uncomfortable for him to walk onto a drug rehab floor, where there were some people in pretty rough shape, but it didn't show. He handled it really, really well. Everyone was talking to him and asking him a lot of questions, but he was totally cool.

When he first walked in and saw me, he said, "Damn, you look good." I told him I'd been running, playing rac-quetball, and eating right. Then we just shot the bull. He told me everyone in the organization was behind me and that they were all asking about me. I said, "Tell them I'm doing great." The only thing that bothered me was not being able to throw. By this time each off-season, I'd be outside throwing a hundred passes a day. He told me, "Don't worry about throwing. You take care of things in here. I'll handle the rest."

There were two things I hated most about being in the clinic.

One was morning rounds. Every day, the doctor and nurse would come into my room and ask a lot of questions. It was the same routine for seven weeks. How do you feel today, Brett? "Feeling great." Any problems last night? "Nope. I worked out. I ate. I slept good." Any urge to do anything? "No." Are meetings going okay? "Yeah, fine. Just boring. I'm ready to go home." This went on and on.

It was even worse when my first doctor left after two weeks. The new one used to be hooked on Percodan. I guess he was a mountain climber and he fell off a cliff and that started it. Well, I'd fight him on everything every day. I was just sick of answering the same questions over and over. They'd document everything you'd say, so I tried to be careful, but it wasn't easy. That's probably one reason I didn't get out sooner.

The other thing I hated was meeting with what I called the Parole Board.

Once a week, you'd meet with four doctors, a nurse, and the NFL's doctors. They were letting other patients go home on weekends, patients who'd been in there less time than me. After two weeks, I told them I missed Mother's Day and I wanted to go home to visit. They'd get all quiet and go over their notes. It was like a scene straight out of *Shawshank Redemption,* where the old guy always goes in to see if he's getting out of prison and the parole board always says no.

Finally they'd look up at me and they'd say, "No. We don't trust you. We don't think you should go home. You'll probably do something." I told them I wasn't going to do anything. I just wanted to go home for Mother's Day. I knew how hard all this was for my mom and I wanted to cheer her up. So I said, "C'mon. Let me go home." They said no. That's when we started arguing. We went back and forth.

Now, never before in my life had I gotten verbally abusive with anybody, but finally I was like, "Screw this. You guys are unbelievable." A nurse was sitting there and she said something smart and I turned and started cursing her, too. They all just sat there and took it. I guess it wasn't the first time someone had an outburst in front of them.

Finally I turned around and slammed open the door to leave. I swung it so hard, the knob went right through the wall and put a big hole in it. A few of the patients went in later and circled it with a black Magic Marker and wrote, "Remember this!" Every time I saw it from then on, I would laugh.

The doctors said, "You're going to have to pay for that." I said, "Screw you. The NFL is paying for it. I'll put another one in the fucking wall if I feel like it."

That was the most frustrating time for me. I felt like they were really trying to be hard-asses with me. It was a concerted effort to get tough on Brett Favre. They wanted to make a point with me. They were going to make me an example.

Man, some of those meetings got ugly. I kept telling them I was ready to leave. I told them, "The longer you make me stay, the worse it's going to be."

They didn't care.

This went on for seven weeks. I told my doctor in psychotherapy about my outbursts. He said, "I agree with you. I think you're ready to leave." So I said, "Tell them that." He said he couldn't because that would violate our doctor-patient confidentiality.

He said, "You just need to go with the flow." He was right.

After that, I started telling the Parole Board that I was a drug addict and I needed help. I told them what they wanted to hear. Sure enough, a week later they said, "We think you're ready to leave."

I was like, "Hallelujah!" I got my things together, filled out some paperwork, and told everyone, "I enjoyed meeting y'all." I told the doctors and the nurses thanks. Then I walked out the door and was like, "Screw you." I couldn't wait to get out. Now, looking back on it, they were really good people. They were just trying to help me. I know that now. But that day when Deanna picked me up, I couldn't wait to get out.

I was so excited, I called Ron Wolf.

"Ron, I'm getting out. I want you to know that I'm going to the Super Bowl this season with you or without you."

Ron laughed. "Brett, I'm going with you. You can count on it."

I flew back to Diamondhead and the first thing I did was play golf. I hooked up with Scott and our good friend Mark Haverty, and we had the best time. We drove to the local golf course and got after it.

The NFL's substance-abuse program called for me to stop drinking alcohol for two years. Their reasoning is that an addict is nine times more likely to suffer a relapse with his drug of choice if he continues to use alcohol. They say it impairs your judgment.

Maybe that's true, but I had no desire to take Vicodin ever again.

After golf, we stopped at a little restaurant and ate some crawfish and really relaxed. I hadn't had a good time like that in a long time. Then we drove home.

Two days later, I guess it was July 1, I flew back to Green Bay.

Scott came up with me to work out. Deanna and Brittany were already there.

It was good to be home. Right away, I kept asking Deanna to marry me. Finally she said yes. I think I wore her down. She cried and said, "My old Brett's back."

Deanna had doubted whether I was serious about getting married, so she hadn't gone ahead with any plans, which made things pretty hectic for her. In one week she got the dress, the rings, and the church. She walked right up to Father Getchel at St. Agnes Catholic Church in Green Bay and said, "Will you marry Brett and me next Sunday?" He was glad to do it. Brittany was thrilled. It was on such short notice, we kept it really small.

Kent Johnston, my good friend and the Packers' strength coach, was the best man. His wife, Pam, was the matron of honor. My mom and Deanna's mom flew up for the ceremony. Neither of our dads came. I think they both felt like, "What's the big deal? It's about time after all these years." Everything went smoothly. After the ceremony, Brittany was so excited, she turned to Deanna and said, "Mommy, you've made me so proud." We honeymooned in Kohler, Wisconsin. There wasn't enough time to go off to Hawaii or some exotic place. Training camp opened in two days.

The first day I showed up at the team's headquarters on Lombardi Avenue, right after I arrived back in Green Bay the first of July, everyone treated me great. They acted the same as they always had toward me. They knew I wasn't any different, except for my goatee—which I later shaved off—and the fact that I wasn't drinking beer anymore.

The NFL was testing me a couple of times a week and I didn't want to screw up. I'd just drink O'Doul's when I went out, which wasn't very often. I didn't want to push it. I didn't want people to think I was back to partying and taking the painkillers again. Then if I had a bad game, which is going to happen, I didn't want everyone wondering if it was because I was back on the Vicodin.

On the first day of training camp, the Packers set up a press conference for me. The media wanted to see how I was doing after the rehab, which was fair enough. This press conference was nothing like the first one back in May. It was much easier. I was back to being my old self. I felt good and I was in great shape. Besides, the cat was out of the bag. I didn't mind talking about it. I was excited about it. Mike sat next to me at the press conference. No one coached me on what to say. Mike said, "I'll nudge you if there's something I need to interject." I said no problem.

We started by reading a statement I had prepared. It was pretty straightforward.

"I suffer from a dependency on painkillers. Upon completion of my in-patient treatment program, the expert on prescription medication abuse [at the Menninger Clinic in Topeka, Kansas] informed me and the Packers' team physician that I no longer have a dependency on Vicodin or any pain medication.

"Further, it has been rumored that my problems also involve alcoholism. The same specialist stated unequivocally that I do not have a problem in this area, namely that I am not an alcoholic. While there are certain questions that I am able to answer, due to the nature of the league's substance-abuse program, there are certain areas which must remain confidential.

"I realize that while I am in this program, I must abstain from alcohol. I am aware that I have an obligation, not only to myself but also to my fans and team, to comply with the rules while in this system. Believe me when I tell you, 'This is going to be hard.' But I have faced tougher trials and succeeded.

"I will not allow myself to be defeated by this challenge. In conclusion, I hope you understand that due to the nature of the program, I will not be able to answer some of your questions to your complete satisfaction. However, let us not lose sight of your main focus—playing football.

"I also realize that during the course of the season, questions will come up regarding this particular time of my life. I hope you understand that I choose to dwell on what lies ahead for the Packers on the football field, rather than rehash the past two months of my life."

Then came the questions. How many pills were you taking? Who was supplying them? Mike intervened on several occasions and said, "We aren't going to answer that." He probably saved me from myself because I was willing to tell everything. I didn't feel like I had anything to hide, but Mike was just looking out for me and the team.

When I did answer questions, I was totally honest. I told the media that I found out trying to deal with drug addiction by myself leads to rock bottom. It leads to losing your family, your job, and your life. Everything you've worked hard for. I told them that it's hard for me to realize that I'm only twenty-six, what with all I've been through. I knew a lot of good things had happened to me, and a lot of bad things, too. I had grown up a bit through rehab. Now I could look myself in the mirror and tell myself things and know I was telling the truth. I was growing up. I was making that turn.

Someone asked if I was worried about suffering a relapse. I said no. I could see the doubt and the skepticism in some of the reporters' faces. It pissed me off. I thought, "The hell with you," and I let them know it.

"All I can tell people is if you don't believe me, bet

against me because eventually they'll lose. I'm going to beat this thing. I'm going to win the Super Bowl.''

It took six months and a lot of hard work, but I proved to be right.

# 3

# SUPER BOWL XXXI

The Las Vegas bookies made us a two-touchdown favorite to beat New England in Super Bowl XXXI. I liked that. At least they were giving us helluva lot better odds than most people gave me back in July when I came out of drug rehab.

I read what people were writing in the preseason football magazines. Back then, mostly all anyone did was doubt me and write negative stuff. Can Brett Favre come back from drugs and carry his team? Can he prove that the Most Valuable Player award he won in '95 wasn't a fluke? Can he beat the long odds?

The media made it sound like it was a million miles from Topeka to New Orleans. That really helped motivate me. The whole time I'm thinking I'm no different than I was in '95, only a little less buzzed up. I felt fine. I worked out hard. I was on a good diet. I was in great shape. I was ready for the '96 season no matter what anyone said.

Then I went out and proved it.

I broke my own NFC record by throwing thirty-nine

touchdown passes to win my second straight Most Valuable Player award. The team went 13–3 to win its second straight NFC Central Division title, something the Packers hadn't done since Vince Lombardi and the 1960s. On offense, we scored more points than any team in the league. On defense, we allowed the fewest. The last team to do that was Don Shula's unbeaten Miami Dolphins in 1972.

Could I make it back from the Vicodin? Hell yeah.

It was funny how when I arrived in New Orleans for the Super Bowl, writers would come up to me and say, "I can't believe what you did. That was amazing." Well, it wasn't to me. I knew we could do it all along. I was supremely confident. That's why I predicted we would make it to the Super Bowl back in July. I wasn't guaranteeing a victory like Joe Namath did with the New York Jets in '69. I'm not really that kind of person but I am confident. I know what I can do, and if people don't want to believe me, that's their problem. I've been a battler my whole life. I wasn't about to stop now.

Well, after two weeks of practices, meetings, and media hype, the big day was finally here. At first, the day of the Super Bowl didn't seem much different than any other road game. Frankie and I woke up in our room at the Fairmont Hotel, which is where the Packers were headquartered, and we went downstairs for breakfast. I grabbed an omelet and went back up to the room until our team meeting at ten o'clock.

Then we broke down into individual meetings and watched twenty minutes of film. By now there wasn't much preparation left. It was all pretty boring. I knew the game plan inside and out. I sure as heck better. I had two weeks to study it. After Mike went over our first fifteen plays he'd scripted, I went back to my room. Dad stopped to pick up some tickets and wish me luck. We shot the bull and Bus came by to say hello and wish me good luck. Then I hung out in my room until the pregame meal at one.

The first team bus left at 1:30. I took the second bus at 2:30 and hopped into the front seat next to Sherman Lewis, our offensive coordinator. I always take the second bus. It's a superstition thing.

I was pretty anxious to get to the Superdome. Then I looked out the bus window. I couldn't believe it. Everything was green and gold. Packers fans were jammed thirty, forty deep along the road. It was like a home game and Mardi Gras rolled into one. It was really an awesome sight. I had the chills going through me. For the first time all day my heart started pounding.

Right then I knew this was going to be the biggest game of my life.

I asked Sherman how the mob of Packers fans outside the bus compared with what he saw when he was an assistant coach with the 49ers. Sherman said, "It ain't even close. This would just blow them away."

That was pretty nice to hear.

Up to now the day was sort of dragging. I was pumped. Then I got to the locker room and everything slowed down again.

I got to the Superdome almost three hours before kickoff, which was an hour earlier than we usually get to the stadium. It felt strange having so much time to kill. Actually it sucked.

We had to sit around and wait while the league put on its dog-and-pony show before the game. I guess they've got to have commercial time to pay for the TV contract.

In the meantime, we were doing our own dog-and-pony show in the locker room. It sure as hell wasn't too serious in there for such a big game.

LeRoy Butler was walking around with a camcorder and everyone would look into it and shout, "That shit be bringin' it, Hoss." Wayne Simmons started saying that during the season. We were talking in the locker room one day about the 49ers' defensive tackle Bryant Young, and Wayne told me to look out because "That shit be bringin' it, Hoss."

After that it just stuck.

It was still two hours until the kickoff and I was bored, so I got on my cell phone and started calling around to set up a postgame victory party. I was pretty confident we'd win and I figured it was a good idea to have something lined up. I made a few calls and got in touch with Scott, who rented a room with a balcony at Mike Anderson's Seafood Restaurant and Oyster Bar on Bourbon Street.

After I got the details finalized, I walked into the training room to get my ankles taped. It might not sound like a big deal, but getting my ankles taped is a process that has evolved into a pregame ritual for me during my five seasons in Green Bay.

Kurt Fielding, one of our assistant trainers, always tapes my ankles. I'm superstitious about it and he knows how I like them taped, so why change? When he's finished, he takes a black felt-tip marker and writes on the tape his prediction of the outcome of the game and my statistics for the game.

Before the Super Bowl, Kurt wrote down a "W" for a win. He always predicts a victory. Then he wrote that I'd be 24 of 35 for 272 yards and four touchdowns. Kurt factors in the opposing defense, the weather conditions, and how I practiced all week. He does that shit for every guy he tapes, and he tapes about a third of the players.

Kurt said he started predicting players' stats in 1988. The first guy ever was a rookie receiver out of Auburn named Scott Bolton. He was a twelfth-round pick who played for one season. I don't think Kurt predicted that. Kurt continued it with quarterback Don Majkowski and so on.

Sometimes Kurt's predictions are so close to my final statistics it's scary. There are times when he's only 2 yards off on total passing yards. Lots of times he'll hit the touchdown passes right on the nose. He used to be a little more erratic because, well, I was a little more erratic.

Now he's gotten pretty consistent. I completed 14 of 27 passes for 246 yards and two touchdowns in the Super Bowl, so I didn't make him look too bad.

After I got taped, I killed time by telling jokes. Bad jokes.

Here's one I told to Jim McMahon, our backup quarterback, who has a pretty sick sense of humor:

"A guy having trouble getting a date asks his buddy for advice on how to attract beautiful women. The buddy says, 'Go to the grocery store, buy a potato, and stick it in your Speedo. Then walk slowly along the beach.' The guy comes back the next day and says it didn't work. The buddy says, 'I'll come to the beach tomorrow and see what you're doing wrong.' The next day he goes to the beach, sees his friend, and says, 'You dumb fart! The potato goes in the front.'"

Like I said, bad jokes.

McMahon didn't care. He laughed anyway. Jim was one of the smartest guys I'd ever been around. He did a lot to keep us loose in the locker room before the Super Bowl.

Jim started by throwing footballs at the nameplates over the lockers. He'd wind up, fire, and boom! He'd knock the nameplate off. He hit the first two, which brought some cheers, and then he missed three straight, which brought some boos. Mike heard us from the next room and opened the door to see what all the racket was about. Everyone was like, "Shut up. It's Coach." We were like a bunch of Boy Scouts on a camping trip.

McMahon sure doesn't act his age, which is what, one hundred and two? The more games we'd win during the season, the more Jim would be telling us about what to expect in New Orleans and the Super Bowl. Jim was the Super Bowl MVP with Chicago in '86, when the Bears crushed New England in New Orleans, and he was a hell-raiser. He told us one way to rile up the media was to drop our drawers and moon 'em. He also told us where to go to look at naked women and so forth. He was trying to be helpful, I guess.

Then there was Don Beebe, our backup receiver, who had been to four Super Bowls and lost four Super Bowls with Buffalo. Don's a really religious guy, so his approach was totally different than Jim's. He didn't want to lose a fifth Super Bowl, so he'd be reminding us about being in early and staying off Bourbon Street. Don would say, "Look, I've been to four of these and I know guys goofed off in Buffalo and we lost all four. Well, I don't want that to happen here, so save all that drinking and chasing women and being crazy for later. There's plenty of time for all that stuff after we win the game."

Jim would look at Don and say, "Aw, shut up and sit down. These guys aren't going to pay any attention to you." Then everyone would laugh, including Don, who took it all in stride. It was pretty funny. Don was like God and Jim was like the Antichrist. We had a devil on one shoulder pad and an angel on the other, each whispering advice in our ears.

I admire Don and Jim. Don is like thirty-two years old and he still runs a 4.2 40-yard dash. He's faster than light. It's totally amazing. Then there's Jim, who is thirty-seven and probably in better shape than most of the guys on the team. And we got along good. Our personalities matched. I knew it must've been a tough position for Jim to be the backup quarterback. I'm sure he would've loved to be playing. Who wouldn't? He could easily have told me to piss off when I asked him for help, but he didn't. He was always really helpful. If I was a backup quarterback, I'd probably tell the starter to look for a certain coverage and I'd be lying just so he screwed up and I could get into the game. That's the way I am right now. I'm sure it'll change when I get older. Then I would try to be like Jim. He knows his football. He knows what works and what doesn't and he gives more advice than he takes credit for. Jim retired after the Super Bowl. He was a helluva quarterback. I'll miss him.

Well, everything was pretty low-key in the locker room until right before we were supposed to walk out onto the field for pregame introductions. That's when we popped some smelling-salt capsules—which we do before every game to clear our heads—and all of a sudden the butterflies started flying in my stomach. That hadn't happened to me since the fifth grade. I couldn't believe it.

I told myself to stay cool, but I was way too excited for that.

Right before we left the locker room, Mike stood up and said, "Men, this is what we've worked for since that first meeting in training camp. We're here for one reason and that's to win the Super Bowl. It was a long, hard road. It's why we worked so hard in training camp. It's why we went through all the ups and downs, just to be here in this position we're in right now. So don't let it slip away. Enjoy yourself and remember this moment forever. Now let's get out there and *get after it!*"

My heart was pounding.

I glanced around and everyone looked like they were in a state of shock.

Before a regular-season game, guys would be goofing off until right before we would run out onto the field. This time it was different. It was strange. It was like you didn't want to say anything to anyone, they were that intense.

Andre Rison was crying.

Tears were streaming down his cheeks and he was saying, "This is what it's all about. I can't believe I'm here. A few months ago I'm trying to find a team and now I'm starting in the Super Bowl."

Reggie White was getting really emotional on us. He had this look of determination and pride and intensity that I'd never seen before. It was an awesome sight.

Our nose tackle, Gilbert Brown, was real quiet in the locker room, but all of a sudden when it was time to come running out of the locker room, he was a new person. He was shaking and doing God knows what with that big 350-pound body of his. Wayne Simmons came out and, man, he was so intense, I don't know what the hell was going on inside his head.

I was watching all of this and thinking, "This is pretty cool."

When I got on the sidelines, I was so excited I started throwing rocket balls. I was a little worried I'd launch my first pass into the upper deck or maybe through a damn wall the way I was pumped up.

As it turned out, my first pass couldn't have been better.

We kicked off, forced New England to punt, and took over at our own 45. On the way to the huddle I'm thinking, "We've got great field position. Let's make it count."

On first down, our halfback, Edgar Bennett, ran off left tackle and picked up a yard.

On second down, I stepped up behind Frank Winters to look at New England's defense. I couldn't believe my eyes. Here it was, only my second snap of Super Bowl XXXI, and the Patriots were going for the damn jugular. Their safeties, Lawyer Malloy and Willie Clay, were easing and cheating up to the line, which most likely meant one thing.

Their linebackers were blitzing.

Right away I'm thinking, if I audible to another play and I'm wrong, it's going to be third-and-long, maybe worse. But if I'm right and I audible to the perfect play against the blitz and we hit on it, this will be bigger than any play we've ever had.

It would give us an early lead and do a lot to prove everyone wrong who said, "Favre starts wild in the big games" and "Favre can't throw with a soft touch" and "Favre can't read defenses properly."

The hell I can't.

Mike sent in a play called 322 Y Stick, which is designed to hit our tight end, Keith Jackson, on a 4-yard out. The problem is it also sends Edgar Bennett in motion, which means we don't have the right protection to pick up the blitz. So even though it's a quick pass to Keith, the defense may still get through to me.

I had about two seconds to decide whether the Patriots were blitzing or just faking it. In the handful of films I'd studied, they never blitzed this early in a game. It wasn't one of their tendencies. Then again, their linebackers looked guilty as sin. They were trying to look all innocent, but they weren't too convincing. They were acting like they were whistling and rattling change in their pockets on some street corner. The more they tried to hide the blitz, the more it showed.

Well, I wasn't buying it.

I audibled to a play called 74 Razor in which Andre
Rison lined up wide left with Antonio Freeman in the slot
on the same side of the formation. It was only the fifth
time in five years that I audibled to Razor. Three times it
worked. Twice it didn't. It was a play the defense wouldn't
expect, especially on the second play of the Super Bowl.
Then again, if Andre was covered, I was up shit creek
without a paddle.

When I audibled, everyone on offense picked it up including Andre, which was pretty good since he'd only
been with us a half dozen games. A few weeks earlier I
may not have audibled in the same situation because
Andre may not have recognized it.

But now I was confident he'd do the right thing, which
he did.

He lined up across from Otis Smith, the Patriots' right
cornerback, and spun him around on a hard inside move.
Then he shot past him by a good 5 yards. In the meantime,
Edgar picked up Ted Johnson, the Patriots' middle linebacker, who was blitzing. Now all I had to do was put the
football on the money.

Now, 74 Razor isn't a difficult pass, but it isn't an easy
one, either. It's a touch pass just like the ones I'd seen Joe
Montana throw to Jerry Rice a million times. So I laid it
out there and Andre caught it in stride at New England's
20-yard line. Then he duckwalked into the end zone for a
54-yard touchdown.

I went bananas.

I pulled my helmet off and started acting like it was the
first touchdown pass of my life. I was embarrassed when
I looked at the replay, but that's the way I felt. It was the
second play of the Super Bowl, the biggest game of my
life, and here I am hitting on a huge touchdown pass. I was

also happy for Andre, who went from being an outcast to a hero in one play.

Some people thought I was showing off or hotdogging it or whatever when I pulled my helmet off. If I'd had time to think about it, maybe I would've been calm and cool, but hell, I was fired up. I ran 15 yards toward the Patriots' sideline and then all the way back across the field to our bench. I don't even remember taking my helmet off.

The touchdown to Andre was the perfect beginning to a great win. We beat the Patriots 35–21, but it wasn't easy. I give New England credit. We had them down 10–0 but they came back to take the lead. It didn't last long, though. I hit Antonio Freeman for an 81-yard touchdown to put us ahead 17–14 on the next series.

The Super Bowl was one of my most enjoyable games ever. I felt so clear and so at ease, it was like when you hear about Michael Jordan being in a zone and never missing. Well, that's the way I felt.

Before the game I was worried I'd be too late with reads or too anxious to make plays, but it was completely the opposite once I got onto the field. I was hitting the second and third receivers with no problems. I felt like everything was moving in slow motion, it was so clear.

The 81-yard touchdown to Free, the longest touchdown from scrimmage in Super Bowl history, is a perfect example. I stepped to the line and saw Malloy, their strong safety, trying to play bump-and-run on Free out of single coverage. There was no way he'd be able to stop Free, so I audibled to a different blocking scheme that gave me maximum protection.

And all week long Willie Clay was saying he could read my eyes. Sure, Clay had picked off a few of my passes when he was with the Lions, but I really didn't believe he had something on me. And even if he did, why say it? I would never say, "I think Willie Clay isn't going to be a factor," even if I believed it. There's nothing to gain. All it did was remind me to look him off, which is to say, make him think I was throwing to the other side of the field. It gave me just enough room to stick the ball in there to Free.

Clay wasn't the only Patriot who did a lot of talking all week. We were making positive comments and they were making negative ones. They'd say things like, "We know we're fourteen-point underdogs, but we're the better team and we're going to prove it."

Well, that's a good way to think if you keep it to yourself. If you don't, it only pisses off your opponent, which isn't a smart move when you're an AFC team and your conference hasn't won a Super Bowl in forever.

I also got sick and tired of hearing that the Patriots had an edge in coaching. Bill Parcells is a great coach, but so is Mike Holmgren. I think it frustrated Mike a little bit, which isn't like him. He'd come in and tell us, "Look, I'm the coaching underdog here, but you guys are fourteen-point favorites so it's up to you to get it done."

It pissed me off that the Patriots were trying to take the focus off the game by putting it on Parcells. We knew what the Patriots were trying to do, and Parcells is really good at it, but I think it takes more than that to win a Super Bowl. In my opinion, the whole "Parcells is leaving" issue was a convenient excuse if they lost.

Well, we didn't need any excuses. We played a pretty complete game. Offense. Defense. Special teams. Once again all three contributed in a big way. I thought we were in pretty good shape when I ran for a touchdown to put us up 27–14 at the half.

Mike Prior, a safety, made an interception to give us the ball at our 26. Then I hit Keith for 10 yards and Free for another 22. After that, Dorsey Levens took over. He ran

the rest of the way in four carries to get us down to the
Patriots' 2. On first-and-goal, I rolled left to throw to our
tight end, Mark Chmura, Chewy, but he was covered so I
took off running. Todd Collins, a linebacker, was closing
in so I reached out and got the ball across the corner of the
goal line just as he was taking me down. It was beautiful.
That was one time I was glad I'd worked so hard during
the off-season. I figured I added an extra step, and without
it, I don't think I'd have gotten into the end zone.

Even though the Patriots still had some fight left in 'em,
I was pretty sure the game was ours. I was certain when
Desmond Howard ran a third-quarter kickoff back 99
yards for a touchdown. It gave Desmond a Super Bowl rec-
ord of 244 return yards and earned him the Most Valuable
Player award.

Before the game, Bus predicted I'd be named the
game's MVP. I told him it would be nice, but first, I just
wanted to win. I think three or four years ago I wasn't
quite as productive because I wanted to do it all myself.
Maybe I was a little too selfish. It was like when Desmond
got tripped up at the 49ers' 5-yard line after that big punt
return in the NFC divisional play-off game in Green Bay.

If that were a regular-season game, I'd have been like,
"Great. I'll just throw for a touchdown and pad my stats
because we're going to win anyway."

In the play-offs it's totally different. When Desmond
started to trip, I felt like going out onto Lambeau Field and
throwing him across the goal line, I wanted him to get into
the end zone so bad.

It was the same with Dorsey in the Carolina game. He
had a huge day catching and running and I couldn't have
been happier for him. Actually I was happy that Desmond
won the MVP. I would've been happy if someone like Gilbert Brown or Sean Jones or Eugene Robinson or Dorsey

or Edgar won it because I'd had enough fame and all that stuff during the course of the season. After Desmond's touchdown there wasn't much left to do but sit back on the sidelines and let Reggie and the defense mop up.

Everyone in the place knew Reggie was going to put heat on Drew Bledsoe, but the Patriots decided to block him one-on-one anyway. Bad move. Reggie iced the game with a Super Bowl record of three sacks down the stretch. When he racked up his last one in the fourth quarter, I stepped into the huddle and said, "Well, men. We're Super Bowl champs."

I felt strange after the game.

I came into the locker room and thought huh, we just won the Super Bowl, but at that moment I was feeling like it was anticlimactic. The game is hyped so much that it's tough to know how to react after you win. Maybe it was because we knew we were going to win for quite a while before the game ended.

I went to the back of the locker room so there wouldn't be a horde of reporters around me when I came out of the shower. It was so loud in there and so hectic, I couldn't even hear Mike's postgame speech.

I asked Gordon "Red" Batty, our equipment man, to pack up my gear so I'd have it for the Pro Bowl that week. I had just won the biggest game of my life and I was worrying about my gear. Believe me, I totally enjoyed the game and I was excited, but it was still strange.

Winning the Super Bowl meant so much to me and I worked so hard to attain the championship and then bang! It was over.

I talked with some teammates who said they tried to cry after the game but they couldn't. I was the same way. I felt like I should be crying and getting real emotional and all that but I couldn't. Who knows? Maybe it was because after all the ups and downs that I went through, I could finally relax and not have to worry.

When the postgame interviews were finished, all the players were saying let's get dressed and go celebrate. They didn't want to hang around and neither did I, so I got showered and took Deanna to the Packers' victory party at the Fairmont Hotel. The organization went all out. They spent about $20,000 to throw what turned out to be a helluva party. I'd never seen everyone so thrilled and relieved and grateful for a championship as everyone who attended this thing. We stayed for a couple of hours and then went over to Mike Anderson's to party some more with family and friends.

I remember it was about three in the morning and I was throwing colored beads to Packers fans down on Bourbon Street. There must've been a thousand fans standing down there and I was leading them in chants of "Go Pack Go" and "We're No. 1." I was wearing a Green Bay fireman's helmet and throwing my empty drinking cups to the crowd after I finished a drink. Deanna and I stayed until about four in the morning.

The victory was the perfect way to cap an interesting week in New Orleans.

Personally I think the NFL should make New Orleans the permanent site of the Super Bowl. That's nothing against San Diego, which is a beautiful city and host to Super Bowl XXXII, but I'm biased. I've been to enough Mardi Gras celebrations to know my way around the French Quarter and all the fun to be had. I know New Orleans inside out. I grew up only sixty miles away. The food's great. The atmosphere is fun. The Superdome is a great place to play. It's a really convenient city to get around in.

All in all it's hard to beat.

Then again, my familiarity with New Orleans complicated some things.

For one thing, I was driving Chewy and Frankie nuts.
Whenever we went anywhere, I'd say, "Let's go here and
do this. Let's go there and do that." I was a pretty annoying tour guide. Finally Frankie says, "Dude, I know you've
been down this way before but let us see things ourselves.
Or are we going to have to hear this shit all week?" That
was Sunday night. We'd arrived that afternoon. Hey, I was
excited. This was even better than playing a regular-season game in New Orleans because we got to stay for a
whole week. I wanted to show them the town and if they
didn't like my tour-guide act, screw 'em. I kept right on
talking.

Getting enough tickets for relatives was another problem. New Orleans was so close; everyone wanted to go to
the game. I got as many tickets as I could, something like
twenty-five I think, but it still wasn't enough.

My mom did a great job of handling that whole situation, so I didn't have to worry about it. She held a ticket
lottery so no one's feelings would be hurt. Then she stayed
on the phone all week trying to find extra tickets. The last
I heard she came up with something like forty. It was impossible to make everyone happy, but Mom came close.

New Orleans had one other drawback.

Every time I fly down from Wisconsin to Louisiana, I
get sick. It could be three degrees below zero in Green Bay
and I'm fine, but I can go to New Orleans and it could be
seventy-five degrees and I'd still catch a cold.

I felt one coming on at practice Monday. It was sixty
degrees in Metaire, where the Saints' headquarters are located. We practiced outside for the first time in three
months. The sun felt good but my sinuses didn't. They
gradually got worse as the week went on.

I had planned to drive over to Kiln after practice Wednesday with Frankie and Chewy, but I felt like shit and the media were making such a big deal out of it, it wouldn't have been worth the hassle.

Mom and Dad had thirty-five newspaper reporters and ten television camera crews show up at the house on Monday. It was a zoo.

I was disappointed but I decided I was better off staying in New Orleans.

By Thursday's practice, I was feeling really lousy. It was seventy degrees but my body felt like it was freezing, so I headed straight for the hot tub. I was aching all over and the hot tub felt great. That night my temperature shot up to 102 degrees. I was worried. I waited my whole life to play in this game and now I was sick.

I called Dr. Gray, our team physician, to get some antibiotics. I took them, and in the middle of the night, I woke up in a sweat. I guess my fever finally broke because the next morning I was fine. The night before the game, I slept great. I fell asleep around ten with the TV clicker in my hand and I felt pretty good when I woke up.

One of the week's big stories—and a pretty big pain in the butt for me—was the news that I was drinking alcohol again. Well, I was, but I didn't think it was news.

The NFL told me in December that my status in its substance-abuse program had been changed from behavioral-referred to self-referred, meaning I was cleared to drink alcohol. The league didn't want to make a big deal out of it and neither did I. I wasn't planning on going out and getting drunk during Super Bowl week.

I had a few drinks during the course of the week, which was no problem, except someone saw me and the *Green Bay Press-Gazette* decided to call Bus. He told the newspaper that I was okay to drink, which was true, but that he hadn't seen it in writing from the league, which also was true. The league wasn't too thrilled with Bus's comments, so it put out a statement of its own. It said the NFL wouldn't rule on my status until the off-season.

I just wanted the story to die—it was a distraction I didn't need—so when anyone asked me, I said I hadn't been drinking. Shit. The league's substance-abuse program is supposed to be confidential, so I figured whatever I was doing in my spare time wasn't anyone's business anyway.

Well, the media bought the NFL's statement and the story eventually died down, for which I was grateful. It didn't stop me from having a few drinks on Friday night, but it reminded me to be a bit more discreet. As badly as I wanted to do it, I didn't think it would be a good idea to walk down Bourbon Street with a beer in my hand.

For the most part, the Super Bowl was a great experience.

I'd known for more than a year that the game was going to be played in New Orleans. When I found out, I told family, friends, teammates, everyone, "We've got to get there." It's so close to my hometown. I was thinking, what are the odds of a kid from little itty-bitty Kiln, Mississippi, making it to the NFL, much less getting a chance to play in a Super Bowl right down the street? They can't be good.

Yet here I was, living a dream, and it was everything I thought it would be. Best of all we won. It was a huge relief. If I never win another Super Bowl, at least I can say I won one. I don't ever have to worry about it again. It was something that a lot of great quarterbacks have never done. Dan Marino. Jim Kelly. John Elway. They're all great but they haven't done it, so I felt very honored.

I've also got to admit it was nice to be able to say, "I told you so," to everyone in the media who doubted me.

And there were plenty that did. I think it's fine for people to voice their opinion. If you take a stand, take it. If you think Brett Favre can't be as good as he was in '95 because of the drugs or whatever, that's fine. Go ahead and report it. But when I prove you wrong, be man enough to admit it. Don't come around sucking up to me after you write that shit. That's bull.

The main thing is I knew it was going to happen. I knew we were going to get to the Super Bowl. It was the perfect situation. It was close to my hometown and I knew my family and friends would be there. Everything had to fall into place and it did, and I knew it would. I just felt it. And I knew there was no way I was going to cut myself short. It's why I was so dedicated, why I worked so hard, why I did whatever I thought I had to do to get us to the Super Bowl. That way, if for some reason we didn't make it, I could always say that I did everything I possibly could. I didn't want to leave any doubts.

# 4

## CHILDHOOD

I had four dogs when I was growing up. One was a collie named Fluffy. Another one, a Saint Bernard, was named Whiskey. Then we had Bullet, who was a German shepherd. The last one was a chocolate Lab we called Lucky, who, it turned out, wasn't so lucky. Neither were the others. Alligators ate them all. Maybe we should've named the dogs Delicious—at least that's what the gators living by my house thought they were. Of course, losing a dog to whatever was swimming around in the mucky river water that ran in front of our house wasn't any big deal. It was just part of life when you're a kid growing up on the Rotten Bayou just outside of Kiln in southern Mississippi.

My home was about twelve miles from the Gulf of Mexico and so close to the Rotten Bayou that we could spit into it off our deck. My folks still live in the house where I grew up. I can't imagine them ever leaving. Why would they? That hundred-acre parcel of land, surrounded on three sides by the river, is as near to heaven as a couple of country people can get without shaking hands with Saint Peter.

Both my parents were teachers. Dad, or Big Irv as I call him, taught physical education and drivers education at Hancock North Central High School. A lot of kids in Hancock County learned how to do push-ups and how to parallel-park under Big Irv's direction. Most people in these parts, however, know Dad as a football coach. Dad coached football for twenty-nine years. All three of us boys—Scott, me, and Jeff—played quarterback for him at Hancock. My little sister, Brandi, probably would've, too, if Dad could've figured out a way to slap shoulder pads and a helmet on her and slip her onto the field without anyone noticing. Problem is, Brandi would have been noticed, she's that pretty. As a teenager she was named Miss Teen Mississippi.

Dad was a pretty good athlete himself. He was a helluva football player and good enough baseball player to pitch college and semipro ball. He has a way about him that makes people think he's tough. Well, he is. When Jeff was a senior, all the seniors on the football team had T-shirts printed up that said, "Hammer Time." That was Dad's nickname and it fit.

Mom taught special education at the school. I've never asked her if she knows what a down-and-out is, but she doesn't miss a thing when it comes to football or life. Mom's the kind of lady who speaks her mind, and if you don't like it, well that's too bad. She's also real protective of the whole family, and if you don't believe it, just say something bad about the Favres or the Frenches around her. Then get ready to duck.

Now, Mom is tough, but she also has a streak of compassion that runs deep. She had a heavy hand if we got out of line, but Dad was the disciplinarian. When Mom went into town to go shopping, we'd beg her to take us with her because the second she left, Dad would work our tails off. It was like being in the military. Dad would grab the rakes and say, "Let's get after it." He didn't want to be mean when Mom was there. She'd be like, "Irvin, leave those boys alone."

Ever since I can remember, Mom would be up at six in the morning getting breakfast cooked. It was never anything easy, either. It was always eggs, pancakes, biscuits and gravy. She'd do that every morning. When we were in high school, she'd make an extra-special breakfast on Friday mornings. She'd have a breakfast buffet going in the kitchen. We called it Touchdown Breakfast because we'd have a game that night.

I got spoiled. I went to college and it was either Pop-Tarts or cereal.

Dad likes to say that I got my strong arm from him and my smarts from Mom.

I'm just happy I got my good looks from Mom, although she can throw it pretty good, too. I'll never forget the time she showed me her arm strength firsthand.

When she wasn't teaching in the summer, she worked as the director of lifeguards at Diamondhead. Mom told the lifeguards not to call her if it rained. She said she'd let them know whether to come in to work. Well, she was in the kitchen making a pastrami sandwich and it started raining. Sure enough, the telephone rang and it was one of the lifeguards wondering if he should go to work.

Mom wasn't too thrilled and she let him know it, but I thought it was pretty funny, so I started making faces at her while she was on the phone. Now, I'm twenty-two at the time, but Mom didn't care. She got tired of me making those faces and all of a sudden she reached back and fired that pastrami sandwich at me. Hit me right in the head, too. Hmm. Maybe I did get more than just my good looks from Mom.

I like to kid my parents a lot but they're really special people. The way they raised us, the love they gave us, the time we spent as a family, it was so incredible. It still is. Because both Mom and Dad were teachers, I rode to school with them every day for twelve years. So did Brandi. So did Jeff. So did Scott. And when we played football, we played football for my dad. When we played baseball, we played baseball for my dad. We spent an unbelievable amount of time together.

My parents never missed a game I played in, whether it was a Little League baseball game, my first football game, all my high school games, or even my college games. They were there. I started in forty-three college games and they were there for every one. When you're little, you don't give that much thought, you just think that's the way things should be. It wasn't until I was older that it struck me how lucky I was.

One day I asked Mom, who grew up an only child, why it was that they made such an effort to be at every game. Mom just looked at me and said, "My dad missed my high school graduation. I didn't want any of you kids to feel that hurt."

Mom and Dad were always there for us kids and that means something.

We never had a lot of money growing up. Dad made $6,000 his first year of teaching, and that included coaching both football and baseball. Still, there wasn't much we missed out on. You could say we took life by storm from the get-go.

Mom was seven months pregnant with me in August 1969 when Hurricane Camille roared through the Gulf Coast. Camille really tore up the area, causing something like $1.5 billion in property damage. I think I was destined to cause just as much of a commotion. I certainly was big enough. When I was born October 10, 1969, I was twenty-one inches long and weighed nine pounds, fifteen ounces. Definitely a keeper. After the delivery, Mom's doctor came into her hospital room and shook his head.

"He's a big one, Bonita," the doctor said, smiling. "Right now he's back in the nursery doing push-ups."

Okay, so maybe I wasn't lifting weights at birth but I was getting into mischief before I could walk. When I was ten months old, I got my hands on some prescription medicine at home and almost killed myself. I swallowed like fifteen Percodans. My folks rushed me to the hospital, where I had to have my stomach pumped out. Other antics I pulled were just as hard for my folks to swallow. And a lot of those have to do with where I grew up.

Legend has it that the Rotten Bayou got its name because Indians dumped their old pelts in the river, causing it to stink. I don't know if that's true or not, but I do know that there's enough swimming around in that dark river water to make a fella think twice about going skinny-dipping. Not that any of those Rotten Bayou critters with big teeth stopped us, they just made the swimming—and the living—more interesting.

On Saturdays I watched *Tarzan* on TV like every other kid I knew. I loved that show because Tarzan always seemed to be wrestling around in the water with alligators or man-eating snakes or something else that could kill him if he didn't whip it first. What Tarzan did seemed as natural to me as walking barefoot in summer. I saw gators and snakes all the time. I thought every kid in America did. Tarzan's world was just like my world, and if I wanted to I could've jumped into the Rotten Bayou and wrestled just about anything Tarzan did. Of course, there was one time the alligators didn't wait for me to come to them.

One day Scott and I were home alone after school throwing rocks into the river. I was maybe eight at the time. Scott's three years older than me and whatever he did I did. To this day we are as close as two brothers can be. Well, combine my natural instinct for getting into things and Scott, shoot, he was worse than I was. Anyway, on this day we're messing around outside, seeing who can hit a pine tree with a rock across the river when we spot three alligators swimming around.

That's when I got the notion that it would be fun to feed them. We went inside the house, got some cookies, and threw them down in the water for the gators to eat. Well, we found out fast that gators like cookies. For the next few days we fed those gators as many cookies as we could find. After a week of this we had those gators trained. We'd get home from school and the same three gators would be waiting for us to feed them. We thought this was cool, until the day Dad came home early from coaching football.

Dad was pretty strict about things, especially when it came to his boys trying to make pets out of alligators.

By the time Dad pulled into the yard the three alligators were tired of waiting for their daily cookies and had started walking up the bank from the river to our house. I guess they thought they might have to help themselves. Dad spotted them and nearly lost it. He glared at Scott and me. But not for long because those gators were hungry and were headed our way. Dad ran into the house, grabbed his shotgun, and blasted a few shots over the gators' heads. I didn't know gators could move that fast. They hightailed it out of the yard and back into the river.

Scott and I weren't anywhere near as quick.

Dad turned on us and we froze like a couple of idiots.

"You boys ain't been feeding those gators, have you?" Dad asked, even though he sure the hell knew what we'd been up to.

Scott and I looked at each other. We knew Dad was pissed. Our imaginations worked fast trying to come up with something that would keep us from getting a licking. But all we managed to come up with was to deny everything.

"No, we ain't been feeding 'em," I said, praying Dad wouldn't take off his belt right then and there and whack my backside. "They just came up that hill on their own."

Dad knew we were lying. I just hoped he was thinking that Scott, being the oldest, should've known better. That was about all I had going for me. I braced myself for the worst. But Dad surprised me. He just walked away disgusted. It was a look I would become familiar with in the years to come. That was the last time we fed the alligators. But hardly the last time we got in trouble.

We grew up a close family, emotionally and physically. You could hardly swing a cat without hitting one of my relatives. My Grandma Mee-Maw lives in a trailer across the clearing from my parents' house. Next door to the trailer is a small house where my Aunt Kay-Kay lives. Aunts, uncles, cousins, they all lived nearby. And most of them were characters. Mom's late father, Bennie French, owned and ran a tavern on the beach. Grandma Mee-Maw used to tell me that Grandpa was an acquaintance of famed gangster Al Capone. Bonnie and Clyde, she said, also stopped by the bar on their way to Louisiana when they met their Maker. Grandma Mee-Maw ran the bar after my grandfather died. My middle name is Lorenzo, the same as Grandpa's.

After school when I was little we'd drive out to the bar

and run around or ride our Big Wheels around in the bar. Everybody in the place knew us. We were hell-raisers even back then.

I go back there today and all those people are like fifty or sixty years old now, but they still say, "I remember when you were running through my damn legs and punching people in the balls."

My grandfather built most of the family buildings back in 1943 with money he was making at Bennie French's Tavern. Grandma Mee-Maw, who's nearly eighty years old, sold the tavern a while back, but she still cooks some of the best gumbo, shrimp Creole, and red beans and rice on the Gulf Coast.

The first thing you have to know about Kiln is how to pronounce it: It's *Kill,* no "n." Why? Probably for the same reason that "Favre" rhymes with "carve." That's just the way it is; and the way my hometown is slow. And small. There isn't much to see in Kiln. As a matter of fact, you'd probably not know you're in Kiln even if you were smack-dab in the middle of it. About all there is, is a yellow caution light surrounded by a few businesses. The closest thing we ever had to a speed bump was a dead raccoon in the middle of the road. There isn't a town park or a maze of city streets. Mostly we just have red clay roads that wind their way off into the backwoods. The roads aren't numbered, either. Which is fine for everyone around here because we know where we're going. Forget the map, my dad tells visitors flying in from the north. If you're coming from New Orleans, you get off Interstate 10 at Exit 13, drive a ways, take a right at Dolly's Quick Stop, go a bit farther down a dirt road, take a right on Kapalama Drive, go a little ways more, and turn right at the second dirt road. You can't miss the place. It's at 1213 Irvin Favre Road.

They named the road after my dad. The roads used to have numbers but the police wanted to give them names so they could find people easier in case of emergencies. And since we're the only ones living on the road, they named it after Big Irv back in the 1970s. Problem is, they misspelled his name. So the road sign reads "Irvin Farve Road." Nobody's bothered to fix it. Why? It wouldn't change anything. Everybody knows my family lives down there.

Curley Hallman, my football coach at the University of Southern Mississippi, once described Kiln as "a place that's kind of like *The Dukes of Hazzard* minus the demolition derby." Coach Hallman wasn't that far off. Hell, I know people who can tear down a car engine by the time they're eleven or twelve. A lot of people here work on cars all day, party at night, and wrap it all up with a few barroom brawls.

People might be a little wild but they're loyal.

When the Atlanta Falcons traded me to the Packers after my rookie season, Atlanta's coach, Jerry Glanville, called me uncoachable. "Brett's the kind of kid you would kick out of kindergarten," Glanville said.

That comment didn't sit too well with folks in Kiln. Gladys Haas, my kindergarten teacher, who's about ninety years old now, wrote a letter to the local newspaper that tore into Glanville. She called me a model student, one she was proud of. Not many people know that I went ten years without missing a day of school.

A lot of people tell me they enjoy watching me play football because I look like I'm having so much fun playing. They tell me that I look like a little kid out there. And in a way, I take that as a compliment. I like the fact that I can still enjoy life like a child can enjoy life. I always loved the magic of being a kid, the feeling that anything is possible. Growing up, there always seemed like something special was happening, something I figured would last forever. I actually believed in Santa Claus until, I don't know, the fifth or sixth grade, which is kinda old, but I didn't want to believe that there wasn't a Santa Claus. It may sound kind of funny but I wanted to believe in Santa Claus for as long as possible because it was so much fun. Once you find out there's no Santa Claus, it kind of takes some of the magic out of Christmas.

When we were kids, Dad used to hide all our presents out in the shed or down in the barn or wherever he thought we wouldn't look. Jeff was the ringleader when it came to hunting for Christmas presents. He'd be telling us that he knew where Dad had stashed things and he'd go off digging in closets and all over the house looking for them. But I wouldn't want to find anything because, you know, the surprise part of Christmas, the magic part, was what I enjoyed the most. I'd wake up at three in the morning on Christmas Day and run right to the Christmas tree set in front of the big window in our living room to see what I had. It used to drive my parents nuts. They'd be trying to sleep and I'd be bouncing around the house.

Because of football, I haven't been back home for Christmas since 1989. God, I'd love to go back just one more time; to be in my old bed, to wake up in the middle of the night to see what toys Santa left for me under the Christmas tree. Just one more time. I know it wouldn't be the same, but still, it's hard to let go of some things.

The magic of Christmas stays with me today. I still think just about anything is possible. When you're a kid growing up in Kiln, Mississippi, you better think that way.

Because we lived in the country, there were never a lot of kids hanging around. Living in Green Bay, I can look out my front window and there's kids playing all the time.

My daughter, Brittany, goes over to someone's house down the end of the block and they play. I never had that luxury. But I did have two brothers. And sports.

When I was one year old, I got my first football uniform, including the helmet and shoulder pads, for Christmas. I got a baseball uniform shortly afterward. We always had a ball of some sort that we were throwing around. One of our favorite games was playing football in the yard. It was brutal. We used to take a hose, water down the yard, and put our football pads on. Then we'd get after it. We'd be flying around in the mud, knocking the crap out of each other. We played tackle football with whoever was around. Usually it was just the three boys. Noses got smashed. Fingers got mangled. There'd be blood. But there were never too many fights. There was a lot of arguing and a lot of shoving. We'd get pissed at each other, but that was it. We'd argue and the next day we'd be right out there again like nothing ever happened.

One game we made up as kids to pass the time was called goal-line. Scott and I would play defense and Jeff would play offense. We gave Jeff the ball 5 yards from the goal line and he had to try to score in four plays. And there was no running around us. Jeff had to run through us to score. We used to beat the shit out of him. God, we played that game all the time. Scott was in college and we'd still play it. Here's Jeff, about thirteen, and his two big brothers pounding on him. We busted each other up pretty good. But that's what we did for fun.

Because Scott was older and such a good athlete, I always looked up to him. And we always seemed to get in trouble together. It's a wonder neither of us got killed. One time when I was nine, Scott and I were goofing around with our BB guns and I shot him. In the face. It was an accident but Scott was still mad because it hurt like crazy.

See, we were outside shooting at trees. Well, you know with a BB gun you can shake it and hear the BBs rolling around inside. That's how you can tell how many BBs you have left. When you shake the gun and you don't hear anything, that's when you know you're out of ammo. So we're outside blinking away at things and I shake my gun. Nothing. I shot it four or five times and there's nothing but air. I was sure there weren't any BBs left. That's when I had an idea.

"Hey, Scott," I said, placing my BB gun under his chin, "you want to feel the compression of my gun on your face?"

Scott didn't blink. He just looked at me. "Go ahead and shoot," he said. "I dare you."

So I did. Poof! Guess I was wrong. There was one more BB in my gun. And now it was lodged in Scott's chin. But not for long. Scott dug the BB out with his fingers and ran off to tell Dad I shot him on purpose. I got whipped good for that one.

About a year later Scott was chasing me around outside. I can't remember what we were fighting about, nothing too serious, just brother stuff. We were always running around, hollering, chasing each other. Ours was not a quiet house. This time as Scott was after me I ran inside our barn and up into the loft. Scott was down below teasing me and threatening to come up after me.

"You better not," I said, picking up a brick, "or I'll throw this at you."

"I'm not afraid," Scott said, dancing around below me. "You couldn't hit me if you tried."

Scott should've known better than to dare me. I threw the brick hard. I missed and hit the ground. But a chunk of the brick flew up and hit Scott underneath the left eye. Christ, I thought I killed him. My folks rushed him to the hospital, where they stitched him up. It was always like that for Scott and me.

When I was sixteen, my parents bought new carpeting for the house. Scott and I took the old carpet and piled it up outside near the house. This, we figured, was going to be fun. I grabbed a football and Scott ran pass patterns. I threw him passes just long enough so that he had to dive into the carpet to make spectacular game-winning catches. It was great fun, until I led Scott a little, too. I threw long, and instead of Scott diving into the carpet, he dove right through the front window of the house. Smash! Glass flew everywhere. I thought he was dead for sure. But there wasn't a scratch on him. He bruised his hip a little bit, that was about it. The window, on the other hand, was totaled.

Mom never had to worry about us getting into too much trouble. I mean, we did manage not to kill each other. That's because we were mostly with Dad. He dragged us off to football or baseball practice every day. All of us. God, it was incredible to watch my dad coach at Hancock. I remember being a little kid, five or six years old, going out to watch the high school football practice thinking, "Someday I want to be just like those guys." In my eyes the players were gods. They were as big as trees and as strong as horses. They pushed the blocking sled back and forth on the practice field as if there was nothing to it. After practice I'd get a running start, lower my little shoulder, and drive into the sled—boom! That big sled threw me back on my butt like I was a bug.

Despite how big those players seemed to be, there was my dad, Big Irv, a squat but powerfully built Choctaw Indian, chewing their asses out. Nobody messed with him. I'd watch as he whipped my heroes into a team. I couldn't believe he was yelling at these grown-ups the same way he yelled at us at home. I remember standing on the sidelines thinking, "My dad has got some nuts."

By the time I was in the second grade sports were my life. If Dad's team lost I'd cry. If my two favorite pro teams, the New Orleans Saints or the Dallas Cowboys, lost I'd cry. Roger Staubach of the Cowboys and Archie Manning of the Saints, man, those were my two favorite players. I liked the Saints because they were so close to us, about sixty miles away. I really pulled for them, but they broke our hearts every year. I liked the Cowboys because they were so damn good. Roger Staubach, Drew Pearson, Robert Newhouse, Randy White, I knew them down the line. I was passionate about those teams. One year, the Cowboys lost to the Redskins in what seemed to me the most important game of the year. Afterward I went into my bedroom closet and cried my eyes out. It was the most painful feeling in the world.

Now I cry if the Cowboys beat us.

As far back as I can remember I was always bigger than other kids my age and I always played with older kids. When I was six years old, I played with the eight-year-old all-star baseball team. When I was thirteen, I started on the fourteen- and fifteen-year-old all-star baseball team. In the eighth grade I started on the high school baseball team at third base and led the team in hitting. When I was fourteen, I played for my dad on a sixteen-to-eighteen-year-old team. I really wanted to be back with my buddies playing in the league that was my age, but Dad said sorry, you're going to play with us. He knew the competition would be good for me, and he was right. By the time I got to college and later into professional football, playing with older guys was nothing new to me.

From a young age I knew I had something pretty special in my right arm. When I was in grade school and at

Dad's football practice, I'd be on the sidelines throwing as far as the high school quarterback. I knew that I had something that other kids didn't. I used to dream that my arm would take me somewhere special someday.

The first organized football game I played in I was in the fifth grade. Our team was scheduled to play in a jamboree, which is four teams playing round-robin. Believe it or not, Dad, Mr. Punctual, decided he had to get a haircut that Saturday morning. He would only go to one barber, nobody else. I don't know why. Dad wore a flattop. Not exactly a hairstyling challenge. So on the morning of my very first game I'm sitting in a Gulfport, Mississippi, barbershop in full uniform waiting for my dad to have the finishing touches put on his flattop. The jamboree was in Bay Saint Louis, a half hour away. I was not a happy fifth grader.

Our first game had already started when we got to the field. I was mad, but I was also nervous. My coach put me in right away at split end. On the first play I catch a pass, but when I get tackled, I fall on the ball and get the wind knocked out of me. There's nothing fun about having the wind knocked out of you, especially when you're in the fifth grade and you're sure you're going to die. I'm lying on the ground gasping for air, and nothing's happening. When I do catch my breath again, I start to cry. It was awful. I managed to get up and back to the sidelines.

"I hate playing split end," I told my coach. "I want to play quarterback."

Hell, I think he probably felt a little sorry for me, what with my near-death experience. The second game of the jamboree I played quarterback. I ran for two touchdowns and threw for another one. It was great. On the sidelines the cheerleaders were jumping around, cheering and going crazy every time I did something good. I looked over at them and I thought to myself, "Hey, quarterback is a cool position. It sure would be nice to play this for a long time."

The only bad thing about playing quarterback in grade school was that I didn't look the part. The problem was my helmet had a bar right down the middle like a line-backer's helmet. My helmet looked like something Ray Nitschke would've worn. In the seventh grade I took a hacksaw and cut the bar off. Enough of Nitschke, I wanted to look like Roger Staubach.

Growing up with a coach as your father made life sim-ple. In high school it was wake up in the morning, eat breakfast, and talk football. After school there was prac-tice. At home there was dinner and more football talk. I didn't party in high school. I was at home on Friday nights doing push-ups and sit-ups. My dad didn't make me do that, but somewhere along the way, I developed a strong commitment to that type of discipline by just being around him, by talking with him, and by watching him coach.

My dad was a pretty good athlete himself. Dad grew up in Gulfport, a block away from the football and baseball field. There wasn't much to do back then except play sports, so that's what he did. I think that because he played football and baseball, he knew as a coach how the game should be played. And he let his players know. My dad told me the same thing he told all his players: "If you get hurt, get off the field. If you can't crawl off the field, then I'll come out and get you. But don't give me any of that crybaby stuff where you're acting like you're dying out there. Don't pretend you're hurt when you're really not because you won't get any sympathy from me." To my dad, football was a physical and demanding sport. I learned a lot about toughness from him. Sure there are going to be times when you're hurting, but the same thing is true in life. Sometimes you get hit hard, and sometimes you don't feel like getting back up, but I always have, on and off the field.

A lot of kids would come up to me and say, "Ah, man, I'd hate for my dad to be my coach." They saw how hard he was on me. But to me, his rules and strictness were a good thing. Dad wanted me to concentrate on football, work out, run, do all that stuff.

On Friday nights after football games other guys would go out and party. Me, I'd go home to the back room and do push-ups, sit-ups, lift weights. I did that every night. But I *wanted* to do it, too. Dad just kept me focused. I knew I had to work harder than everyone else does, partly because I wasn't the most gifted athlete. Scott was a better high school quarterback than I was. Same with Jeff. But I was competitive. I wouldn't stop. I wouldn't let anyone beat me, I was so competitive.

I was a back-talker in high school. I thought I knew how things should be. There were times when Dad would tell me things and I'd look at him and say, "Screw that, I'm not doing that." He'd just look at me, set his jaw, and say, "Screw that, you *are* doing it." And I would.

Dad was competitive. He wanted to win and he'd do just about anything to motivate his team. He'd write letters to his own players, pretending they were from the other team. They'd say stuff like, "You no-good so-and-so, we're going to whip you." And the players believed it. We'd get so mad we'd want to kick some ass.

I was all pumped up to play for my dad my sophomore year but I came down with mononucleosis. So when the doctors told me I had mono the second day of practice, that was it. I was out for the season. The problem was that my spleen was enlarged from the disease and I was told that on contact it could explode and that I would bleed to death before I'd ever make it to the hospital. Hell, I didn't even know where my spleen was. I figured I didn't need to have it explode to find out. Turned out, mono was the best thing to happen to me. I was a skinny, skinny kid. Going into my sophomore year, I thought I was going to be a star, but I was kidding myself. I weighed only 160 pounds. On a windy day I was in trouble of getting blown over. I was tiny.

With nothing else to do but eat and work out, I put on about twenty-five pounds. And more than anything else I was hungry to play. The mono made me aware of just what playing football meant to me. I never had to sit out before and I didn't want to go through that again. By the time I was a junior I was so anxious to play I felt like a little kid.

When Ty Detmer was my backup at Green Bay, we got talking about high school football. He told me he threw for something like 6,000 yards in high school. I just looked at him. Damn, I threw for 800 yards total. But that's because we just didn't throw the ball much in high school. Dad ran a wishbone offense most of his coaching career. All three of us boys played quarterback and Dad stuck with that offense even though he knew we could all throw. The fact was before Dad started coaching Hancock, the team sucked. They lost something like thirty-six straight games at one point. And the games weren't close. There were scores like 71–0. It was terrible. So when he took over, he decided that instead of going nose-to-nose with teams, he would use a little misdirection and some option. That's when he decided to go with the wishbone. And we had some success with it. My junior year we switched to the Wing T and I threw maybe six or seven times a game. Tops. We went 8–3 my junior year and 7–4 my senior year. I don't know that we would've been any better if we had thrown more. We had two guys run for 1,000 yards, so we were pretty good.

The 838 Power Pitch, man, that was the play. I had the lead block and I'd go after whoever was in the way. We didn't have plays where you'd block a certain person. Hell, I'd come around the corner and whoever was in the way, I'd knock the shit out of them. To this day I still love to block and tackle. That's how I learned to play from my dad. Of course, I was pretty big, about six-two, 190 pounds, and I lifted weights. I was a lot stronger than I am now. I was benching 300-something pounds. I couldn't bench 300 pounds now to save my life.

Besides quarterback I played safety and punted. At safety I was slower than Christmas, but I hit anything that came my way. And I was a pretty decent punter. I had a strong leg, but it was my arm that got me attention. Back then I could really fling it, but I was wild; no touch at all. In practice guys would run little 5- or 10-yard routes and I would throw the ball as hard as I could. Bam! I'd bounced one off their chests or their helmets. There was no way they could catch those things. One time in a game my junior year I threw a touchdown pass to Tommy Lull so hard that when he went up in the air to catch it, it knocked him back two feet. I had a little to learn about touch.

There was a lot I had to learn, and not all of it was on the football field. I was never one for causes in high school. I'm more active in things now, but I'm still not big on politics or elections. I always figured things would happen the way they should happen whether I got involved or not. That changed a bit my senior year, the last time I've ever voted in an election. It was right before our homecoming game. At Hancock, the only people who could vote for homecoming queen were the senior football players. As I remember, there were only eight seniors that year, and only two were black. Color wasn't an issue on the team. Except that year. Hancock was a small school; there were only about a hundred kids in my class. Everyone on the homecoming court was a friend of mine, including Jackie Bush, who is black. No big deal, only there had never been a black homecoming queen at Hancock High School and Jackie was a candidate.

It was getting near the time when we had to vote for a queen. I was listening to some of the white guys sitting around the locker room saying things like, "Don't vote for that black girl" and "We don't want no black homecoming queen." I really don't think the guys meant to be racists about it. They were probably more scared than anything else. What would everyone think? To me, that was stupid. Don't get me wrong, there are black people I don't like. But there are white people I don't like, either. It has nothing to do with the color of their skin. It has to do with the person. It's that simple.

I remember Reggie White picking on me in Green Bay for being from Mississippi. He said he wouldn't ever visit me down there because he would be lynched. I know Reggie was just giving me a hard time; Lord knows I tease *him* enough. I told Reggie that my best friend in high school, Beno Lewis, is black. I know Reggie was just kidding, but I think he was surprised to hear that. But that's the perception about Mississippi, that everyone is a racist. It just isn't true.

Anyway, I talked to the guys on my high school team. I told them that not to vote for Jackie just because she's black wasn't right. I spoke my mind: "Jackie's a good person," I told them. "You all know her and you know it's so. So why not vote for her?"

Well, it turned out she won. Who knows, maybe I convinced the five or six white guys to vote for her. Like I've said, I've never been a real big activist for change. I'm not what you would call a civil rights leader. But I do know that I did the right thing. I'm sure Jackie Bush had no expectations of being named homecoming queen. And I'm sure everyone else didn't think she could, either. For a long time after that homecoming game, people talked about how Hancock High got a black homecoming queen. I thought: "Hey, it's about time."

From being a little kid to being a senior in high school, it seemed like my entire life was about rules. Everything was about discipline. For one thing, I could only talk fifteen minutes on the phone. Of course, that changed once I met Deanna.

There's another reason I'm grateful for having Scott as my brother: It was at his sixteenth birthday party—a surprise party Mom put together—that I met Deanna Tynes. I knew Deanna before the party, I mean, everybody knows everybody in Hancock County. I thought she was cute. She was a year older than I was with dark brown hair and beautiful green eyes. She was easy to notice all right, I just never really did anything about it. I was thirteen years old and I knew a lot more about sports than I did girls.

On Scott's birthday, Dad took Scott, Jeff, and me to a New Orleans Saints game. While we were gone, Mom set up the party. She had invited both the boys' and the girls' basketball teams, and Deanna, who was a helluva guard for the girls' varsity team, was there. Scott was surprised and we all had a good time, but as the evening wore on, the party kind of broke up a bit; kids splintered off into their own little groups. I noticed that Deanna went outside to shoot on our basketball hoop. It was getting dark but we had a light by the hoop, so I watched her for a while from inside the house. I worked up my courage to go talk to her while finishing off a hot dog. Outside I kind of flirted with her, if you can call taking the ball away from her flirting. We were both sort of shy and embarrassed, typical teenagers. But we were both athletes, so I think that made things easier. I took the basketball and started dunking, you know, showing off in front of her.

After a while of talking and shooting around, Scott and his girl and Deanna and I got in the car and went for a ride. It was dark by now and we went to the cemetery of all places. I never liked the cemetery or the dark, but this time it wasn't so bad. My hand brushed against Deanna's and it was like, "Whoa!" And I pulled it back real quick. After a while, I gave her a little kiss on the lips. I think we even held hands for about five seconds, but I was pretty darn nervous the whole time.

So began one of the great romances of our times. Well, it was great for us anyway. And even when it didn't seem so great, it sure wasn't boring.

Our first date was a Dedeaux dance. Dedeaux was this small town, not much more than a bump in the road with a quick stop. But it had this big ol' building where they held dances. Dedeaux dances, man, those were big-time back then. Everybody went. There was a DJ and they served Cokes and chips. It was strictly blue jeans and T-shirts. The first song we ever danced to was "Time Will Reveal," a slow song, naturally, by a group called Debarge. Life that night was just about as good as it gets.

We were both jocks, so we had a lot in common. Not only was Deanna a good basketball player—she was named all-conference and all-district her junior and senior years—she was a good fast-pitch softball player, too. She also took karate for three years in high school; not a bad thing to take when you're hanging around the Favre clan. Usually we just hung out together, talking and playing some kind of sport. I was a pitcher on the baseball team and for fun Deanna would catch me. That's how we would spend our time together. I didn't ease up either, just because she was a girl. I'd just fire fastballs at her. I knew her hand had to be on fire but she didn't let on. Hell, she was as hardheaded as I was. One day Dad's watching me pitch to Deanna from inside the house and he comes running out all hot and bothered.

"What in the hell are you doing, Brett?" Dad yells at me. "You're going to kill that poor girl. Don't throw that dang thing so hard."

I stopped my windup and looked at Dad.

"Why?" I shouted back. "She's catching 'em, ain't she?"

And you know, it seemed that no matter what I threw at Deanna, she could handle it. And believe me, I threw a lot of curves at her, and I'm not just talking about sports.

Deanna and I were almost inseparable in high school.

The thing is, she lived about fifteen or twenty miles away from me, so we spent every night on the telephone. That's about the time the fifteen-minute rule went by the wayside. Deanna and I talked nonstop every night. It was always about the future, and how great it was going to be. Mostly it was me bragging on how I was going to get a big football scholarship to Mississippi State or some other big school.

"You know, Deanna," I'd be whispering into the phone, "it's going to happen. You watch. I'm going to play big-time college football."

"I know you will, Brett," she'd whisper back.

Then I'd tell her how I was going to be so good that the college's alumni would buy me a car. A big one, too. And how I was going to play professional football someday. Deanna would always say, "I know you will." She was my biggest fan.

I remember Deanna telling her mom, who was a huge pro football fan, that I was awesome and that I was going to play professional football someday. Hell, Deanna had never even watched a pro game on TV. But she believed in me.

"Mama, Brett can throw the ball eighty yards," Deanna would tell her mother.

"Don't be silly, dear," her mama would say, "pro quarterbacks can't throw it that far."

But Deanna knew. Probably better than I even did. We'd talk and talk and talk on the telephone late into the night. We'd get so tired we'd fall asleep on the phone talking about our dreams.

My favorite song at the time was a tune by Phil Collins called "Against All Odds." That song pretty much characterized not only my sports career but also my relationship with Deanna. Because we were so much alike, both so strong-headed, we got in our share of fights. There were plenty of times that I had to work hard to patch things up. I'd put little notes on her car or in her school locker, trying to smooth things out. My junior year I wrote this poem to Deanna.

Roses are red/Violets are blue
You're my sweetheart/And I love you.
I love your smile/I love your hair,
Your presence is/Known with the gentle air.
Your hair is black/Your eyes are green
And I still love you/Even when you're mean.
You're a beautiful girl, I must say/I like to be around you, every day.
To end this poem, I want to say/That I love you now and will when
The skies are grey.

Ah, the innocence of young love. But you know, that's pretty much how it was back then. And how it still is today.

# 5

## COLLEGE DAYS

Coming out of high school, I was recruited by all the big schools in the area. Auburn. Alabama. Ole Miss. Mississippi State. Louisiana State. Now, when I say recruited, it was nothing more than a form letter or maybe an assistant coach stopping to say hello while he was passing through. No one ever followed up on anything. To those schools, I was just a name at the bottom of a very long list. In fact, the only guy who showed any genuine interest was Mark McHale, the offensive line coach at Southern Mississippi, which may explain my fondness for offensive linemen. Anyway, Coach McHale met my dad when he was on a recruiting trip the summer before my senior year at Hancock North Central. They talked some football, hit it off, and stayed in touch.

My senior season was a lot like my junior year. I was a hard-hitting safety with decent range and a quarterback who ran more than he threw. I averaged three pass attempts a game, but I could hand off with the best of 'em. My statistics weren't much to brag about. I passed for 460 yards and eight touchdowns as a senior. I wanted to play quarterback in college, but the reality was I'd probably wind up at safety, which is where I lined up in the Mississippi High School All-Star football game in Jackson.

I thought I could be a good college quarterback, but the problem was nobody had ever seen me throw. In high school, we operated out of the wishbone and the Wing T, neither of which will ever be confused with the run-and-shoot. By the time spring rolled around my senior year, not a single four-year school considered me much of a prospect at quarterback. The best offer came from Alabama, whose coaching staff thought I might make a fairly decent safety and special teams player. I thought about going there, but I didn't want to give up on my dream before it even had a chance. Naturally Dad figured I could play quarterback in college, too, so he called Coach McHale at Southern Miss to see if they might be interested. By now the recruiting period was over and there was no film of me throwing a football, so Dad told Coach McHale to come down to Hancock one afternoon to visit. Dad said, "I know you can't work him out, because that would be an NCAA violation. But suppose you stopped by just to shoot the bull with me. Suppose on your way out of my office, we happened to stop by the practice field. Suppose Brett just happened to be out there throwing a football."

Coach McHale said, "I suppose I better come down and take a look." He agreed to make the one-hour drive from Hattiesburg, probably as a favor to my dad more than anything. The next day, Coach McHale happened to show up during fifth period. By some amazing coincidence, I happened to be out there on the practice field really winging it. Dad was no dummy. Well, Coach McHale's jaw nearly hit the ground when I whistled one about 65 yards. He

told Dad, "Damn, we don't have anyone on our entire roster who can throw it that far." That was the first time he
actually saw me throw. Right then, he was convinced
Southern Miss ought to give me a scholarship. There was
only one problem. They didn't have any scholarships left
to give.

So there I was, five days before the signing deadline,
debating which two-year school I was going to attend.
When it came right down to it, only three schools offered
me a scholarship at quarterback. There was Delta State in
Cleveland, Mississippi, Mississippi College in Jackson,
and Pearl River Junior College in Poplarville. I told myself,
"What the hell. I'll go to Pearl River for two years, play it
out, and hope some four-year school offers me a scholarship." That was how my future shaped up until I got a
telephone call three days later. I was baby-sitting at my
aunt's house when Coach McHale called. He said, "Brett,
do you still want to play at Southern Miss?" It was a good
thing I was sitting down because I'd have fallen flat on my
face. I said, "Yeah, Coach. Hell yeah." Coach McHale said
a kid from Florida had backed out and he convinced Jim
Carmody, the head coach at USM, to offer me their final
scholarship. Southern Miss had six quarterbacks on the
roster, so I'd be seventh string, but at least I'd get a chance
to show the coaches what I could do at quarterback. That
was all I ever asked for to begin with.

The freshmen were scheduled to arrive six days before
the upperclassmen, which was very thoughtful of the
school officials. It gave us time to handle such pressing
concerns as taking a physical, locating a cool bar to hang
out in, and being assigned a jersey number. Well, my number was 10. That was my favorite number. I wore it from
fifth grade through my senior year of high school. I told
the equipment manager that and he said, "No, you can't

have 10. That's Reggie Collier's number and more than likely it's going to be retired. We're not giving it to anyone."

When I was growing up, two of my heroes were Roger Staubach and Terry Bradshaw, so I said, "How 'bout 12?" He said no, it was already taken.

Well, my brother Scott was always 11, so I said, "I'd like to have 11." He said no. That was already taken, too. Finally I said, "Well, what number *can* I have?"

He said they had one left. Four.

I said, "Four? I don't want 4. That's stupid."

He frowned. He said they had one hundred players on the roster. He said take it or leave it. I took it.

Well, it was the best thing that ever happened to me. It fits Brett Favre. There aren't many 4s out there. Southern Miss used it to promote me for the Heisman Trophy my junior year: "Favre 4 Heisman." I didn't win, but I loved the slogan.

The freshmen participate in what's called "double days" before the upperclassmen hit town. We'd work on offense in the morning and defense in the afternoon. I did both. My goal was to make the traveling squad. The top three players at each position traveled, so I figured I had a chance at safety. I was a lot smaller then and I moved pretty well. Quarterback was another story. We had Ailrick Young, Simmie Carter, David Forbes, Michael Jackson, Jay Stokes, and one other guy. I was seventh string.

My first chance to show my stuff came on the scout team. We were supposed to give the defense a good look and I was just killing them. Throwing bombs. Completing outs. All that stuff. The coaches were saying, "God dang, this guy ain't bad." I was still seventh string.

My next big chance came during a game commonly refered to as Suicide. That was when the freshmen would play against the upperclassmen. The rookies versus the big boys. The idea basically was for the freshmen to go out there and get killed. Michael Jackson, who is now a terrific receiver with the Baltimore Ravens, started at quarterback for the rookies. He was a great athlete and the coaching staff expected Michael to be USM's quarterback for a long time. Now, Jackson could run and he could throw, but he wasn't very accurate and he was playing pretty awful. After a couple days, the coaches said, "Brett, get in there." I played, and played well against the big boys. I threw for two touchdowns against the No. 1 defense in one scrimmage. From that day on, I worked my way up the depth chart. First, a couple guys got hurt. Then the coaches switched Jackson from quarterback to receiver. Before I knew it, I was third string and climbing fast.

We opened the season with a 38–6 loss at Alabama. The most exciting thing about that game was seeing 75,000 fans in the stands at Legion Field in Birmingham. It's pretty awesome. The second-most exciting thing was thinking I might go in with the third-team tight ends and offensive linemen near the end of the game. They didn't put me in, though. Coach Carmody was thinking about redshirting me, which meant I would have to sit out my freshman season, but still have four years of eligibility. That would've been okay, but I had a feeling I would play as a freshman. What I didn't know was it would be that week.

After the Bama game, Tulane was up next. Ailrick Young started at quarterback and was playing okay, but we were getting our asses kicked. Simmie Carter replaced Ailrick in the second quarter, but he wasn't doing much, either. At halftime, Coach McHale told Coach Carmody to put me in. Coach McHale said, "Hell, he can't do any worse." I could tell Coach Carmody liked the idea, but I didn't really think I was going to get into the game. Besides, I felt like shit. Chris Ryals, my roommate and a freshman offensive lineman, and I played a game called Quarters the night before in our dorm room. The rules for Quarters are pretty basic. You get a quarter—we didn't have any change, so we used a washer off the sink—and try to bounce it in the other guy's beer glass. If you get it in, he drinks. If you don't, you drink. You get the idea. We went through a case of Schaefer Light that night. It was the beer of choice because we didn't have any money. Six bucks a case. Not bad. Back then, I thought all beer tasted the same. I made one awful mistake that night. I tried to keep up with Chris, who is a monster. He stands six-eight and weighs 310 pounds. I paid for it the next day against Tulane.

It was 110 degrees in Hattiesburg and I was about to throw up on the sidelines from the heat and the game of Quarters the night before when Coach Carmody turned to me and said, "You're going in." My balls were in my throat and I said, "Are you for real?" I was seventeen. A true freshman. He said, "I'm for real. Get in there." Wow. I tugged on my helmet and trotted into the huddle. I looked around and the offensive linemen were all seniors. These guys were twenty-one, twenty-two years old. Big fifth-year seniors. They said, "C'mon, Favre. You can do it." We were down 17–3 to Tulane, but they still believed in me. That was because I wasn't a total stranger to them. I would hang out at the North End Zone and the Judge's Chambers whenever they asked me.

Now I was calling the shots in the huddle. I was nervous as hell, but things couldn't have worked out much better. I drove us down the field on our first series, even though I didn't know the offense all that well. I'll never forget my first touchdown pass. We ran a little bootleg where you fake one way and roll out the other. I just knew it was going to work. Well, when I rolled out, Chris McGee, a senior receiver and one of our leaders, was wide open. I threw a balloon and the ball just fluttered down. It was an awful-looking pass but he caught it and I went crazy. There have been a lot of touchdown passes since, but that was my first and I acted like it. I ran over to Coach Carmody and jumped on him and hugged him. He was so excited, he hugged me, too. We were like two little kids out there. Hell, there really was one little kid out there. Me. I threw another touchdown pass and we rallied to win 31–24. It was a great day.

The next week, Coach McHale sat me down and said, "We're going to start you." We were playing Texas A&M in Jackson. The Aggies were coached by Jackie Sherrill, one of the best of all time, and they were ranked in the Associated Press Top Ten. It was no big surprise that we got beat that day, 28–14, but I played pretty good. I started every game the rest of that season. I completed 79 of 194 passes for 1,264 yards and fifteen touchdowns, which was a school record. Not bad for a seventh-string quarterback.

That probably makes my freshman year sound pretty carefree, but actually it took a while to get adjusted to college life. At first, I thought it was pretty cool to be away from home for the first time. Mom and Dad were always pretty strict with us. I would never even dream of drinking or staying out late in high school. I had to be home by ten o'clock on weekends. Unless Deanna and I had a date, most weekends I wouldn't even bother going out. In college it was different. I was my own man. I could get up, go to class, and stay out all night if I wanted to. I didn't have to ask Mom and Dad anymore.

Sure enough, I got homesick. That might sound stupid, but it was true. I was only seventy-five miles north of the

Kiln, but I missed it something awful. I missed Mom and Dad and Jeff and Brandi and Mee-Maw and Kay-Kay. I missed Scott, who was attending Delta State. I missed home-cooked meals. I called every night. I was a home-body at heart.

Luckily, between classes and football and my roommate, I kept pretty busy.

Chris Ryals, my left tackle, was actually my second roommate. My first roommate was a linebacker from Slidell, Louisiana, named Alan Anderson. We lasted all of two weeks. We got along as friends, but not as roommates. Shoot, I thought you could get along with anyone. Well, Alan had some annoying habits. One thing he did was talk constantly to his girlfriend, Vanessa, on the telephone. He'd have a big dip in his mouth that made him sound like he had a speech impediment. He'd sit on the phone for hours saying, "I love you, Vanetha." Good Lord. It made me about puke. I sat there thinking, "To hell with Vanetha. Get off the damn phone already."

Finally I figured out a way to get Alan to move out. When he was out partying one night, I took tacks and stuck them through the cover sheet on his bed. I had about five friends hiding when he came into the room. He got undressed, hopped into bed, and started to scream. He was going, "Ouch! Oh! Uh! Ouch! Shit!" It tore him up. Everyone was laughing their ass off. Everyone except Alan. He was pissed. He said, "I'm going to put a snake in your bed." I said, "Okay, Alan."

The next day he moved out. When I see him now, we hug and talk about old times. Alan's a great guy. He just wasn't a very good roommate. Chris Ryals, on the other hand, was the greatest roommate. He moved in and we hit it off perfect. He was from Purvis, Mississippi. A great guy. Chris would . . . talk . . . real . . . slow. You wouldn't know it, but he was smart as a whip. A perfect 4.0 in computer engineering. We roomed together for four years at USM. Coach McHale said we were inseparable. Well, we were. When we were sophomores, our beds really sucked. We were too big to be comfortable in bunk beds, so we decided to get two king-size mattresses and box springs from home and push them together. That way we had plenty of room to sleep and still get around the room. People would come in and say, "God, do you guys sleep together?" No. He was way on one side and I was on the other. We never knew the other guy was there.

Every Monday night we would go down to the North End Zone and eat chili dogs, drink pitchers of beer, shoot pool, and watch *Monday Night Football*. The End Zone was a great bar. It was the players' hangout. Our jerseys were up on the wall and the owner was a helluva guy. Man, I would eat about twenty chili dogs, they were so good. And best of all, they were free, which was key when you're a college student.

When I wasn't at practice or the North End Zone, I was trying to learn the offense. We ran the I-formation. It was toss sweep and off-tackle stuff with drop-back passing mixed in. I didn't understand the passing game very well, so it was difficult. Now I look back and think it was pretty simple. When you passed, the backs would split and block for you. In Green Bay, there are guys going in motion, guys going out for passes in every direction and about four or five different protections. At USM, it was basic. We'd run plays like 75 XYZ Cross. The 75 was the protection. X and Y would cross. Or 75 Right Z Hook. The Z receiver would run a hook. Like I said, it was pretty basic, but coming from the Wing T, it seemed fairly complicated.

By my sophomore year, I had developed a decent command of the I-formation and it showed. We went 10–2 under first-year coach Curley Hallman, including a 38–18 victory over UTEP in the Independence Bowl. I set single-season records for passing yards (2,271), total offense (2,256), and touchdown passes (sixteen). I threw just five interceptions in 319 attempts for a 1.57 interception ratio, which was the lowest in the nation among the top fifty passers. Coach Hallman was very supportive of me and started pushing me as a Heisman candidate going into my junior year.

He told reporters, "If you go back at the end of last year and look at the top players in the country, and that's what the Heisman Trophy is supposed to represent, then you have to throw Brett's name in there with the best ten. The mark of a truly great player is that he makes the other players around him look a little bit better. And Brett has that kind of quality about him."

That was a really nice thing for Coach Hallman to say, especially because I knew he meant it. Before he came to USM, he coached the defensive backs at Texas A&M. He remembered me having a pretty good day against them as a freshman. But most of all, he remembered my composure.

"We came after him hard all day and never got to him," Coach Hallman said. "I'll never forget that. I could tell then that he was something special."

Coach Hallman also knew something that only a handful of my relatives and closest friends knew. Deanna was pregnant. I found out during the summer before my sophomore year. We reacted like any young couple. We were scared.

I tried to concentrate on football while we were sorting everything out, but it was tough. I wasn't myself. Instead of being happy-go-lucky and carefree, I was pretty somber. A million things were going through my mind. Would I have to quit school? Was my football career finished? Where would I get a job to pay for the baby? Not surprisingly, I wasn't playing very well when fall workouts started. I was pretty distracted, to say the least. My reads weren't sharp and my passes were all over the place. I was pretty down.

It didn't take long for Dad to know something was wrong. Occasionally he would drive up to Hattiesburg from the Kiln to watch me practice. He could tell I wasn't myself. He suspected that Deanna was pregnant, but he didn't say anything to me. He figured I would tell him when I was good and ready, which I did the next weekend at home. Dad and I were sitting in the living room talking and I just blurted it out. It was the hardest thing I had ever done in my life. Well, he didn't say a word. He just got up and went to the kitchen and started doing the dishes. That's what Dad does when he gets upset. He does the dishes. While he was in the kitchen, I sat there thinking about all the times Dad and I would be together when I was in high school and he would say, "I know you really like that girl, but whatever you do, don't go getting her in trouble."

That was the closest Dad ever came to telling me about the birds and the bees. Now, sure enough, I'd gone out and done exactly what he told me not to do. Well, when he finished with the dishes, he came back into the living room and sat down next to me. He looked me straight in the eye and said, "I'm not going to preach to you. I'm not going to scold you. All I'm going to say is that I expect you to step up and be a man about this. Your mom and I will do everything we can to help, but this is your responsibility, okay? Now, how are you going to handle this?"

Whew! I felt like a two-ton weight had been lifted from my shoulders. Deanna was off somewhere telling my mom at the same time. When we all got together, we sat down and had a big discussion. Abortion was not an option. We were raised Catholic, so there was no way that was going to happen. Hell, it wasn't our baby's fault. We talked about me dropping out of school, quitting football, and getting a job, but I didn't want that and neither did Deanna. We figured that would only make things worse. Naturally we talked about getting married. Deanna didn't think we were ready and I agreed. We had seen too many friends get pregnant and then get married because "it's the right thing to do." Yeah, right. Then two years later they're divorced. Or they stay together but they're miserable, which doesn't do them or the child much good.

We thought about what people might say because I got Deanna pregnant. I said, "Well, who cares what people say?" Besides, no one is stupid. If you get married and have a baby seven months later, people figure it out. If we got married, it was going to be because we wanted to, not because we had to.

Dad said, "I don't think you should get married unless you really want to, and frankly I don't think that's what either of you want." Mom felt the same way and Deanna's parents agreed. No one said, "Well, you better get married because it'll look bad if you don't." Today, neither one of us regrets our decision. We're happily married and we have an adorable little girl. We couldn't imagine life without Brittany.

I'd be lying if I told you being a teenage parent was easy. It wasn't. Deanna and I tried living together but it didn't work out. We were just too immature. We were like a lot of other young couples. Money was tight and we argued over stupid things. I moved out but we stayed in touch. I talked to both Deanna and Brittany all the time. We just didn't live together.

Thankfully with Deanna being a great mom and our parents helping us out, I didn't have to quit football. In some ways, having Brittany helped my game. It settled me down. Well, a little, anyway.

We opened my junior year on the road against top-ranked Florida State. The Seminoles were loaded with talent. Nobody in the country gave us a prayer. The Las Vegas bookies made us 27-point underdogs. We didn't care. We were coming off a 10–2 season, we had some decent talent, and we were in great shape. Coach Hallman worked our asses off to get us ready for the Seminoles. He ran us to death and it paid off. The game was in Jacksonville, Florida, on September 2. It was brutally hot and humid. It must've been 120 degrees in the stands. It was so hot, the stadium's security officers had to take about a hundred people to the hospital for heat exhaustion. Well, the heat was our best friend. Apparently Florida State Coach Bobby Bowden didn't make his players run much. The Seminoles were so talented and so deep, they thought they didn't need to bother.

The gap in conditioning showed, especially along the line. Our defensive front was knocking their offensive line off the ball. The Seminoles' asses were dragging. Our offensive line blocked great, too. I threw two interceptions, but I also threw two touchdown passes. I came through when they needed me. I completed 21 of 39 passes for 282 yards. One of my touchdown passes came over the head of LeRoy Butler, currently the Packers' strong safety. To this day, LeRoy gets pissed when I talk to him about it. It was a little rollout play and LeRoy, a cornerback then, came up to hit me. When he got close, I just lobbed the ball over his head to tight end Anthony Harris for 6 points and the game-winning touchdown with twenty-three seconds to play. It was awesome. Once we got the lead, we hung on, hung on, hung on. About midway through the fourth quarter, we went from thinking, "We can't possibly win this game" to "We're going to win this game." After the touchdown to Harris, Chris Ryals turned to me and said, "Can you believe it?" I just smiled and said, "Hell yes!"

The plane ride back to Hattiesburg was unbelievable. We mimicked the Seminoles' tomahawk chop all the way home. There were twenty thousand people waiting to greet us at the airport, which is more than we got for home games. When we got to the North End Zone, the craziness continued. Every time ESPN would show highlights of the upset, we'd all start tomahawk chopping and chanting, "Hey, oh! Hey, oh!" We were riding high. When the rankings came out on Monday, the *Sporting News* had us twelfth in the nation.

We didn't stay there long. We lost the next three games and finished 5–6.

I was disappointed with our record in '89, so I was determined that my senior year was going to be special, which it was, but not before a couple of trips to the hospital.

In May, I had bone spurs removed from my right elbow. Actually that was a good thing because the surgeon did such a great job, I was throwing better than ever.

In July, I had this little head-on collision with a tree and the tree won. It was a beautiful Saturday and Scott, USM linebacker Keith Loescher, and I had spent it fishing on the Gulf. It was about 110 degrees and we were sunburned. We stopped fishing around seven o'clock, just before sundown, and headed for home. I was going to hit the shower and catch a movie with Deanna, who was playing in a softball tournament that day. I was driving alone in my brand-new white Nissan Maxima, and Keith and Scott were following me. I was going about 70 mph, which was a lot faster than I should've been going. I'd driven down that road a million times and I guess I took it for granted. I was about seven-tenths of a mile from my parents' house when my right front tire hit some loose gravel on the shoulder. I corrected the steering wheel, but because I was going so fast, the car shot across the road. My Maxima hit a culvert, slid down an embankment, flipped three times in the air, and smashed into a pine tree. The bumper skidded off the bark as it slid down the side of the tree. Scott said you could've driven a dump truck underneath my car, it was that high off the ground. I was knocked out cold.

When I came to, there was glass all over. Scott was bashing in the front window with a golf club to get to me. He thought I was dead. The automatic seat belt probably saved my life. My car had hit the tree with such force, the seat belt snapped. But instead of being thrown from the car and killed, I ended up in the backseat. When I looked up and saw Scott, I asked if I'd been in a plane crash. I couldn't see anything but glass and trees. Scott and Keith tried to lift me out of the car, but my back was killing me. Eventually they slid me out onto the road. Mom rode to the hospital with me in the ambulance. All I kept asking her was, "Am I going to be able to play football again?" Every bump in the road was painful. I winced. She just said, "Honey, I don't know." When I got to the emergency room, the doctor told me I had a fractured vertebra, a lacerated liver, a severely bruised abdomen, and lots of abrasions. He said, "There is no way you're playing football this year."

Well, that ticked me off. I said, "Just watch me."

It was July 14. The season opener was in six weeks.

The accident was nasty. My side hurt so bad, I couldn't

move for a week. I was in intensive care for three days. I couldn't get out of bed. A nurse had to come in and bathe me. Mom or Dad would clean me up after I went to the bathroom. Talk about parents making the ultimate sacrifice for their kid. Everyone was real nice to me when they heard about the car wreck. I got phone calls from the head coaches of other teams. Hell, I didn't even know they knew me. Gene Stallings, the coach at Alabama, even called. It was pretty funny. He called right after I'd taken some pain medication, so I was out of it. He wished me a speedy recovery, and I said, "Thanks, Coach." Then I took a nap, but when I woke up I was pretty excited. I told everyone Bear Bryant had called to see how I was doing. The nurses probably thought I'd sustained a head injury, too. Bear Bryant had died years before.

I went home after five days and everything was going fine for three weeks. Then my stomach started hurting again. I mean hurting real bad. I would eat, but the food wouldn't pass. I'd throw it back up and then I'd be okay. The doctors said it was just a reaction to the trauma. I said, "Screw that. I'm dying. Something's wrong here." I went back to the hospital and the doctors discovered that thirty inches of my intestine had been crushed and died. The doctors said I didn't have to worry because I had eight feet of the stuff. So thirty inches wasn't so bad. I'd joke that without it, "I could shit a little quicker now." Actually the unexpected intestine surgery on August 7 was nothing to joke about. It kept me from returning in time for our season opener against Delta State. I weighed 226 pounds the day before the car wreck. When I went back to Hattiesburg in mid-August, I weighed 192. I had lost thirty-four pounds in six weeks. I was weak as a kitten and skinny as a scarecrow. And if it wasn't for Mom's home cookin', I'd have been in a lot worse shape.

I was in no condition to play against Delta State. Then again, Delta State was in no condition to play against USM. We beat the hell out of them. The final was 12–0, but it could've been worse. Next up was Alabama in Coach Stallings's first game at Legion Field in Birmingham. The big talk all week was "Will Favre play?" I looked awful, but I was strong enough to practice a little bit at least. Coach Hallman came up to me on Friday and said, "Brett, can you play?"

I said, "Sure."

He thought that was great news. He also thought Alabama didn't need to know it. So he decided to start John Whitcomb, a redshirt freshman, at quarterback. Then after the first play, I would come running into the game. It sounded pretty hokey. I liked it.

Everything went according to plan. John took one snap, I ran onto the field, and 86,000 Bama fans were actually clapping for me. I'd never heard of Alabama fans treating an opposing player like that. When I got into the huddle, all of the guys had tears in their eyes. It was a great reception, right up to the snap.

The first play was a pass. I dropped back, threw, and got drilled. I was laid out flat. The whole place went silent. Everybody was thinking, "Oh, man, he busted his stomach open." Larry "Doc" Harrington, our head trainer, came running onto the field. He leaned over me and said, "Oh, God, Brett. What's wrong?"

I couldn't breathe. I was about to throw up.

"Doc, I got hit in the balls."

"Oh, good," Doc said. "Stay down."

And I'm saying, "No. Not good."

Then Doc does the old conventional lift-up method for ball resuscitation. Now, everybody in the stands sees that and knows what the hell is going on. They start laughing.

I went to the sidelines, threw up, and came back into the game. Well, it didn't take long for the Alabama fans to quiet down. Jim Taylor, our place kicker, nailed field goals from 45 and 53 yards. Kerry Valrie, a senior safety, returned an interception 75 yards for a touchdown. And Tony Smith, our running back, scored on touchdown runs of 4 yards and 3 yards. Interestingly Smith was the player the Atlanta Falcons selected with the seventeenth pick in the 1992 NFL draft, the pick they acquired by trading me to Green Bay.

The Crimson Tide outgained us 442 yards to 195 yards in total offense, but we still came away with a 27–24 upset victory. I was pretty weak, but I managed to complete 9 of 17 passes for 125 yards and an interception. I was sacked twice, but I survived. Alabama Coach Stallings was pissed. He thought we pulled one over on him by not saying I was going to play. And I guess we did.

The next week we were at Georgia and the Bulldogs had us down 18–17 with two minutes to play. I drove us to the Georgia 25-yard line before we stalled with fifty-four seconds to play. Taylor came on and attempted a 42-yard field goal. He hit the hell out of it, but the damn ball hit the right upright and bounced back onto the field. We didn't get down, though. We won five straight after that before losing to Virginia Tech 20–16 in Blacksburg, Virginia. We closed out with wins over Southwestern Louisiana and a monster road upset of Auburn, 13–12. We were 8–2, which was good enough to earn a berth in the All-American Bowl. I was named the game's Most Valuable Player, but we lost to North Carolina State, 31–27. We were a total of eight points away from an unbeaten season.

I was invited to the East-West Shrine game and played well enough to be named Most Valuable Player. I finished my career at Southern Miss with school records for yards

(8,193), pass attempts (1,234), completions (656), completion percentage (53.0), and touchdowns (55). I was most proud of my interception ratio (2.9), which ranked among the all-time career best in NCAA history.

Several NFL teams considered me a fairly high draft pick, but they wanted to see me up close, so I held a pre-draft workout in Hattiesburg. About twenty coaches and scouts showed up. Ron Wolf. Lindy Infante. Ken Meyer. June Jones. Mike White. I thought it was real impressive that all these guys were coming down to work me out.

It was the first time I met Mike Holmgren.

I had what I considered a really good workout. I made all the throws. I showed pretty good agility. My accuracy was decent. I felt good about it. Afterward, Coach Holmgren came up to me. I knew he was the quarterbacks coach of the 49ers, which was pretty impressive. All the coaches and scouts said hello to me, but Mike was one of the few who took the time to sit down with me in the stands. He told me, to be totally honest, that the 49ers weren't going to select a quarterback. They had Joe Montana and Steve Young and Steve Bono. They didn't need one. "We're pretty set there," Mike said. "But for future reference, if I ever need it, I wanted to work you out and see for myself. Somebody will probably take you fairly early. I wish you luck."

As the draft drew near, there were conflicting reports regarding when I would go. June Jones, the quarterbacks coach with Atlanta, said he thought the Falcons would take me with the thirteenth pick. They held the fifth, thirteenth, and thirty-third picks. A scout with the Saints told Bus he thought I was going to go in the top fifteen, but he didn't think I could move out of the pocket well enough to go that high. Shoot, that's what I do best.

Ron Wolf, the Jets' scouting director, came to Hattiesburg to watch film of me after my senior season. He was in the film room for about an hour when he came out and told our sports information director he wasn't too impressed. Our SID said, "That's because of his car accident. Check out the film from his junior year." Wolf turned around, went back in, and took another look. He liked what he saw.

When draft day came, I was nervous. I was hoping to go high, maybe in the top fifteen, but my name wasn't called. Dan McGwire went to the Seattle Seahawks in the first round. We were on the same team in the Senior Bowl, so I knew what he could do. He was big. If people were looking for a big, robo-type quarterback, that's what they got. He was six-six, six-seven, 240 pounds. He didn't have as strong an arm as me. He wasn't smarter than me. He didn't move as well. He wasn't as good as me, but then, I didn't think any quarterback in my class was better than me.

Todd Marinovich went to the Los Angeles Raiders in the first round. Weird dude. When the Raiders played the Kansas City Chiefs in the play-offs one year, he drew a little mustache on the guy on the Raiders' helmet. I thought that was pretty cool. I liked him. But he's out of football. Now he's playing in a band up and down the West Coast, eating cheeseburgers and junk food because his dad wouldn't let him when he was growing up.

The Falcons took Bruce Pickens, a cornerback from Nebraska, with the fifth pick. Then they took Mike Pritchard, a receiver from Colorado, with the thirteenth pick. The teams kept picking and my name kept sliding. When the first round was over, I was pissed. A lot of teams that told me they were going to take me in the first round had lied. Finally Atlanta took me with the thirty-third pick. At that point, I was just happy to get drafted and get it over with. Besides, I thought Atlanta would be a good time. Wolf, who was with the New York Jets at the time, ended up taking Louisville's Browning Nagle with the next pick.

# 6

# THE EARLY YEARS

I was running late.

I'd been out partying the night before and I forgot to set the alarm for my first (and last) team photo in Atlanta. I was supposed to be there at nine in the morning. But between oversleeping and the midmorning traffic, it was about ten o'clock when I finally showed up at One Falcon Place, the team's headquarters in Suwanee.

On my way into the parking lot, I noticed Jerry Glanville's van was already on the way out. I pulled my truck next to him and rolled down the window. I explained that I got caught behind a wreck. He took one look at me, shook his head, and said, "You are a wreck. This will cost you $1,500." Then he rolled up his window and drove off.

That summed up my career in Atlanta.

The only time I ever did anything that impressed Glanville was right before a game against the Rams at Anaheim Stadium. I told one of my teammates I could throw a football into the upper deck. Glanville overheard me and said, "I'll bet you $100 you can't." I told him he was on. Then

I reached back and fired a football into the upper deck. It was a lot farther than it looked, but the ball cleared the railing. Glanville reached into his pocket and pulled out a hundred bucks. We were never going to be best buddies.

I played all right in the exhibition season. I completed 14 of 34 passes for 160 yards, two touchdowns, and one interception. Then I sat the bench behind Chris Miller and Billy Joe Tolliver. I was never quite sure why Glanville picked up Billy Joe in a trade with San Diego early in the regular season. June Jones, the quarterbacks coach, told me it was because they didn't want to rush me in there.

No chance of that. I played in just two games and threw five passes. Two were intercepted. It didn't bother me. I figured my chance would come soon enough.

After the season, June said the Falcons planned to keep me around a long time, and if not, I was going to play somewhere for sure, no matter what happened as far as trades and stuff. I guess it never occurred to me that June might be trying to tell me something. That was in early February. A week later, I was traded to Green Bay.

I was at my parents' eating crawdaddies and drinking a few cold ones when Ron Wolf called. He'd just acquired me in a trade with Atlanta. He sent the second of the Packers' two first-round picks in the '92 draft, the seventeenth overall, to the Falcons. He seemed genuinely pleased to get me. He said he expected big things.

I heard what Ron was saying and I really appreciated it. But I was shocked Atlanta gave up on me. I knew Glanville wasn't thrilled with me, but I always figured he was smart enough to give me a chance there anyway. I was wrong. When I look back on it, I enjoyed my time with the Falcons. My teammates and coaches were great. The only thing I didn't like, aside from the $1,500 fine, was not being able to get off the bench.

Oh, well. I had a fresh start. I didn't want to dwell on the past. I told myself it was great that Ron and the Packers thought enough of me to send the Falcons a first-round pick. It boosted my confidence, especially after sitting the bench for a year. I was excited about coming to Green Bay.

There was just one problem. I had to find out where it was.

Getting to Green Bay proved to be no big deal. Staying there was another matter. I failed my physical.

Clarence Novotny, the team physician, discovered what the Seattle Seahawks already knew. My left hip was degenerative. I suffered from vascular necrosis. It's the same condition that put a premature end to Bo Jackson's NFL career. The blood stops flowing to the bones in that area and they slowly rot out. I injured it in the East-West Shrine game after my senior year. It was the only reason the Seahawks drafted McGwire instead of me that year. Their management didn't want to take a risk.

Ron felt different.

He was determined that I was the Packers' quarterback of the future. When Dr. Novotny informed Ron that I had failed my physical, he studied the chart, got a second opinion, and said, "No. We're not failing him." The necrosis didn't put me in any danger on the field. It just meant Ron was willing to risk a first-round pick against the chance that I might be finished after a couple years. He could've voided the trade with Atlanta and gotten back his pick, but he didn't. He believed in me. I knew I had a bad hip, but I didn't know the Packers had failed me until a few years later when one of our assistant trainers showed me my medical chart. Across the top it read, "FAILED PHYSICAL." In Dr. Novotny's opinion, I'd probably be out of the league in four or five years. In Ron's opinion—which is the one that matters most in Green Bay—I was worth the gamble anyway. It turned out he was right, although I must admit my first two months with the Packers weren't smooth sailing.

I celebrated my own arrival in Green Bay by partying the night before my first minicamp practice in a Packers uniform. I've always been a sucker for really good country music, and it just so happened that Brooks and Dunn, Reba McEntire, and Travis Tritt were performing at the Brown County Arena, which is just across the street from the Packers' indoor practice facility. The way the night went, I might as well have slept at the arena and walked to practice the next morning. Talk about a hangover.

Shoot, it all started innocent enough. A gal at the front desk of the Best Western I was staying in said she had extra tickets to the concert. I didn't know who Brooks and Dunn were at the time, but I had met Travis Tritt in Atlanta. I figured it would be fun to go to the concert and get together with him afterward. I didn't particularly want to go to the concert alone, though, so I invited Nolan Cromwell, our special teams coach.

Well, we went to the concert and had a big time. We walked around the arena, drank some beers, and got to go backstage with Travis. After the show, he invited us to party in his bus. It was awesome. I partied until Lord knows how late.

The next morning I paid the price.

I felt like shit and I threw the same way. The ball was going all over the place. To make matters worse, the receivers weren't used to catching a football with that much velocity. I was skipping passes at their feet. I was bouncing them off their helmets. Their hands. You name it. I didn't feel too bad, though, because Don Majkowski, the starting quarterback, wasn't doing any better. He was coming off a shoulder injury and his passes weren't any better than mine. Besides, we were both new to the offense.

Neither one of us really knew what was up.

I don't know if Mike ever knew I was out drinking the night before, but it didn't take long for Steve Mariucci, our quarterbacks coach, to get wind of it. Or should I say, to get downwind of it. Mooch smelled alcohol on my breath, so he pulled me aside after practice. He said, "You can't do that. You've got to tighten up. This whole organization has a lot invested in you." At first I thought he doesn't know me. What gives him the right to tell me what I need to do? I just got here. Well, the more I thought about it, the more I realized Steve was right. That wasn't the way for an NFL quarterback to act. Right then I made a vow. No more partying the night before a minicamp opens.

That was in April.

I've kept that promise ever since, except for one time in 1993 when I showed up at practice too hung over to participate. We had beaten Denver on a nationally televised Sunday night game that week. It was our bye week that weekend, so Mike scheduled a short Friday morning workout and we had the rest of the weekend off.

It just so happened that Travis Tritt and the country band Little Texas were playing at the Brown County Arena on Thursday night. So a bunch of us went to the concert and had a great time. Afterward, Little Texas asked if I wanted to go on their bus and I was like, "Hell yes." I got into the bus and it started moving. They drove us over to the Holiday Inn, which is where they were staying in town.

Wow, that bus was awesome. It had an entertainment center, a living room in the back, everything. I was sitting on this long couch just shooting the bull with the band when one of the guys said, "Get up a minute." He flipped up the seat and there was a cooler full of Labatt's Blue Ice underneath it. Hell, I was sitting on a gold mine and didn't even know it. Well, we partied until about three in the morning, then the band packed up its stuff and said they had to get on the road that night. So I'm like, "See y'all." And I give 'em a hug and they drive off.

That was great, except here I am, standing in the Holiday Inn parking lot with no way to get home and I'm thinking, "What in the hell am I doing?" It's 3:30 in the morning and we've got practice the next day. I rode to the concert with Chewy and Frankie, but we got separated, so I figured I better call a cab.

Well, I'm waiting and waiting and finally I see a cab outside, but the cabbie is nowhere to be found. Apparently he'd gone inside to find me, so I jump in the cab and get on the CB. I'm going "Breaker One Nine" and talking shit. I was pretty drunk.

Finally the cabbie comes out and says, "Get off the CB."

I did and he took me home. I thought I'd set my alarm for 7:30 so I could get up for practice, but I must've forgot. I'm sleeping on my couch fully clothed when the phone rings. I ain't answering it. Then I hear the voice on the answering machine.

"Hey, dumb shit. It's Frank. We've got practice in five minutes. Get your ass over here."

Click.

All in one motion I'm up. I didn't even brush my teeth. I had my clothes on, my watch on, and I'm up and out the door in one breath. I drive to Lambeau Field, hustle into the locker room, and grab my jersey, my helmet, my shorts. I didn't even bother dressing. I just jumped back in my truck and drove it to the practice facility across the parking lot. I pulled it around the back and got dressed

right there. No taping. No nothing. And I come running
into practice. My eyes were bloodshot. I'm sure I stunk.
Mariucci asked where I was. I told him my alarm didn't
go off and he's like, "I don't want to hear it."

Guys were dogging me when I came onto the field, but
I was just laughing. I was still drunk. I took a few snaps
and I'm bouncing passes. I'm high. I'm low. Finally Mooch
says, "That's it. Out."

So I stood in the back of the line and didn't take any
more snaps.

It wasn't a big deal because we had a bye that weekend
and it was a once-in-a-lifetime thing. As funny as it was,
I'd never do that again. It's the only time I've ever shown
up for practice less than totally ready to perform. That's
only happened twice, once before the bye week in '93, and
back on that April day before my first minicamp.

When our June minicamp rolled around in '92, I was a
model citizen. I studied the playbook, worked hard, and
tried to be sharp on every throw. I was feeling pretty good
about things and I was making friends on the team.

Esera Tuaolo, a second-year nose tackle, and I really hit
it off. We both came from pretty big families, we enjoyed
music, and we liked to laugh. I decided to invite him
down to Mississippi to hang out with me and my family
for a week. Esera, who is Hawaiian, had never been down
South before, so I figured he'd get a kick out of it.

Well, the first night we went to a bar in Hattiesburg.
It was one I'd hardly ever gone to. It was called Ropers
Nightclub, a country bar, and I got about twenty guys together and we went over there. It was perfect. It was five
dollars for all you could drink and it was Ladies' Night.
We were drinking Alabama Slammers. I don't know what
goes into those things, but boom! We were slammin' 'em.

We got there about eight and the bar didn't close until

four in the morning. We knew it wouldn't be long before we'd be on our way to oblivion. It was a big bar and it was jam-packed. We were just hanging out, relaxing, when Deanna, my girlfriend, walked into the place. She was still going to college in Hattiesburg and was upset because I came to town without calling her. I went over to talk to her, but man, I was smashed.

We started to argue, over what only the good Lord knows, when the next thing I knew, some guy came up and hit me. He was going to take it upon himself to be a tough guy—even though Deanna had no idea who he was. He was just a little ol' fart, but he sucker-punched me. I went down and then I jumped up and grabbed him. Right then I noticed I had blood all over my face. It all happened so fast Esera and the other guys couldn't get over there quick enough. All they knew was that there was this fight on the other side of the bar. Finally they must've gotten curious or something and they walked over. There was this huge pile of bodies and they're looking at it and all of a sudden, I came out from the bottom of it.

They were like, "Damn, Brett. What are you doing down there?"

Then the cops showed up.

I wanted them to arrest the guy who hit me. The cops tried to calm me down, but I was pissed off. They said, "If you don't shut up, we're going to arrest you."

I said, "That's typical." So they arrested me.

Then Deanna—she's defending me by this time—starts yelling at the cops and they arrest her for cursing. She hadn't hardly said anything. So then I pointed to Esera and said, "He's with me. I guess that means you're going to arrest him, too." So they arrested him. Then my little brother, Jeff, started bitching about them arresting Esera.

He said, "Why arrest him? He didn't do anything." Naturally the cops arrested Jeff, too.

We ended up with four of us in custody.

I was charged with public drunkenness, disorderly conduct, and profanity. Jeff was cited for interfering with a police officer. Esera was charged with disorderly conduct. Deanna was charged with profanity and interfering with a police officer.

On the ride to the police station, I told the cop he ought to be ashamed of himself for handcuffing a girl. I said some other things, too, and finally he told me to shut up. So I said, "Why don't you just pull over and drop your gun? We'll take these cuffs off, step out of the car, and I'll whip your ass." Lucky for me the cop just kept driving.

Esera, Jeff, and I sat in the drunk tank for four hours.

Deanna sat in the lobby.

We didn't talk much in the cell, except Esera kept saying we were going to be in big trouble. He was afraid Coach Holmgren might fine us, or worse, cut us. I told him to quit worrying about it. I told him nobody would find out about this. Well, the next day the brawl was on the front page of the *USA Today* sports section.

Everybody knew about it.

My agent, Bus Cook, got us out of jail for fifty bucks apiece. I had blood all over my T-shirt and two black eyes from getting punched in the nose. The news about the fight was everywhere, and on top of that my family was furious.

My folks were embarrassed, especially my mom. I think Dad was upset more because Mom was mad than anything. If she hadn't been so ticked off, he probably would've accepted it, chalking it up to boys being boys. But Mom kept saying I was a pro quarterback who had just got traded, and just when things were looking up, I had gone out and got arrested. I heard what she was saying, but I suppose I was too naïve at the time to think it would really affect anything.

I knew it would take Mom and Dad some time to simmer down, so I figured there was only one solution. Road trip. I told Esera and a couple of buddies, "Guys, it's time to load the truck up. We're heading to Florida for some fun in the sun."

When we got to Fort Lauderdale, I called home and Dad told me to call Coach Holmgren. He wanted to talk to me right away. My stomach did a somersault. Finally I got in touch with him. He was vacationing in California. He wasn't too happy with me.

Mike said, "We just can't have this. You can't play for me and do all the things you did all your life." I tried to explain to him what had happened, but he said my side of the story was irrelevent. He said I was in all the newspapers for fighting. The whole conversation lasted about ten minutes. It was short and not too sweet.

Mike told me to take care of myself and, before I forgot, I should give a call to Ron Wolf, our general manager. More somersaults.

I was really nervous while I was dialing. When I got Ron, I asked him how he was doing and he said everything was okay. He asked me how things were and I said things were fine. Then he said, "Let me ask you something. Did you kick the guy's ass?"

I said I didn't get a chance because the guy suckerpunched me. Then he said, "Goddamn it, Brett. If you're going to fight 'em, you got to kick their ass."

Talk about two totally different conversations.

After I hung up with Ron, it was real quiet in the hotel room. The guys were sitting there looking at me, wondering if I'd gotten fined or worse. The mood was way too serious. Nobody was saying anything, so I reached into the cooler, pulled out a cold one, and poof! I cracked it open. The guys let loose a cheer and we were back at it. Hell, I thought it went pretty well with Ron. I felt good about myself again. Now, in the back of my mind, what Mike said woke me up a bit. I knew he was right. He's coached the best. Montana. Young. BYU. Super Bowls. MVPs. I knew he'd been around great players, great organizations. I knew he knew what he was talking about.

As hardheaded as I was, I knew I had to change. I just wasn't going to change that weekend.

Besides, I didn't figure there was any hurry. Don Majkowski was the starting quarterback. He had that name that stuck in everyone's mind. The Majik Man. He was a good quarterback. A nice guy. Talented. You could tell his arm was never the same after he got hurt in 1990 and had shoulder surgery. I felt like in time, I would get a chance to play, but he was smooth in the huddle. He was the starter. I didn't see that changing, at least not early in the 1992 season. I was wrong.

Minnesota beat us 23–20 in overtime in the season opener and Tampa Bay hammered us 31–3 the next week. I played the second half against the Bucs and was awful. I threw an interception and was sacked four times. About the only memorable thing I did was complete a pass to myself. The ball got batted into the air and I caught it. The play went for a 7-yard loss. It summed up how we played that day.

We didn't look much better the next week at home against Cincinnati. Midway through a scoreless first quarter, Don got sacked by Tim Krumrie and tore ligaments in his left ankle. Mike turned to me and said, "You're in." I was nervous. Everybody kept coming up and saying, "You'll be okay. Just go out and play." I went out and played, all right. I was all over the place, like a chicken with his head cut off. The Bengals led 17–3 after three quarters and it didn't look good, but I wasn't about to give up.

Our chances improved when Terrell Buckley returned a punt 58 yards for a touchdown and I hit Sterling Sharpe from 5 yards out to make it 20–17. After the Bengals added a field goal, we had one last shot. We took over at our 8-yard line with no time-outs and 1:07 to play in the game. The Bengals were playing man-to-man coverage the whole day and whipping us good, so when they came out in zone coverage on that last drive, I couldn't believe it. I hit Sterling up the sideline for 42 yards and eventually drove us to the Bengals' 35-yard line. We called 2 Jet All Go, where we send four receivers up the field. I looked hard and pumped at one of the safeties to keep him in the middle of the field and then I threw it to Kitrick Taylor up the right sideline. I was so scared I thought I was going to throw it halfway up into the seats. When I threw it, I closed my eyes and I was just listening for a cheer. I didn't have to wait long. Kitrick caught it and we won 24–23. I was running around the field looking for people to hug. Just my luck, I found 300-pound guard Ron Hallstrom. I head-butted him with my helmet and split open my forehead. I had blood running down my face but I didn't feel it.

I played pretty wild but had found a way to get it done, which is my trait. I knew there was no way I was going to sit the bench again. I had too much fun that day. This was where I belonged. I knew if I prepared harder and harder each week, things would work out. Mike didn't say much after the game. He told me he was proud of me and that I played well, but I had a long ways to go. I agreed. I just didn't know how long.

I started the next week and we beat Pittsburgh 17–3. I used a pump fake to beat Rod Woodson, the Steelers' All-Pro cornerback, for a 76-yard touchdown to Sterling. It was awesome. I was more giddy than mature. I ran down the field and jumped on Sterling. I wanted to celebrate with everyone else. I did that for a couple weeks before Mike called me into his office. He told me, "You're hitting our guys low. I'm not worried about *you*—you're too far out of it to get hurt—but you're going to end up hurting someone else. If you do it again, I'm going to fine you $5,000."

That was the end of tackling my own guys.

It was just one of many changes Mike demanded of me.

For the next two and a half seasons, from 1992 through the midway point of 1994, we had our moments. I was baffled as to why I was so up and down. Mike was frustrated more than anything. He's a real professional. Very rarely does he come in and joke around with the guys before meetings. He is bright, intelligent, and very regimented. It's boom, boom, boom at practice. Even if we screw something up, he keeps us on a tight timeline and that's it. What that teaches you is to get it right the first time. Well, I couldn't get it right the first time. The offense was very overwhelming. Atlanta's offense was easy by comparison. When I got to Green Bay, the playbook was a foot thick. The verbiage was unbelievable. It was a totally new language. You've got Brown Right Slot A Right 2 Jet Dino Wash All Across. That's one play. Red Right 22 Texas. Brown Left Tight Close F Right Sprint Solid Z Quick Drag. That's two more plays. There are hundreds of them. Just when you think you've got it, they flop the formations, and you have to learn it the other way. Then you've got to read the defense and apply it to what you're doing.

Now I'm to the point where Mike can throw in a new play and, click, the concept is there. I know what's going on. It took a couple of years to get the hang of that. A couple of long years. There were times, especially during the exhibition season in '92, when I would call just an off-the-wall audible and the play wouldn't even be close to being completed. I'd go to the sideline and Mike would say, "Why did you do that?" Most of the time I didn't have an answer. I didn't know why I did it, so I'd say, "I thought I saw something." Then he would say, "Well, fuck, Brett. In this game you can't think you saw something. You've got to see it." When you're young and you're learning, you tend to think you see the blitz coming when the reality of it is the defense is sitting back in a normal coverage. Mike calls it seeing ghosts. Those first couple seasons I'd swear Casper was playing free safety. Mike found no humor in that.

When I screwed up in practice, he'd get pissed off. He would raise his voice, curse, bitch, and complain. He was bursting my ego the whole time. We were grown men and I was being embarrassed in front of fifty guys on a daily basis. I was like, "Screw him." I wanted to do it my own way and the hell with him.

I thought there must be a better way.

There wasn't.

That sunk in over a couple of years. Mike was the coach and he knew what he was doing. He knew he had to be hard on me. Looking back on it, it was the right thing to do. That didn't make it any easier at the time. I always knew Mike was really pissed at me when he wouldn't talk to me. I'd pass him in the hallway and he wouldn't even look at me. I guess he felt like if he started talking to me, he'd just lay into me for screwing up the day before and he didn't want to do that. He had no problem verbally abusing me in front of everyone at practice, but he wouldn't do it in the hallway. He would just give me the cold shoulder and we'd start all over again the next day at practice.

I didn't think I'd be around long. Mike was bitching at me right and left those first couple of seasons. I figured one day he would come in and say, "Screw it. I've had enough. Favre's outta here."

It turned out Mike's capacity for patience was huge. More than I first suspected. Harping on me was just his way of getting me to where I am today. It's not an easy thing to admit, but as tough as he was on me, I'll be forever grateful.

Now when I look back, I'm not surprised I was so hot and cold. I hadn't played in Atlanta, so essentially I was a rookie. This is an extremely difficult offense to be consistent in, especially at such a young age. I was twenty-three when I took over in Green Bay. That was the youngest any quarterback ever started in this system. Joe Montana. Steve Young. Steve Bono. They all had the benefit of sitting and watching for a few years before they took over. I never had that luxury. I was learning on the fly and it showed.

In '92, most defenses laid back and waited for me to make mistakes. That allowed me to get comfortable enough to have some success. I threw eighteen touchdown passes, compared with only thirteen interceptions, and it was good enough to make the Pro Bowl.

The next season was something else. Defenses stopped sitting back and started attacking. They blitzed everyone from everywhere. I was shell-shocked. My confidence suffered and I started throwing too many interceptions. Casper the Ghost owned me. I threw twenty-four interceptions and my quarterback rating of 72.2 was a career low.

To make matters worse, the fans had come to expect more because of what I'd done in '92.

They didn't realize I was still new to the system. I was learning in front of sixty thousand fans and my mistakes were replayed over and over. There wasn't much patience in Green Bay. The fans had been waiting thirty years, which is one helluva long time, for a winner. They didn't want to have to wait another thirty years. The average fan figures you're making a lot of money so they expect you to do it right now. It doesn't work that way. I was trying too hard. Instead of letting the system work for me, it was working against me.

Now if I make a mistake, I remember to be patient. Back then I was always trying to make up for the bad things with a touchdown on the next play. I was forcing the issue. When you're going through that, there is no way to take a step back and realize what's going on. That's why I think young quarterbacks need to sit and watch and learn for a year. Then when they get their chance, at least they know what to expect.

There's a fine line between struggling and stardom. For two and a half seasons, I did a tightrope act on that line. There was no consistency. It was good play, bad play. Good play, good play, bad play. The team was the same way. We finished 9–7 in '93 to become the first Packers team since 1972 to make the play-offs in a nonstrike season. It was also the first time the Packers had back-to-back winning seasons since 1966 and '67. We were making progress, but it was slow. We finished the '93 season by going win, loss, win, loss, win, loss, win, loss. It was one long roller-coaster ride.

My personal life was about the same.

I lived in an apartment my first three seasons in Green Bay. I was lonely. Scott lived with me for part of my first season. So did Mark Haverty, a good friend from back home. The next year it was Clark Henegan. We had met at Southern Miss and roomed together one summer. We got along great and he didn't have much going on down in Mississippi, so he came and lived with me. He would run errands, hang out, clean the apartment, and cook. His specialty was Chicken a la Clark. Or Beef a la Clark. Or Pork a la Clark. He'd just use the same gravy and switch the meat.

It was a bachelor's life.

Deanna and I still talked all the time on the phone, but we weren't making any long-term plans. Everything was pretty much on hold with us, even though I still considered her my girlfriend. The only real game plan I had in my life was the one I tried to execute on Sundays. Everything else was easy come, easy go.

Personally I was living for the moment.

Professionally I was disappointed with the way I played in '93. The inconsistency was driving me crazy. We won six of seven games in one stretch during the second half of the season, but I was still learning and struggling. I threw four interceptions in the regular-season finale at Detroit. We lost 30–20 and it cost us the NFC Central title. A headline in the *Milwaukee Sentinel* read, "Favre's Mistakes Difficult to Excuse."

Everyone was frustrated, including me.

The next week we opened at Detroit in the play-offs. This was my chance for revenge and I made the most of it. We were losing 24–21 with less than a minute to play and the ball at the Lions' 40-yard line. I called Red Left 25 Okey Double Squareouts at the line. It was supposed to put Sterling on the left side, except he was tired from the previous play, so he stayed on the right side. Detroit rolled up the cornerbacks, so they're in double coverage and you can't throw an out. The receivers are supposed to adjust and run fade routes. I dropped back and looked left for Sterling. He wasn't there. So I looked for Ed West over the middle. He was covered, but I noticed the safety was cheating way inside. He was watching me and he didn't think I could throw it behind him.

When I saw that, I turned, wheeled, and threw it. Sterling was wide open up the right sideline behind the safety. We won 28–24. Revenge was sweet, even if it didn't last too long. We lost at Dallas 27–17 the next week. What's new? I played pretty good, completing 28 of 45 passes for 331 yards and two touchdowns. After the game, some guys were excited we only lost by ten points. I wasn't. I knew we still had a long ways to go to catch Dallas. I also knew some people doubted me.

I rolled into the '94 season convinced we were going to be really good. I was right, but not before we hit on some hard times early in the season. I'd have a great game and then a bad game. One week I'd be on. We'd be calling the right plays and it was perfect. The next week, we'd call a play at the line and I was still learning and still making mistakes and I played that way. I thought we should be better and I started pressing.

The bottom nearly fell out in week 7 at Minnesota. I got hit in the first quarter and bruised my left hip. I tried to play, but I could hardly walk. At halftime, I told Mike I thought I could go back in. He said he was staying with Mark Brunell. Well, that was it. I thought Mark would be the guy the rest of the season. We lost 13–10 in overtime and our record dropped to 3–4. Mike was pulling his hair out. He had about had enough of me.

I met with Steve Mariucci, our quarterbacks coach, the next day. Steve said Mike was thinking about replacing me. A couple of assistant coaches felt the same way. I wasn't surprised. I could tell by the way they acted toward me in practice. If I made a play, no one said anything. If Mark made a play, they'd go, "Good throw, Mark."

Steve said he fought to keep me in there and Mike agreed to stick with me. I don't know if Mike was just trying to get my attention, but it worked. I was pissed. We had that weekend off—we'd played the Vikings on a Thursday night—and I went home to Mississippi. I did a lot of soul-searching and when I came back I had one goal. I was going to be the best quarterback in the NFL.

The challenge turned out to be good for me. I was a different quarterback when I returned. It's hard to explain, but everything started coming together for me. I was seeing things a lot clearer. I started understanding my division better. I started realizing what plays worked and what plays didn't. It was a snowball effect.

Ever since then, I've been the best quarterback in the league.

Someone showed me my statistics before and after that Minnesota game and it's incredible. Before that, I had a 21–17 won-lost record with 46 touchdowns, 44 interceptions, and a 78.5 passer rating. Since then my record is 30–11 with 101 touchdown passes, 33 interceptions, and a 98.4 passer rating.

It was like day and night.

We won seven of our next ten games, including a 16–12 victory over Detroit in the play-offs. The game was at Lambeau Field and our defense played great. We held the Lions' Barry Sanders to negative yardage. That was when I knew we were coming together as a team. We lost the next week at Dallas, but I felt we were heading the right direction. After that nightmare at Minnesota, I never looked back. I truly felt like I was going to be the NFL's next great quarterback. That confidence made a ton of difference.

The 1994 season was critical for another reason. That was the year, in my opinion, that I became the leader on offense. Until then, Sterling was the guy. The first time I challenged him was during training camp. I had signed a four-year, $19-million contract extension in the off-season and Sterling was envious. One day in practice, I threw two bad passes in a row to him. One was high. The other was low. He came back to the huddle and said, "For $19 million, you ought to be able to put it right on my hands." I was so pissed I started shaking. I told him, "Shut the fuck up and catch the ball." Everything got real quiet. I thought we were going to fight right there. Well, Sterling didn't say another word. He just stepped into the huddle and listened for the next play.

It was strange. Midway through the season, Sterling was hurting with a hamstring injury. He couldn't practice and he could barely run well enough to play in games. Sterling's production dropped but we were winning. I was getting more comfortable in the offense all the time, so I was going to whoever was open. The low point for Sterling came when we beat the New York Jets at Lambeau Field. Early in the second half, Sterling's hamstring was so sore he limped off the field.

That week Mike asked me if Sterling and I were fighting or something. He wanted to know why I wasn't throwing the ball to him. I said we weren't fighting; it was just how it was going in the offense. Hell, I want to complete passes and throw touchdowns more than anyone. I'd never say, "Screw Sterling, he's wide open but I'm going to go to someone else." Mike said, "Well, you need to try to get him back in the game a little bit." I said, "I'll do what I can do, but I'm just playing."

We played Buffalo, Dallas, and Detroit, and Sterling caught six touchdown passes in those games, so I guess you could say I got him back into the game.

It was at that point that my game really started to come on, and it set the stage for a special 1995 season.

I started playing like I knew I could and so did the team. I threw for thirty-eight touchdowns and a league-high 4,413 yards to win the NFL's Most Valuable Player award. One of my fondest memories was of a play that occurred during a 35–13 win over Tampa Bay. We were inside the Bucs' 10-yard line and the play was supposed to be a rollout right and a toss to tight end Mark Chmura in the corner of the end zone. One problem. Chmura got knocked down at the line. Another quarterback might have thrown it away and tried on the next down. Not me.

I did a 180-degree spin and, at the same time, glanced over the field. I caught a glimpse of Robert Brooks near the back of the end zone and threw the ball back across my body. It barely got there over one defender and ahead of two others. When I got to the sidelines, Mike grabbed me and said, "Did you know what you were doing?"

I said I did and Mike said, "That was the best play I've ever seen in my life." Coming from him, that was quite a compliment. I was like, "Whoa!" My chest came out a little bit. It was the kind of play that helped me win the MVP award.

We also made huge strides as a team. We went 11–5 and we won the franchise's first NFC Central Division title in twenty-three years. We hammered Atlanta 37–20 in a wild-card game at Lambeau Field. After the game, I'm walking off the field thinking one thing: I hope we play San Francisco next. That's what everybody was talking about. That's who everybody wanted. That's who Mike really, really wanted. It was his hometown and his old team. We figured it would mean a lot to him if we knocked them out of the play-offs. It didn't take long for us to find out how badly he wanted it. It happened the first thing Monday morning. We sat down for the team meeting and Mike walked in.

Now, he and Reggie White have this deal going. If Mike curses, he gives Reggie's charity a hundred bucks. Anyway, Mike comes into the room, looks around, and the first thing he said was, "We're going to beat these fuckers."

We were shocked. Mike said "Here" to Reggie and handed him a hundred dollars. Then he looked around and said it even louder. *"We're going to beat these fuckers!"* and he forks over another hundred bucks.

I was like, "Whew! We're getting ready to kick their ass." After the meeting, everybody was fired up and saying how we were going to get the 49ers. That really sparked us. I came out of that meeting thinking, "Mike's right. We can win. We can beat San Francisco."

People might be surprised that we still, most of us anyway, have the desire to win. To the little kid inside us, it still means something. Too much is said about the money we make, the endorsements, all that crap. Honestly, when I came into the league, if they'd have told me the highest-paid quarterback was making fifty grand and they were going to pay me thirty grand, I'd have taken it. Come game time, I'd play no different than I do now. I'd dive and block and tackle—I'd do all that crazy stuff. That's football and I love it. The motivation is still there. I don't think it's that difficult to reach us if a coach has a way of doing it. It's why Mike pulled out those hundred-dollar bills. He wanted to motivate us and it worked.

We went out to San Francisco and beat the defending Super Bowl champion 49ers 27–17 even though no one else gave us a chance. I had one of my best games ever. I completed 15 of 16 first-half passes and finished with 299 yards and two touchdowns. One of my favorite plays of all time was where I dropped back, fell down, got up, and hit Keith Jackson for a 38-yard gain over the middle. I'm still not sure how I did that.

That game solidified my relationship with Mike.

Afterward, I went up to him on the airplane and we sat and bullshitted. We recapped everything that happened in the game and the season. Mike said, "I'm real proud of you. We've come a long way. We're going to be in this for the long haul." It was one of those "as you go, I go" conversations. When I walked back to my seat and sat down, I felt like everything was off my shoulders. For the first time, I felt like the Big Guy was at ease with me. I thought about how tough he had been on me, but also about how fair he had been. To go through what we did those first couple of years, and to stick by me and say, "Okay. Give him time. He'll develop into what we're looking for." Well, that meant a lot to me.

# 7

# THE 1996 SEASON

If there's one team in the National Football League I'd like to embarrass, it would be the Dallas Cowboys. I think just about everybody in America, except for the Cowboys' fans, would like to see Green Bay beat the hell out of Dallas.

I know I would. I've lost seven straight games to the Cowboys at Texas Stadium and I'm sick of it. The loss that hurt the most was the one that ended the 1995 season. We were shooting for the franchise's first Super Bowl appearance in twenty-eight years and we led 27–24 going into the fourth quarter. Things were looking pretty good, and then all of a sudden it was the same old shit.

Emmitt Smith runs for his third touchdown. Troy Aikman passes to Michael Irvin for a big gain. I throw a terrible interception and it's over. We wound up losing 38–27 and it hurt. After the game I walked off dejected.

The Cowboys were dancing around and celebrating up on the platform for the postgame awards presentation. I could see how happy they were and I felt lousy. We had no one to blame but ourselves. We beat San Francisco the week before and then we breathed a sigh of relief. We felt that was our Super Bowl and whatever happened in Dallas the next week didn't really matter. But it does matter.

You only get so many opportunities in life.

I still wish I could go back and change everyone's thinking, starting on the plane coming back from the San Francisco game when everyone was partying and having a good time. Hell, I was right in the middle of it. I was thinking, if we go to Dallas and lose, so what? We already did more than anyone thought we could.

Now I know that's the wrong way to think.

If we had said we should beat Dallas, we should kick their ass, then we could've gone to the Super Bowl that year. But we didn't think that way. We went into Texas Stadium and screwed around and let the game slip away. We just let them take control. People said later that we got cheated. We didn't get cheated. We played them as tough as we could, but late in the game we just didn't believe we could win.

Yeah, we came back against them because we were talented, but mentally we didn't see ourselves winning. We were ahead with ten minutes to play and we let it slip away. I knew it was over when I rolled out to my right and got picked off along the sideline. Mark Ingram was supposed to keep running and I wasn't supposed to throw it to him in the first place, so we both screwed up. When Mark stopped running, Larry Brown turned around and the ball hit him right in the chest. I should've thrown it to Chmura in the flat but I didn't.

Then the Cowboys went on a 99-yard scoring drive that broke our backs.

After the game in the locker room, everyone was saying, "Damn. How'd we lose that game?" But they were all looking at the next person instead of looking at the guy in the mirror. That's when I knew mentally we didn't think we could really do it. I think other players knew it then, too.

On the way back to Green Bay we talked to each other. That was when we decided we'd never let that happen again. We'd never go into a game wondering if we could really win. We meant it, too. We believed in it. By the time the plane touched down, we knew we'd be back and we'd get past this game.

That feeling stayed with us going into the 1996 season.

I felt totally confident, more confident than I ever had been. It was probably because of what had happened with the drug rehab and all that. I was really no different than I'd ever been except maybe in better shape and mentally a bit clearer. And I was another year into this offense and another year into the NFL. And we were a better team. We were only a couple days into training camp, but already everything just seemed better.

Then the car accident happened.

It was about six in the morning when the phone rang in my dorm room out at St. Norbert College. At first I thought it might be Frankie Winters's wife. She'd call sometimes early in the morning before the kids got up. Frankie picked up the phone and said, "Oh, God." Then he handed it to me.

It was Deanna.

She said Scott had been in a bad car accident. He was driving a van and he got hit by a train at an unmarked railroad crossing near my parents' house. I knew exactly where she was talking about. Scott was seriously injured, but he was going to make it. Mark Haverty, one of our best friends, wasn't so lucky. He was killed in the accident. When I hung up, I was numb.

I practiced that day but my mind was on Mark.

The next day Deanna and I flew to Mississippi for the funeral. I can't tell you how tough it is to bury one of your best friends. It was like it wasn't really happening. I tried to be strong and I told the guys at the funeral, "I'm going to get us to the Super Bowl. I'm going to do this for Mark." They said it would be great. It would give everyone—including the Havertys, who are really close with my family—something to help take their minds off what had happened.

When I got back to Green Bay, the first day of practice was tough. I tried to act like nothing had ever happened, but I was quieter and the guys knew it. For the next couple weeks, Deanna was my source of strength. She knew Mark and she knew what I was feeling, but she also knew I was strong and there was nothing I could do to change what had happened.

Frankie Winters and Chewy are good buddies and they both knew Mark, too. We spent a lot of time in the dorm room talking about him and Scott, who was having a tough time dealing with everything.

Scott was legally drunk the night of the accident and a judge sentenced him to fifteen years in prison, with fourteen years suspended and the other to be served under house arrest. So Scott can serve his time at home, but he can only go to and from work. The sentence could've been a lot worse, but Mark's father, Lester "Buddy" Haverty, spoke up at the sentencing. He told the court, "Scott is considered another member of my family. Any further punishment to Scott, especially incarceration, would just be further punishment to everyone involved . . . Lord knows, everybody has been punished enough for this."

At times, my mind was elsewhere during practice.

I had to find a way to get the accident out of my mind,

but I couldn't. I wanted to be there for Scott and I couldn't forget Mark because he was a part of my life. Sometimes you don't fully realize it until a person is gone. Mark was a great friend who never asked for anything but my friendship. I never realized how close I was with him until he was dead. You can't forget good friends. You can't forget family, either. You can't forget the things you went through together because that's what carries you through the rest of your life.

I felt guilty at times.

I knew that could just as easily have been me riding with Scott. Hell, if I'd been home instead of at training camp, it probably would've been me.

Even though we were staying at St. Norbert, I'd go home each night after meetings to spend time with Deanna. We would just sit around and talk about everything.

We talked about our new home in Green Bay and the privacy it gave us. We talked about Mark. We talked about the season. Hell, she was so excited about it, maybe even more than I was. She'd say, "God, we're going to do it this year. We're going to the Super Bowl." She was like that the whole season.

It was good for me to hear that.

A month later, our family was hit with more bad news when my sister, Brandi, was accused of taking the wheel in a drive-by shooting in Slidell, Louisiana. Brandi didn't shoot a gun and nobody was hurt, but the two people she was with pled guilty to illegal use of a weapon and were sentenced to six months in prison. Brandi entered the district attorney's diversionary program, where she's under one year of supervised probation. If she keeps out of trouble, which I'm confident she will, everything is going to be okay.

At the time, though, it was a lot to deal with. I knew it

was especially tough on Mom and Dad. They worked so hard to raise us right and then when things happen they feel like they should've done more. I think they did a great job. Every family has problems, it's just that ours are more public because of what I do for a living. I tell Mom that, but I don't know if it helps. I think some of that just takes time.

That's how it was for me after Mark's death. I was out of it for a while, but slowly I started to snap out of it. I mean there's nothing I could do, so I had to try to move on. It was the same with the painkiller addiction.

Everyone on the team pretty much knew what I'd been through during the off-season. I thought Mike did a good job when he addressed the team early in training camp. He said, "I don't want to harp on it, but we know Brett got hooked on painkillers and it can happen to any one of you. Pills got in his hands some way, whether it was from teammates or outside sources. The trainers documented what they gave Brett, so there was no problem there. So if you guys are sharing pills, it needs to stop. I can't be with each and every one of you, but it needs to stop. You've got to know how serious this is."

Everyone got the message.

Now if someone offers me pills or asks me for pills, I know what to look for. Now if someone goes up to a team-mate and says, "Can I get a Vike?" it's like, "Hey, wait a minute. Go to the doctors because I don't want to be the culprit."

Mike only talked about it that one time.

After that, our whole focus was football and Mike spoke to us with more confidence than ever before. It was like the first year he expected to have a winning season. We went 9–7. Then the second year we made the play-offs. The third year we advanced further into the play-offs. The fourth year we got within a game of the Super Bowl.

And now the 1996 season was here and we were here for only one reason: to win the Super Bowl. Mike never said it was Super Bowl or bust, but that's what he was saying in so many words. I think everyone agreed. We had enough talent.

I really liked our nucleus and I really didn't care what Dallas or San Francisco had because it didn't matter. What mattered is what we did. If we split our road games and win at home, we'll get the home-field advantage and nobody can beat us at Lambeau Field.

Frankie agreed. Chewy agreed. Reggie White agreed.

We kept making that point. Don't worry about what the other teams are doing. The mark of a great team is to control your own destiny. It's a huge leap—the biggest leap of all—and I think we made it in a short period of time.

We were talented in '95 and then we added Eugene Robinson and Santana Dotson on defense and that made us really good. Santana was a good young nose tackle from Tampa Bay and Eugene was a natural leader at safety.

The preseason was going along great until we went to Indianapolis. That exhibition game was humbling. We played just awful, but it was probably good for us. The Colts are pretty good at rushing the passer and I think they felt like it was a challenge to see what they could do against us. We weren't ready.

I came out of that game early and I was happy to do it.

We played like we didn't care. It gave Mike a chance to really lay into us, to tell us we're not invincible. We agreed. We got our asses kicked 30–6 but it was okay.

We had a problem at left tackle with our veteran, Ken Ruettgers, out with a knee injury. We had a revolving door at that position. I cared, but I didn't care. I knew there was no way Rutt would be healthy in time for the season, maybe ever be healthy again, and there was no time to bring in somebody experienced.

We had Bruce Wilkerson, but he is more a right tackle, and we tried Gary Brown, but he is more a guard. So we went with John Michels, a rookie.

John was our first-round draft pick out of Southern Cal. I knew he would struggle early. That's a tough postion and you're up against the NFL's best athletes. John's a little light in the ass, but he's got great feet. Give him some time and a few more pounds and he'll be really, really good.

One thing Mike and our assistants do really well is help out linemen with backs and tight ends on blocking assignments. Most of the time, I never even noticed a difference at left tackle. I knew there were times when John would struggle and I'd have to step up in the pocket and do something but no one was really worried about it.

Then John had some problems in a game late in the season and the coaches put Wilkerson in. I thought it was a good move. It gave John a chance to watch and learn. I don't think any left tackle should come into the league and try to play right away. It's a tough position and it can be really tough on the quarterback if the left tackle doesn't play well.

I'd like to take note of Tom Lovat, our offensive line coach. He's the unsung hero on this team. People laugh sometimes because Tom will occasionally act senile. Like last year, we're getting ready for Dallas and he'll say in a meeting, "Now, Jeffcoat is going to rush hard from this end." And I'm looking through my notes. Jeffcoat? Shit, he's been gone for two years. What are you talking about, Tom? And he'll just say, "Well, whoever is in there. It doesn't matter."

It could be Dick Butkus in there as far as he's con-

After a twelve-year courtship, the big day finally arrived when Deanna and I were married at St. Agnes Church in Green Bay on July 14, 1996. *(Deanna Favre)*

Deanna is used to carrying me. It's good thing she's strong enough for both of us. *(Deanna Favre)*

Our daughter, Brittany, was thrilled our wedding day. Here she's asking me where we're all going for the honeymoon. *(Deanna Favre)*

**E**ven when I was at Southern Mississippi, I had a knack for eluding the pass rush. Here I'm about to unload before the defensive end does. *(Bonita Favre)*

**T**hrowing on the run has always been one of my strengths. *(Bonita Favre)*

**A** good quarterback has to buy time until his receivers get open. *(Bonita Favre)*

The tuxedo looks OK, but I'd rather be in a muddy football uniform. *(Deanna Favre)*

Here I am with my childhood sweetheart, Deanna Tynes, all dressed up for the prom when I was a junior in high school. *(Deanna Favre)*

A special moment on graduation day with Mom, who was as proud as she could be. *(Deanna Favre)*

I wore my game face on picture day as a junior at Hancock North Central. That's me wearing number 10 in the first row, far right. Dad is second from the left in the back row. *(Bonita Favre)*

I was more of a runner than a passer in high school. Here I show my incredible speed on a bootleg to the corner of the end zone. *(Bonita Favre)*

Every time I touched the ball I dreamed of becoming an NFL quarterback, even as far back as the tenth grade. *(Bonita Favre)*

The Favre Clan was stylish in the seventies. From left: me, Dad, Scott, Brandi, Mom, and Jeff. *(Bonita Favre)*

The Rotten Bayou is only a 10-yard squareout from our deck. The alligators that call it home claimed four of our dogs over the years. *(Bonita Favre)*

Here is the Favre team with our mascot, Duke, who followed me home from Atlanta. I brought him home for Christmas and he stayed with us. From left: me, Jeff, Mom, Dad, Brandi, and Scott. *(Bonita Favre)*

I was a big baby, twenty-one inches long and weighing in at nine pounds, fifteen ounces. Here I am at eight weeks old, just loving life. *(Bonita Favre)*

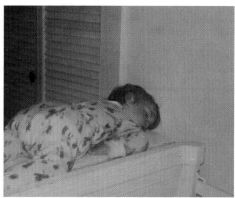

I've always tried to reach new heights. This time I made it all the way from my crib to the dresser before I decided to take a time-out for a nap. *(Bonita Favre)*

When I was a year old, my coach (a.k.a. Dad) gave me my first football uniform and some darn good advice: ''Son, keep your head down and your pants up.'' *(Bonita Favre)*

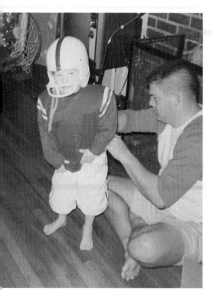

All those years of saying ''cheese'' for my class pictures helped prepare me for the National Dairy Council's milk-mustache ad. *(Bonita Favre)*

**M**y two biggest fans are all set for the big game. *(Deanna Favre)*

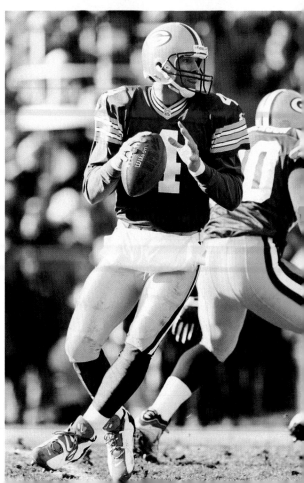

The Packers' brain trust tries to find a way to rally at Kansas City. But not even Coach Mike Holmgren, quarterbacks coach Marty Mornhinweg, Jim McMahon, and yours truly could figure out how to beat the Chiefs that day. *(Mark A. Wallenfang)*

I've been known to do a little Fred Astaire in the pocket while looking downfield. *(Mark A. Wallenfang)*

**F**resh out of rehab with Coach Mike Holmgren at my side, I told reporters, "We're going to the Super Bowl. You can bet against me but you'll lose."
*(Mark A. Wallenfang)*

**T**urn out the lights. It's the same old shit in Dallas. I'm thoroughly dejected on the way to my seventh straight loss at Texas Stadium. This time it was 21–6 on *Monday Night Football. (Mark A. Wallenfang)*

**T**here's nothing like coming out of the tunnel at Lambeau Field to the sound of sixty thousand screaming fans.
*(Mark A. Wallenfang)*

The people back home have always supported me. *(Mark A. Wallenfang)*

**T**he Broke Spoke can be a pretty rough joint unless you're a Brett Favre fan. *(Mark A. Wallenfang)*

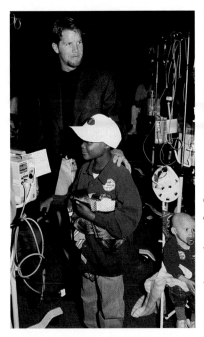

**I** try to reach out to the kids at the Children's Hospital of Milwaukee as often as I can. *(Mark A. Wallenfang)*

**W**hen I visit children at the local hospitals, we both get something out of it. This boy got a jersey and I got a smile in return. I got the better deal. *(Mark A. Wallenfang)*

This touchdown pass to Andre Rison, who isn't in the picture yet, helped us knock off the San Francisco 49ers in the 1996 NFC Divisional Playoff game. (*Mark A. Wallenfang*)

I've had some squirrelly teammates in the past, but this little critter really had me hopping. (*Patrick Ferron*, Green Bay Press-Gazette)

Keith Jackson was one of my favorite weapons while he played with the Packers. We often celebrated touchdowns by getting in each other's face. (*Mark A. Wallenfang*)

Doug Pederson (18), Jim McMahon (9), and I pose for a pregame shot with the gang. That's Ty Detmer to my right and Steve Mariucci to my left. *(James V. Biever)*

Steve Mariucci was not only my quarterbacks coach, but also one of my best friends. *(James V. Biever)*

The Three Amigos are getting ready for a training camp workout. My right-hand guys are Mark Chmura and Frank Winters. *(James V. Biever)*

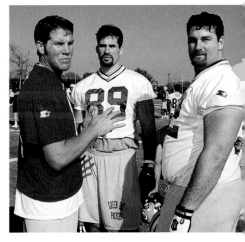

My best friend and agent, James "Bus" Cook, and I make a pretty good team. I take care of business on the field; he handles my business off of it. *(Bus Cook)*

After a forty-six-day stint at the Menninger Clinic, the guys were glad to see me back on the field in time for training camp. *(Mark A. Wallenfang)*

Reggie White tells the dumbest jokes in the world, but they never fail to crack me up. *(Mark A. Wallenfang)*

The Packers were well represented at the 1996 Pro Bowl. Here I am with (from left) Reggie White, Keith Jackson, LeRoy Butler, and Frank Winters. *(Mark A. Wallenfang)*

A lot of things go through my mind when I'm barking out signals. This time, I was hoping Frankie would get a block on the Vikings' John Randle. *(Mark A. Wallenfang)*

I still get crazy whenever we score a touchdown, just like I used to do back at Hancock North Central. *(Mark A. Wallenfang)*

I'm waiting to pull the trigger while Don Beebe beats his man. He did, and I hit him for a 65-yard touchdown pass in a 28–18 win over the Lions in '96. *(Mark A. Wallenfang)*

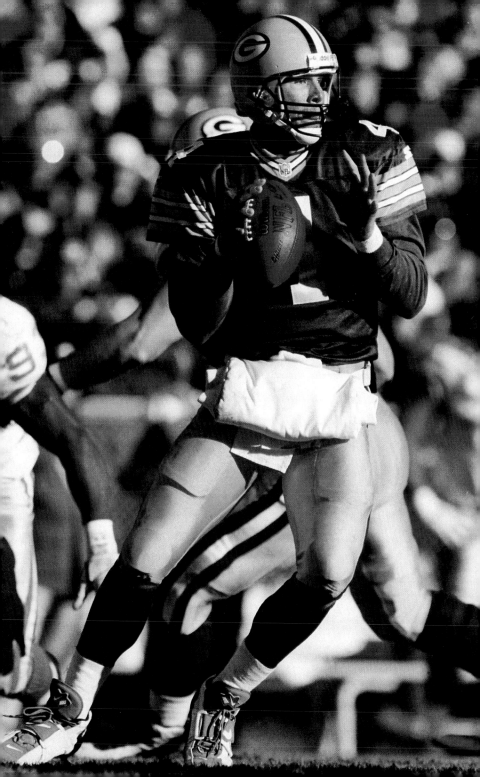

I went nuts right along with the crowd when we won the Packers' first Super Bowl in twenty-nine years. *(Patrick Ferron, Green Bay Press-Gazette)*

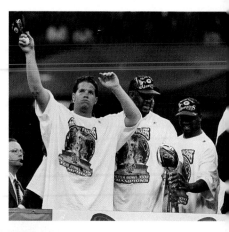

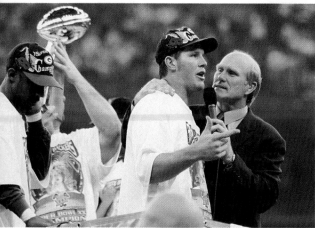

**B**efore I thanked all the Packers' fans for their love and support, I pinched Terry Bradshaw in the ass just to be a wise-guy.
*(Mark A. Wallenfang)*

**T**erry Bradshaw interviews Mike Holmgren after we beat New England to win Super Bowl XXXI. I'm in the on-deck circle with Reggie waiting for my turn at the microphone. *(Patrick Ferron, Green Bay Press-Gazette)*

cerned. He's a cliché a minute. He'll say he wants his offensive line to be like water around a boulder when it
protects the passer. He's talking to his linemen and he'll
say, "Kick their ass! Kick them in the balls! Kick them in
the mustache!" He'll say it all.

Here's how funny Tom is. He's talking about playing
teams with 3–4 defenses this season, "so this week, while
we're preparing for New England . . ." And we'll say,
"Tom, we played New England two years ago." He didn't
care. He just says well, let's pretend we're playing them.
What the hell's the difference? It's still a 3–4 defense. And
he's serious. He's forgetful, but he's a helluva coach.

At times over the past few seasons Tom kept that line
together when there wasn't much to keep it together with.
It was a revolving door, but he keeps on swinging. What
he did with Adam Timmerman at right guard in the '95
play-offs was remarkable. He took a guy with no experience and got him to play at a high level. Same thing at left
tackle.

Tom's coaching has a lot to do with my durability. By
the end of the '96 season, I'd started in seventy-seven
straight games. I think that's the most important statistic I
have because without it the rest don't mean a thing.

I'm going for the record for most consecutive starts by a
quarterback. I think it's 145 by Dan Marino. Ron Jaworski
started in 117 straight and Brian Sipe made it for 109 in a
row. That's not too bad. I'd like to get on that list.

We had a new quarterback coach last season, too.

Marty Mornhinweg replaced Steve Mariucci, who took
the head coaching job at California. Now he's the head
coach at San Francisco and Marty is his offensive coordinator. I'm not surprised by either move. Steve was a great
coach when he was here and Marty picked right up where
he left off.

Marty was young, but he handled himself in a way that I respected. He didn't come in here and try to change things. He just said I had a helluva season the year before and he wanted to build on that.

When the regular season started, I was totally confident we'd go into Tampa Bay and beat them. And I was totally confident that I'd play well, probably more so than ever. Sometimes I feel like I'm in a zone. The Super Bowl was one of those games. So was Tampa in that opener. The feeling is fun. I don't want the game to end. I'd like it to be like that the whole season. Just play that one game sixteen times and everything will be great. A lot of it has to do with what the defense is doing. If I have them on their heels, it's a good feeling. Everyone is running the right routes. I'm throwing it perfect. I'm reading it perfect. When we played Cleveland in '95, it was amazing. I was going to my fourth receiver right away; I could read it that quick. I wonder why I can't be like that every week. Well, no one can because if that was the case, nobody would ever beat us.

We beat Tampa Bay 34–3 and I threw four touchdown passes—three of them to tight end Keith Jackson. All the media questions about our offensive line were answered in that game. I got sacked only once. It was a good way to open the season, the first time we opened that well on offense.

We really got off to a fast start.

We outscored our first three opponents by 110–16. I didn't see that coming, but I wasn't surprised by it, either. Philadelphia came into Green Bay for a *Monday Night Football* game the week after the Tampa game. I knew Philly had a good team and I figured it would be a close game but we dominated them. Then we hammered San Diego the next week and I knew we were pretty good.

There were times in the Philly game when I'd just watch and go, "Damn, that's pretty impressive." I'm standing there on the sidelines watching our defense kick their ass, take the ball away from them, force turnovers. They couldn't piss a drop on offense. I was glad I was playing for the Packers. Then we'd go on offense and it was damn near picture-perfect.

That first *Monday Night* game was pretty exciting. It was real festive. Our fans were fired up and we felt like we earned the right to play our first *Monday Night* game at home in ten years. We won 39–13.

Then we went out the next Sunday and beat San Diego 42–10. Our defense made it easy for me. They really got after the Chargers' quarterback, Stan Humphries. I felt sorry for Stan. I wouldn't want to play against our defense. I had a good game and we put a lot of points on the board, which is what counts.

We were feeling pretty good about ourselves, but then we had to go to Minnesota, where Mike hasn't won since he arrived in Green Bay. Well, here's what happened at Minnesota: the same old shit. Something freaky always happens there. Their defense really pounded me. They played like it was their Super Bowl. But after George Koonce, one of our linebackers, intercepted a pass and ran it in for a touchdown, I thought the game was ours. Then the Vikings came back and they won it 30–21. We were still in the game despite only eight first downs, but they forced some turnovers, which is what they do best.

I was disgusted after the game.

Shit, I couldn't believe it. But then I started thinking well, we'll get them. It's the last game of the season and it's a long wait, but that's okay. I didn't think we'd win all sixteen games and that's what Mike said after the game.

He said no one expected us to be 16–0. Losses are going to happen. We may lose again.

I got sacked something like seven times. I was pretty sore. Every time I play them, I'm pretty sore. I was thankful to get home in one piece. I dealt with the pain by taking some Motrin. I was tired and I went to bed right away. Deanna and Brittany were in there, so I climbed right in with them. Usually I watch *SportsCenter,* but not that night. I didn't even care how the other teams did.

I got up the next day, worked out, and hopped in the whirlpool. That's how I dealt with the pain all season.

The next week, we kicked the shit out of the Seattle Seahawks. Then we beat the Bears and we were back on a roll, scoring a lot of points. After the Bears game we had the San Francisco 49ers coming to our place on Monday night. It was one helluva football game. We ended up winning 23–20 in overtime but we paid a price. We lost our best receiver, Robert Brooks, for the season.

Coming into the game, we knew San Francisco had the best defense we'd faced so far. Offensively, though, we didn't think they could move the ball that well against our defense.

We hit some big strikes early, but we couldn't capitalize on them. I hit Don Beebe down the sideline but he accidentally stepped out of bounds. Then I hit Keith Jackson on a big one and if he scored, it could've been a blowout, but he got tripped up and it turned around and worked against us. We didn't get seven. We had to settle for three and they came back to take the lead.

But we were still doing some things well.

I could see some things that were open if I got a little time to throw. I knew I couldn't drop back five or seven steps and pick the 49ers apart; they were too good for that.

But I was confident Don could do some things. He ended up catching eleven passes for 220 yards.

In the third quarter, he scored on a long play that was controversial. Their safety, Merton Hanks, let him go by about 10 yards and I just threw it. Don dove for the ball and caught it and it looked like Hanks touched him while he was down, but Don got up and ran it in for a touchdown.

Good teams get breaks like that. How many times have we gone to Dallas and they get the breaks? And you go, "Oh, shit." Referees know a good team and if you start making plays, they start expecting them. More than likely if a shitty team makes a play, he's down. If a great team makes it, it's a touchdown.

We needed a field goal in the two-minute drill to get the game into overtime and I thought what the hell, this is what I like. I love the two-minute drill because I've got nothing to lose. It's like the last shot in a basketball game. You miss it, everybody goes, "Oh, damn." If you make it, everybody goes crazy.

I thrive on that.

It's like when you're young and running around out in the yard playing ball. I'm doing it at the line. Squareout. Hook-and-go. We practice the two-minute drill every week. It's the most fun we have at practice. That drive propelled us into overtime and Chris Jacke kicked a long field goal to win it.

We were pretty beat up after that game.

We had a bye week and we needed it. Then we won a couple more games before those back-to-back losses at Kansas City and Dallas. Those losses didn't surprise me. We had everybody hurt and morale was down. Offensively we had been doing so well and now we didn't know if we could do it. Not to mention we were playing two great teams at their stadiums. It was bad scheduling.

It would've been tough if we had everybody healthy. We could've split, maybe, but I don't know who we would've beat.

Kansas City was playing well at that point and they had a great game on offense—probably better than they had all year. We couldn't beat their bump-and-run defense and they rushed the passer pretty well. I was down after that game, but not really upset. I said when we get our backs against the wall, we'll be fine.

Then we went to Dallas, and once again we couldn't piss a drop.

Some of our guys got upset when Barry Switzer, the Cowboys' coach, had them kick that last field goal without much time to play. They were ahead 18–6 and the game was over, but Switzer wanted to give Chris Boniol a shot at tying the NFL record. He made it and we lost.

The last play of the game I threw a pass and rolled out toward Dallas's sideline. The horn blew and I went over and congratulated Switzer and told him he did a great job. Reggie White was upset, but Switzer wasn't rubbing it in.

It was a 21–6 game. They didn't score a touchdown; we scored one. We kicked their ass; they kicked our ass. There wasn't much more to it. Their defense played well; so did ours. We stunk it up on offense and they didn't do much, either. So give the kid the field goal record. How often does a kid get to do that?

I mean, if you're going to be pissed, be pissed at the last six or seven times the Cowboys have beaten us, not at that game. Now, Reggie can do his thing and I can do mine, so there's no beef between us. He was on defense and he felt like they were rubbing it in, so that was his business. I didn't feel the same way.

No big deal.

Well, after that we got healthy again and we went on an eight-game winning streak. Pretty impressive.

We were 8–3 going into the St. Louis game down there, but we were still down because of the Dallas loss. That Doug Evans interception and return for a touchdown to start the second half was huge. It turned us around. It was like the fumble recovery and touchdown Craig Newsome made for us against the 49ers in the play-off game the year before.

We were still struggling on offense and Mike was dejected. We hadn't been doing anything on offense for a couple of weeks but it wasn't his fault. He just calls them. But he told Sherman Lewis to call the plays. They're pretty similar in the way they call them, but sometimes Sherm says screw it and he wings it a bit more. Mike tends to be a bit more conservative.

Anyway, Sherm scripted the first fifteen plays of the second half. It would be hard for anyone to tell who was calling them. About the only difference is Sherm likes to roll out and use play action a bit more. That's about it.

We came back to beat the Rams 24–9.

We're a good first-drive team because the coaches do such a good job of scripting plays. But I still love to call audibles because it's all me. Every once in a while I'll tell Mike a play is going to work. And when it works, your chest just swells up and you can tell everybody, "I told you so." And when it doesn't work, Mike will tell me he's never going to listen to me again. But that only happens about four or five times a year.

Sometimes I think about playing back when the quarterback still called his own plays. That would've been pretty cool. I don't know how good I'd be at it, but it would be fun. That's why I can't wait to be a coach someday and call the plays. It would be razzle-dazzle and all that. And I'd have to deal with some knucklehead quarterback, although I've already dealt with one before.

Me.

And when I'm a coach, I'm going to say to that young quarterback, "Look, I know. I've tried it myself. Now shut up and listen."

It would be tough to call the plays. It's way too technical out there. There are too many defenses to allow that. The fire zones and the man-to-man on one side and zone on the other, this guy dropping off—there's just too much to do.

Every once in a while, I'll call a play and the guys will say, "Oh, shit. That won't work." Well, what the hell do they know? I've got offensive linemen telling me a play won't work and I'm like, just block the play. Everyone's an expert.

Sometimes they'll come back into the huddle after a play and ask why I audibled on a certain play. I'll say I saw something and they'll say, obviously it wasn't the same thing I saw. Linemen really hate it when there's a pass called and they think we should run. They love to run block and hate to pass block.

They get over it.

That stretch of the last five regular-season games included a showdown with the Denver Broncos. Well, it didn't turn out to be such a big deal because John Elway didn't play. I was dejected at first, but then I decided we'd just go out and kick some butt anyway. And we really made a statement that day—with or without Elway. We beat them 41–6. If they would've had Elway, it would've been a different story, like 41–28. I'll give them four touchdowns and it still wouldn't have been enough.

I remember the play when Michael Dean Perry broke

free and I stiff-armed him. Good players make good plays. Good teams make other teams look bad. We made Denver look bad and I really thought the Broncos would make it to the Super Bowl. I threw four touchdown passes that day.

It gave me thirty-four and LeRoy Butler came over in practice and said I needed to do something after I throw a touchdown pass because I do it so often.

"Let's do six-guns," he said.

I said what the hell is six-guns?

"You come over to me on the sidelines, we'll pull out six guns and make believe we're shooting and then we'll stick 'em back in," LeRoy said.

Fine. We did it.

Then he said, "Let's add something to it. Let's tap each other on the left shoulder twice after we put the guns away." So we did that. Then he wanted me to add some more stuff right before the Super Bowl, but he thought it over and said, "We probably shouldn't. You don't have enough rhythm."

I said, "You're right. We're pushing the limit as it is."

LeRoy's always making that shit up. He's got entirely too much time on his hands. He's cool to be around, though. He makes it fun out there. What the hell, I'm out there to have fun, too.

Andre Rison is another hell-raiser. We got him before the St. Louis game after Antonio Freeman was out for some time with a broken arm. Ron and Mike asked me what I thought of Rison and I said, "Go get him." He had been released by Jacksonville and he was available. Andre's a helluva player. Nobody can play bump-and-run coverage on him. He's too damn quick and he can catch, so I said I was all for it. It was the first time anyone asked my input on a personnel decision.

When Andre came in, it was a reunion. We'd been together in Atlanta.

We hugged and he said, "We're going to the Super Bowl. It's you and me back together again, Favre."

The first time Andre showed up in the locker room, the young receivers were like, "That's Andre Rison." It was like me with Jim McMahon. Even though I knew the guy, I still thought it was pretty cool to be playing with him. That's how our young receivers were around Andre.

Andre is a character.

He'll be telling me all the time that he's open and most of the time he was. Sometimes, though, he was open over here when he was supposed to be open over there. But that son of a bitch could get open.

Once he started learning the routes, he was dangerous. He'd be running post routes and they'd be so smooth. He'd run a slant route and the defender's legs would almost break. It was like poetry in motion.

By the time the play-offs came, we were on a roll. Chewy was back from an arch injury. Free was back from the broken arm. Andre knew the offense. Keith Jackson was still all-world and our running backs were eager to dominate.

We beat Denver, Detroit, and Minnesota to close out the regular season. That Minnesota game was fun. It was payback time.

Before the game the Vikings' linebacker, Jeff Brady, said he was going head-hunting at Lambeau Field. Well, we tore their asses off. That type of stuff has always been a positive for us. We don't ever say stuff like that, and when Brady said it, that was really stupid.

In the pregame talk, Mike said, "Okay, on the first play I want William Henderson to knock Brady flat on his ass.

I don't care what you do the rest of the game. I just want you to knock him on his ass.''

Henderson, our big fullback, drilled him.

The rest of the game Brady played like his head was on a swivel. He was always looking around to see who the next guy would be to knock him on his ass. Our guys were really pissed he said that. It was added incentive. It's amazing. That old sticks-and-stones thing works, even with thirty-year-old guys.

After the bye week, we played San Francisco at Green Bay and we knew we were going to beat them, even though we got hit with a monsoon before the game. I was upset about the weather because we weren't going to throw much. I wanted to go out and throw it forty times, but I knew fifteen would be a miracle. And if I completed half that many, it would be an even bigger miracle.

The ball was like a greased watermelon; I couldn't even grip it. My hands were frozen but it was fun. It was like playing goal-line in the backyard at home. We beat the 49ers pretty good, 35–14. It was no surprise.

Steve Young went out of the game early with the broken ribs and the groin pull. I was glad. I'd hate to play against him for four quarters because you never know when that son of a gun will beat you. But I felt sorry for him. I've seen him play when he was remarkable. But he's getting older and it's catching up with him. Then again, he may come back and light it up against us and win the MVP. Mariucci will give him a chance to do it.

It was laid-back after the game.

We had a few people over to the house and kicked back and relaxed. The next day Dallas and Carolina played and we'd face the winner, but I didn't care who won. Bus and Deanna were rooting for Carolina, but I didn't think Dallas could beat us in Green Bay anyway.

Well, the Panthers won and it set up the biggest game in our history since the Ice Bowl. This game was bigger than the Super Bowl because it propels you into the big game and you get to play in front of your own fans on your own turf.

I was a little nervous before the game. I was confident, but I was also anxious to get out there. I looked briefly over the fifteen scripted plays and walked over to our receivers. I told them to concentrate on the ball because it was going to be windy and cold and hard to catch. It was about zero degrees.

We all got the ammonia capsules out and we popped them. We do it before every game. That stuff wakes you up. I don't know if it helps, though. It's more of a superstition thing than anything else.

That's when the rah-rah shit started.

I used to be that way more in college, but now that I'm an NFL quarterback I've got a lot more to think about. Reggie White started it by saying, "Okay, we're going to beat these guys. We're going to beat them."

But Wayne Simmons is shouting, "Fuck that shit! We're going to kick their ass." And he was saying this right after we got done praying with Reggie. Nothing like good old Christ when you need Him.

My demeanor was pretty level.

If I say anything, it's more about how far we've come and to concentrate and somebody will butt in and start yelling, "We're going to kick their ass." I'm a little old for that stuff. I doubt if Dan Marino or John Elway steps into the huddle and says, "Let's make these cocksuckers pay." I doubt it. I think as a quarterback you go through that evolution. You don't want your teammates looking at you going, "That guy's our leader?" I don't want them doing that. I want them thinking I'm on an even plane the whole time.

During the course of a game I'm very talkative. I'm telling our linemen to go down there and block their ass. I'll be in the huddle saying, "Let's go on an eighty-yard drive and jam it down their throats."

It's pretty intense.

Right before the Carolina game, Mike came in and told us that before we went out on the field, he had a special guest to talk to us. He said this guy hasn't been here very long, but he wanted him to say a few words.

Then he said, "Andre?"

I heard Rison go, "What?" He had no idea Mike was going to do this. He had no clue. I was standing on the side laughing, but Andre went with it.

He said, "Bring it up. Bring it up." He got everyone together and he thanked us for making him feel like part of the team and he concluded with a whole bunch of expletives about what we were going to do to the Panthers.

Well, we had a terrific game. We beat them pretty good, 30–13, to get to the Super Bowl for the first time in twenty-nine years. After the game, Mike told the crowd, "We have a great football team and we're not finished yet."

The place went wild. It was like a state of euphoria. It was colder than hell and I looked around and nobody was leaving. Our fans wanted that moment to last forever no matter what the temperature was. It was a total celebration. The Super Bowl and this game were two different games. In some ways, the championship was more fun. Everyone got to celebrate with us.

When I looked up in the stands and saw all that blaze orange and sixty thousand people not budging—not forty thousand with twenty thousand no-shows—I'm thinking this is what it's all about. It was packed and people were enjoying it as much as we were, if not more. People were crying and excited. I didn't get cold at all after the game. Standing on that podium and looking around was like, well, this is it. We have finally arrived. I said to myself, "No one ever thought I'd be here this early, but here I am and I'm going to enjoy it."

And we're going to win the Super Bowl.

# 8

# TEAMMATES

I had barely recovered from our Super Bowl victory party at Mike Anderson's on Bourbon Street when the Packers announced their 1997 minicamp schedule. The first of three minicamps opened less than eight weeks after the Pro Bowl. So much for my off-season. I circled the date on my calendar. Then I put a Ghostbusters slash through it. April 1. "That's perfect," I thought. "April Fool's Day." Talk about bad jokes.

In my opinion, the world would be a far better place with fewer minicamps. Coaches like to think it makes their team better. But if every team in the league didn't have a minicamp, then we'd all be even and we could enjoy the off-season. We need to eliminate minicamps. The NFL is too shrewd to do that, though. Minicamps keep the league in the news year round, which is great for the league. They also keep me in Green Bay year round, which would be fine if you could golf in the snow.

Minicamps do serve one valuable function. They're a great excuse to get together with the guys for three or four days. If you talk to any player who has retired, they'll tell you the thing they miss most is hanging out with the guys. I guarantee it's not the practices. They may miss the games a bit, but more than anything, what they miss is being in the locker room. Goofing off. Joking around. Pulling pranks.

Jim McMahon and I were shooting the bull one day last season. He told me was thinking about retiring. I said, "Well, why don't you?" I mean, he didn't have anything left to prove. He played for fifteen seasons. He won a Super Bowl. He was a great quarterback. He made good money. He could golf every day and hang out with his wife and kids every night.

Jimmy Mac looked around the locker room and said, "I know it, but I'd really miss hanging out with the guys."

I can understand that.

To me, the word "teammates" means friendship. That's what teammates are. They're your friends. And I happen to be lucky enough to have two of my best friends in the world on this team. I don't know how common that is around the league, but I think it's pretty special. During the season Frankie Winters, my center, Mark Chmura, my tight end, and I are inseparable. Guys started calling us the Three Amigos. The way we joke around all the time, it's more like the Three Stooges. We come from different backgrounds, but that doesn't matter to us. We think alike. We act alike. We're all just goofy as hell. We're like little kids in the locker room. That's why we mesh so well.

Frankie is a typical East Coast, Jersey, New York personality. Impatient as hell. Quick trigger. Traffic could be going smooth, but he thinks no one around Green Bay knows how to drive. He'll be bitching and I'm like, "It's perfect. No one's driving slow. No one's driving fast." He's never happy. If I show up five minutes late, he just goes crazy. He'll say, "Dude, you're always late." I'm like, "Geez, it's three minutes." He doesn't care. He'll curse me anyway. He's not scared of anyone or anything. He is one tough s.o.b. and a great guy to have on your side, whether you're in a game or a fight or both. I think he'd give himself up for me. I'd do the same for him. Chmura would do the same for both of us. That's what makes it special. I can trust those guys with my life on and off the field.

Sometimes people have said Frankie and I are like an old married couple, always bitching at each other. I think we're like brothers. You hate each other but if one of you gets in a fight, the other one is right there to back you up. It's like the old saying "That's my dog. If anyone's going to kick it, it's going to be me."

Frankie is like having a 300-pound Mafia hit man on your side. There have been times when I've gotten drilled late in games. The referee won't throw a flag, but Frankie doesn't miss a beat. He won't say anything to the player. He'll just go hit him on the next play, even if the play is over here and the guy is over there. That's the way he is. Aaron Taylor, my left guard, is the same way. If I'm getting hit late, I can hear those guys barking at the defensive linemen. They'll say, "Watch that shit or we'll get you." It's pretty cool when they do that, because you know they mean it.

Frankie is the most underrated player in the league. I'm glad the Packers re-signed him in March. He's one helluva football player. He can really run for a big guy and he's one of the best at scraping the pile downfield. He has a reputation for being a dirty player. I think that's a bunch of bull. A lot of guys quit before the whistle is blown. He doesn't quit until after the whistle is blown. Guys will be standing and looking around and *bam!* he hits them. You don't see that very often, so people look at it as being dirty, but really, that's the right thing to do. There's an old football saying, "If you stand around the pile, you'll get your ass knocked off." They invented that saying because of guys like Frankie.

The first time we met, we were eating lunch at the Midway Hotel in Green Bay. It was during—what else?—my first minicamp with the team in '92. The Packers had acquired Frankie in Plan B from the Kansas City Chiefs that off-season. We introduced ourselves.

"What do you play?" Frankie asked. "Linebacker?"

"Hell no. I'm the quarterback."

"Damn, you're the biggest quarterback I've ever seen."

And I probably was. I weighed about 245 pounds back then. We got to talking and I said, "What are you doing tonight?" He said, "Nothing." Then he asked me and I said, "I may go out." Well, we went out, sucked down a bunch of beer, and hit it off.

We've been roommates ever since.

When we get to the hotel room on road trips, we've got it down to a science. The first thing that happens is Frankie snatches up the TV remote control. Otherwise, I'd drive him nuts because I'm a channel surfer and he likes to watch one show at a time. The second thing that happens is the phone rings and it's Chewy. He'll ask what room we're in. I remember one time I said, "We're in 2072." He said, "Hey. I'm just one floor below you in 2174." I said, "Chewy, that's one floor above us." He said, "You know what I mean. I'll be right over."

Chewy is something else. I think the guy's fairly bright, but you wouldn't know it sometimes the way he acts. When Don Beebe ran a kickoff back 90 yards for a touchdown against the Bears last season, Beebe thanked every guy on the return unit and promised to give each of them $100. Chewy told Don, "Are you stupid? That's $10,000."

That's the kind of stuff he does. It's what makes Chewy Chewy.

I'll never forget the time we flew to Phoenix over the bye weekend in 1993. How could I forget? I still have the Superman tattoo on my left arm to remind me. Chewy's agent flew us out on a private jet. When we hit town, we started partying right away, like at ten in the morning. We were just riding around, drinking and acting smart. Half joking, I turned to Chewy and said, "Let's get a tattoo." He said, "Are you crazy? No way. I would never get a tattoo." A couple of beers later and he's going, "Well, maybe." Then a few more beers and it was, "What kind of a tattoo do you want?"

I thought we should get something different. A Superman tattoo. We went into the tattoo shop and the guy said he didn't have a design of the Superman shield, but that he could try to draw one up. He sketched it out and it looked pretty sharp. It pricked a bit when he stuck me in my shoulder with his tattoo needle, but it was bearable. Then he started on Chewy, man, what a baby.

Here's our six-five, 256-pound, strong-as-an-ox tight end going, "Oh, God. It hurts so bad."

I said, "Aw, shit, Chewy, suck it up."

Well, for the next three or four weeks he was constantly rubbing Vaseline on his tattoo to keep it looking shiny and new. He rolled up his sleeves during games so everyone could see it. And this is the guy who didn't want to get one. He was so proud of that tattoo, it was the best thing he ever did.

It took Chewy a while to make a name for himself in the NFL. That's the way it is with a lot of late-round picks. Chewy was a sixth-round draft pick out of Boston College in 1992. He hurt his back lifting weights and didn't play his rookie season. He never said a word to anyone the whole time. He was real quiet. We weren't even buddies my first year. We introduced ourselves and went our own way.

I remember telling Frankie, "That guy's a stiff. No fun at all." What we didn't know was Chewy was just like us. He came out of his shell during his second season. I don't think too many people believed in him at first, but he works as hard as anyone and once he got his chance, he made the most of it.

When he started playing regularly, it was like having another quarterback on the field. Now, he has said some really goofy things from time to time off the field, but on it, he is incredibly bright. He knows exactly what I'm thinking the whole time. That's uncommon. We're to a point now where I can go to the line, read the defense, and say, "Chewy. Chewy." And he knows what I'm thinking. Usually it's a play where he's got a middle read and I'm thinking of hitting him on the big one. He's able to pick up on that and put it into motion. It's a bond we have. Chewy also happens to be one of the most unselfish players I've ever known.

When Ron Wolf traded for Keith Jackson from the Dolphins in 1995, it could have caused problems. Keith is a Pro Bowl tight end. He's awesome. Chewy could have been upset by the deal. Instead, he took advantage of the situation. He tried to learn everything he could from Keith, who in my opinion was one of the great tight ends of all time. If that would've been me and they brought in a hotshot quarterback, I would've been pissed. That's how we're different. It's what makes Chewy so special. He knew his time would come and it has. Just to show you how hard Chewy works, that first year we got Keith, Chewy had his best season and was named to the Pro Bowl after catching seven touchdown passes.

Frankie, Chewy, and I have taken tons of vacations together. It drives our wives nuts. They're like, "You spend
more time with each other than you do with us." Maybe
that's true. We just really enjoy hanging out together. I've
had both of them come down to the Kiln a couple times
and I think they get a big kick out of it. We're from different worlds. They're both from the East Coast and I'm from
southern Mississippi. One day when they were visiting,
Scott and I took Frankie and Chewy out on a pontoon boat
on Rotten Bayou. Scott and I would point to where we had
seen a ten-foot alligator on the bank the day before, then
we'd dive in and go swimming. I said, "Chewy, jump in.
The water's great." And he said, "You have got to be shitting me. I'm not getting into that water." Frankie was the
same way. They were scared to death of the water, the alligators, the whole works. There is a very good reason for
that. Frank grew up in Hoboken. I don't think they have
water like that in Hoboken. Life on the bayou was totally
different for them. They would never admit it, but I think
they loved it.

People are constantly asking me about Reggie White.
What can you say? He is by far the best defensive player
to ever play the game. He is the ultimate leader. Now, I
have never gotten up and talked at a team meeting. That
isn't my style. But every week, Reggie will get up in front
of everyone at one of the team meetings and stress how
important it is to win the upcoming game. We all know
that, or at least you think you do, but sometimes you forget
just how important it is if you want to make it to the Super
Bowl. Reggie wanted to make it so bad, he didn't want
anyone forgetting the team's goal. Believe me, with Reggie
around, it was impossible to forget. Some players may
have gotten tired of hearing it, but the more you get tired
of hearing it, the more you remember it. Besides, Reggie is

a great talker. He will be rolling along and telling us what
we have to do and then he'll stop and say, "Isn't that right,
Brett?" And I'll say, "It sure is." What? I'm going to argue
with Reggie White?

Reggie is thirty-five years old, but he is still playing like
he's in his prime. You see him getting blocked by two and
three people and you laugh when fans wonder why his
sack totals are down. Look at it. When he's single-blocked,
he beats people. In the Super Bowl, the Patriots decided
to let Max Lane try to block him one-on-one. He embarrassed the kid. You just can't do that with Reggie. You can't
go into a game thinking Reggie is hurting and he's getting
older so you don't double him. That kind of thinking gets
quarterbacks killed. Reggie can still dominate like no
other player in the league. Period. And when you consider
his career, Reggie White is the best defensive player in
NFL history. He holds the NFL record with 165½ sacks
over twelve seasons. I knew he was good when he was
with the Philadelphia Eagles, but now that I've had a
chance to watch him up close since he arrived in 1993,
he's everything I thought he would be and more. The most
amazing thing I've ever seen him do was throw the Dallas
Cowboys' Larry Allen, a 330-pound offensive lineman, to
the turf like he was a rag doll. And that was in the game
that Reggie had an elbow injury. He threw him 5 yards.
Just tossed him in the air. I'm standing on the sidelines
telling myself, "Geez-us Christ! This guy is amazing."

Maybe the greatest thing about Reggie is when you
need him, he comes through. Some of us bitch and complain about what Reggie believes in or doesn't believe in,
but when you need a big play, guys are always saying,
"C'mon, Reggie. We need you." And sure enough, he'll
come through and make a sack.

There are a lot of skeptics out there who wonder

whether Reggie's torn hamstring was actually cured by
God near the end of the 1995 season. The popular story
was the one that said Reggie was lying on the training
table when a flash of light zapped his hamstring. Look, I'm
not going to argue with the guy. All I know is he was injured and then he was healed. It was a miracle. That's all
I can think of. A lot of people ask me what really happened. All I can say is Reggie played and there was no
way he should have been able to. One hamstring was torn
and he still played at what looked like full speed. Hell,
maybe he was only at 75 percent, but I'll take him at 75
percent over anyone else in the league. The miracle thing
has happened to him several times. I say whatever works,
stay with it. Nothing dramatic like that has happened to
me, but if Reggie gets injured again, I'll be the first one
praying for another miracle.

There is something else people need to realize about
Reggie.

He is a down-to-earth guy. When people think of him,
they think of this big man who's awesome and all-world
on the field and a preacher off it. What they don't see is
the guy who imitates Redd Foxx doing Fred Sanford or Ali
or Bill Cosby. He's got a pretty good routine. He's also a
jokester. He'll dump a bucket of ice-cold water on a team-
mate who's going to the bathroom. He also loves to tell
jokes. Reggie has the worst jokes in the world, but we all
laugh because they're so bad. I can't even remember a Reggie joke, because they're so bad, you want to forget them
as fast as possible.

Reggie is a lot better at telling prayers than jokes, but
he doesn't push his religious beliefs on anyone. He is a
licensed minister, whatever that means, and he tells teammates straight out if they want to talk religion, he'll talk
religion, but if not, that's okay, too. That's important.

That's why people respect him. In the locker room, you can curse and tell dirty jokes around Reggie—not that any of us do—and he's right there in the middle of it. He's cool as long as nothing is insinuated or directed toward him. Trust me.

Nobody is foolish enough to do that.

Whenever anyone asks about Edgar Bennett, I tell them he's the best all-purpose back in the league. I've said that a bunch and I mean it. I even pick on Edgar about it. I tell him he's the best bad-weather running back I've ever seen. He gets mad. He'll say, "What about the good days?" I tell him he's good then, too, but under lousy conditions, he's the best. He also has the best hands of any running back in the NFL. When you put him and Dorsey Levens together, I think you've got one of the best running back tandems in the game today. Think about it. They combined for 1,465 yards rushing and sixty-two catches for another 402 yards receiving. That's big-time production. In our offense, Edgar and Dorsey are perfect. They can run. They can catch. They pick up blitzes as well as anyone, which saves me a ton of wear and tear. I wouldn't trade them for any-one. Not even for the Detroit Lions' Barry Sanders, who just may be the greatest running back of all time. Some-times you daydream and think, "What would it be like to have Barry Sanders in the backfield?" Well, I think it would be pretty good, but I also think there is something to be said for having too much. If we had Barry and gave him the ball twenty-five or thirty times a game, that would probably take away ten touchdown passes a year. Maybe we would be totally unstoppable with Barry Sanders. Or maybe we wouldn't be as good. A team's offensive balance is a delicate thing. I think we're pretty damn good with Edgar and Dorsey.

Sometimes Edgar will get frustrated because even

though he has done a lot of great things, such as becoming the Packers' first back to rush for 1,000 yards since 1978—he did that in 1995—all anyone ever talks about is the Cowboys' Emmitt Smith. Some of the guys on the team started calling him Emmitt Bennett because of it. Edgar doesn't let it bother him. In fact, he handles it better than most. He's got the best smile in the world and he's a super guy. We have been dressing next to each other for six years with the Packers. I played against him in college at Florida State.

It's like we've known each other forever.

The same goes for LeRoy Butler, our strong safety and another Florida State guy. LeRoy is what you'd call an instigator. He isn't afraid to pick on anyone in the locker room. He is the one guy who is always joking and cracking on people. When the season reaches the halfway point and the days start to get long, having LeRoy around really brightens up the place. The great thing about LeRoy is that as much as he dishes it out, he can take it, too. A player will crack on him and he may pretend to be mad, but he couldn't keep a straight face to save his ass. He's always got that shit-eatin' grin going. All those little dance steps and hand jive and things that the team does on the field, that's all LeRoy. He is responsible for the whole deal. LeRoy should be listed in the program as our strong safety—slash—dance choreographer.

When it's game time, LeRoy can get after it. He is one helluva player. If he worked a little harder, he would be the best strong safety to ever play the game. The thing is, he's just pretty content to be really good. Hell, he had a great year last year, especially after he got contact lenses so he could see the football. He stopped dropping easy interceptions and started making one big play after another. He finished with five picks and he knocked down another fourteen passes that would've been completed. The nice thing about LeRoy is he isn't afraid to stick his nose in there. He's not a prima donna. He finished with six and a half sacks, which is more than half of the defensive ends in the league. It would be easy to second-guess LeRoy and tell him, "If only you worked harder." Hey, that's just his personality. He is always going to be really good. I guess he could be a little bit better, but you know what? I like him just the way he is.

Eugene Robinson, our free safety, was a great off-season addition. After twelve seasons in Seattle, we found out he could still play. Chalk another one up for Ron Wolf, who made a terrific trade by sending Matt LaBounty to the Seahawks for Eugene. LaBounty is a good defensive end, but we were loaded there, so he would've had a tough time getting playing time anyway. In return, we got Eugene, who solidified our secondary. All the talk going into camp was whether he could still cover ground at thirty-three. Let me tell you, he didn't look like your typical thirty-three-year-old to me. He showed excellent range for a free safety with six interceptions, which was the most by a Packers safety since a guy named Tom Flynn got nine in 1984. He leads all active players with forty-eight career picks, which is a ton. On top of that, he can really carry a tune. You'll hear this sweet sound coming out of the shower or the hot tub and sure enough, it'll be my man Eugene in there singing away. He is fun to be around and he's the consummate pro. We were lucky to get him.

There isn't much to say about our defensive front four except, "Holy shit." I'm glad I don't have to line up across from them. From Reggie to Santana Dotson to Gilbert Brown to whoever plays right end, be it Sean Jones or Gabe Wilkins, it's the best unit in the NFL. Santana's quickness and Gilbert's size make a terrific twosome. Gilbert's big enough to call it a threesome. He's one of the best run-stoppers in the game. I couldn't begin to imagine what it might be like trying to block him. He's that scary.

Craig Newsome and Doug Evans, our cornerbacks, are the best young duo in the league. I wouldn't trade them for anyone. They're fun to watch, they're as nice as it gets, and they're young. At twenty-five, Craig has established himself as a premier left corner. He loves to hit and he doesn't back down from anyone, including the great ones such as the 49ers' Jerry Rice and the Cowboys' Michael Irvin. He's a tough nut. Evans is more out of the mold of the great cover corners. Quarterbacks love to test him, but they keep coming up short. He can make up ground while the ball is in the air. He's that fast. He led the team in passes defensed with fifteen. That's no surprise because he can really haul ass. I get a kick out of watching our corners work against our receivers in practice. They go at it pretty hard and it makes everyone better, including me.

Antonio Freeman, our starting split end, is unbelievable for a young guy. He has all the tools. He's strong. He's fast. He's smart. He's also one of the best double-move guys in the league. By that, I mean he is really good at convincing the corner he is going to run a slant and then blowing right by him on a go route. He can do it by faking an out, too. The double-move is like a knuckleball. Some guys can throw it and some guys can't. Anyone can make a double-move, but some do it better than others. Antonio really sells it. I don't know how many touchdowns I've thrown to Antonio in the back corner of the end zone after a double-move. He has a great knack for it. He led our team with fifty-six receptions even though he missed four weeks with a broken left forearm. He also had nine touchdown catches, which is awesome considering he only started twelve games.

Robert Brooks, who starts at flanker opposite Free, is the hardest-working man in football. He's a lot like Jerry Rice. Super guy. Helluva receiver. Hard worker.

Robert really is one of the best wideouts in the NFL. When the news hit that Sterling Sharpe was going to retire with a neck injury before the play-offs in '94, I told people we weren't going to miss a beat with Robert and he didn't make a liar out of me. He caught eight passes for 138 yards, including a 59-yarder, in our NFC divisional play-off loss at Dallas. The next season, he became my primary weapon. He caught 102 passes for 1,497 yards and thirteen touchdowns as our go-to guy.

I wasn't surprised.

I knew he could step in just by watching how he handled himself in practice and games. I also knew he would do whatever it took to get the job done. That's why I told everyone not to worry when Sterling went down. I think Robert appreciated that and respected me for saying it. That is when our friendship got really strong. A lot of good came out of Sterling leaving.

Robert and I have grown close on and off the field. We're next-door neighbors, and I blame him totally for that. I was looking to move out of my home on Green Bay's west side—just not enough privacy where I was—and Robert suggested I take a look at a house for sale right down the street from his. I thought that would be cool living right next door to Robert, plus I really liked the house when I saw it. It was a beautiful home set on a spacious, wooded lot at the end of a cul-de-sac. The location was ideal. Shit, listen to me. I've looked at so many houses the past couple of years, I'm starting to sound like a damn Realtor.

Anyway, the only problem with the place was the vacant lot between Robert's house and mine. We weren't too thrilled with the idea of someone buying it and building between us, so we went halves on the lot and bought it. We're thinking of maybe putting a tennis court, a basketball court, and a weight room on it.

For now, I walk across that vacant lot to Robert's house just about every day during the season. He juices—he's a health nut, if you couldn't tell by his zero percent body fat—so I go over there and get some juice. We'll go down to the basement and listen to music in his recording studio. He's one helluva keyboard player. A really talented guy. He put together an entire CD in his basement. It's pretty good, too.

When he isn't recording songs, he's working out. He's a genuine workaholic. That's why I have no doubt he'll come back from his knee injury better than ever. When he tore his left knee up in that *Monday Night Football* game against the 49ers, I jogged up to where he was lying on the field.

I said, "How bad is it?"

Robert looked at me and said, "I blew it out."

I told him I was sorry and he just said, "Don't worry about it. Just go out and beat 'em. I'll be back. Don't worry about it. You know I'll be back."

Robert tore the anterior cruciate ligament, the medial collateral ligament, and the patellar tendon. He also chipped some bones, but he rehabilitated it like a demon. And his body heals faster than anyone I've ever known. In March, he was running better than guys like James Bostic and Matthew Dorsett, and they injured their knees six, seven weeks before Robert blew his out. Robert will come back and he'll be quicker than anybody. He'll be full speed again. I have no doubt about that.

On top of that, Robert really wants a Super Bowl ring. He got one this season, of course, but he doesn't really feel like he was part of it. He wants to be contributing on the field. I think he'll have a big season for us in '97.

Robert and I occasionally ride to games together. We don't think it's any big deal, but I doubt Aikman's riding to games with Michael Irvin. We're different. We've got a really close team from top to bottom. That's why we won it all, or a big reason, anyway. We're a good team with great coaches, but other teams can say that, too. What separates us is that we get along so well. There's no arguing or fighting. We're all genuinely pulling for each other and that means so much. I want Reggie or Sean or LeRoy to get a sack. I want Desmond Howard to take a punt back all the way. I want Edgar to rush for 100 yards. I root for all of our players to do well. The whole team is the same way. You can't coach it. You can't preach it. You can't say, "You guys have to get along." It's got to develop. I tip my helmet to Ron Wolf and Mike Holmgren for putting together a team that can do that. We've got great chemistry. Teams like the 49ers and the Vikings have taken trips together before training camp to build closeness. I don't know if that works. To me, I think either you have it or you don't. Now, people may not want to read this, but on paper, I didn't think we were the best team in the NFL last season. I thought that Dallas, at their skill positions, was probably better. But instead of fighting against each other, the way some teams do, we fought with each other. That makes a world of difference. Everyone getting along can be what gets you over the edge to win a Super Bowl. When you put eleven guys together who believe in each other and enjoy being around each other, you can do anything. We proved it.

Naturally it helped to have the support of the entire organization, from the front office on down. Bob Harlan, the president, sets the tone by being down-to-earth and understanding. NFL owners could learn a lot from watching him. He runs the operation not only with savvy and foresight but with great compassion. He cares about people.

When I think of my teammates, I don't just think about the players. The public relations staff, led by my all-time-favorite guy, Lee Remmel, is extremely helpful. So are Linda McCrossin and the other secretaries. How about the job our grounds crew did replacing an entire field in one week before the NFC championship against Carolina? That was amazing, especially for the middle of January.

Gordon "Red" Batty, our equipment manager, has got to be the best in the business. The job he does to keep us from freezing off our asses is amazing. Bryan Nehring, Tom Bakken, and Tim O'Neill, his assistants, are the hardest-working equipment managers in football. They hustle all day, every day, even when it's hot as hell in training camp. When you see them running around out there, it keeps you going. The medical staff is the same way. Pepper Burruss, our head trainer, and I have been through a lot together. He was totally professional the whole time I was going through the addiction. Same way with Kurt Fielding and Sam Ramsden, his assistants. They proved to be true friends by protecting my privacy instead of blabbing all over town.

I hate to start naming names because sure as shit I'll forget someone.

There is one more I have to mention and that's Leo Yelle, Jr., our mail clerk. Leo is forty-two and developmentally disabled, but he is the happiest guy in the world. I loved going down to the mail room and wrestling with him or teasing him. We'd line up across from each other and get down into a three-point stance. Then I'd call out the signals and we'd rush each other. Mostly Leo would just laugh. Teammates would tell me how nice it was that I would go spend time with Leo. I would say, "It's nice of *him* to cheer me up." That was one reason I would look forward to seeing Leo. Whenever I was having a tough day, I'd stop by, and sure enough, he'd cheer me right up. He was doing me the favor. I just heard that Leo won't be back with the team this year. I guess the mail room looked like Christmas every day because of our success and it got to be too much for him. Everyone talks about the team's "key losses" during the off-season. I guarantee you Ron Wolf will find a linebacker and a punt returner. Replacing Leo will be a whole lot tougher.

# 9

# GREEN BAY: THE REAL AMERICA'S TEAM

I was in Hawaii with my agent, Bus Cook, after the Super Bowl this past year when we stopped in a restaurant for a bite to eat. I don't remember the name of the place because we were lost. That seems to happen quite a bit when Bus and I get together. Anyway, we didn't get more than ten feet into the place when a little old Hawaiian lady walked up to me. She stopped two feet in front of me and stared.

"Are you that quarterback for the Packers?" she said, looking up at me through thick glasses.

"Yes I am, ma'am."

"Oh, my God," she said, "we watch you all the time."

Then the woman, who had to be about seventy years old and no more than four feet, eight inches tall, gets all excited. She grabbed my arm and took me over to her table to introduce me to her friends. At the table are three other little old Hawaiian ladies. They're all smiling and happy to see me. I couldn't believe it. I looked over at Bus and he's laughing. Here we are in the middle of the Pacific

Ocean, about as far away as you can get from Green Bay, and four seventy-year-old Hawaiian ladies are telling me how much they love the Packers.

I just about passed out.

When we beat Carolina in the NFC championship game, Packers President Bob Harlan called us "the real America's Team." And you know what, I think we are.

There are a lot of people out there who like the high-profile teams and the razzle-dazzle and the glitter and all that sort of stuff. But the majority of people I meet are tired of seeing players bitch at the referees. They're tired of hearing players talk bad about other teams. They're tired of owners threatening to move the team if they don't get a new stadium or whatever. The holdouts, the contract hassles, all that stuff, it gets old. I think people have been waiting for something different. Then we show up.

We're like the kid who walks through a door and somebody is throwing him a surprise party. It's great.

The whole notion of Green Bay as America's Team really developed a long, long time ago. Green Bay is a small town. The community owns the team. We play outside, on grass, in the cold, the rain, the snow, whatever. It's real football, the way the game was meant to be played. John Madden said that if there is such a thing as a shrine to pro football, Lambeau Field is it. That's because this field and this team are tied to so many great moments in football. People remember the Packers from the sixties just when football was becoming big on TV. Vince Lombardi and all those great teams, people remember. When the Super Bowl started way back when the Packers were there, kicking ass.

Fans remember all that, but until we started winning again, the title of America's Team sort of faded away. In the seventies and eighties the team was pathetic. That's when Dallas latched onto the title. Now we're back and people all over the country are excited again. President Clinton came to see us practice last year and he asked for a tour of Lambeau Field. "I never thought I'd get a chance to see this place," Clinton said.

I think the majority of the country, even fans from cities whose teams didn't make it to the Super Bowl, were pulling for us in that game. The Packers have such a great tradition and that still means a lot. Whenever you hear or read about Green Bay, it's always something about "the frozen tundra of Lambeau Field" or something about "Titletown U.S.A.," or Vince Lombardi, or Bart Starr, or Ray Nitschke, or Paul Hornung, or something about those teams from the sixties. Fans love that stuff. They wanted the Packers to be successful again. I've always loved football, so I knew something about the team's history before I got here. I did a book report in fifth grade on Paul Hornung. I probably got an A on it. I was always good at book reports in school. When I met Hornung, I told him that. He seemed impressed. Although I knew about the Packers, I didn't have a clue about Wisconsin. Until I got drafted I didn't even know where Wisconsin was. I knew it was in the Midwest someplace, but if you had given me a map of the United States without the states labeled, I couldn't have pointed it out. I definitely know where Green Bay is now. When I turn on the Weather Channel in the off-season back in Mississippi, I check out the weather in Green Bay and go, oh shit, it's cold.

My first year in Atlanta we played Green Bay and I thought it was kind of a joke. Green Bay versus Atlanta. There's a battle of titans. How many people are going to tune in for that one? Not too many. When I got traded from Atlanta to Green Bay, I just thought oh man, what am I getting myself into? I didn't know a thing about Green Bay except the Packers weren't that good. But they had this rich, rich history. That intrigued me. I thought man, what if we bring that back?

When I came to Green Bay, I embraced that tradition. I figured that's what I'm here for, to be a part of Packers history. That means everything to me. Like winning MVP or the Super Bowl. I want to etch my name in this team's history. A lot of people just come and go and the only way you can find them is by picking up a program and going through the lists of names of old players. Years from now when people open up a program, I want them to see me on the first page. Lombardi, Starr, Hornung, they'll never be forgotten. I don't want to be forgotten either.

I'd love to be part of a team like the Packers were in the sixties, to win that many championships. Or like the Cowboys or 49ers. If you think of dominance in the NFL, you think of the 49ers and the Cowboys. I would like to be part of that. Just winning the Super Bowl to me is nothing, really. Of course it's a great accomplishment, but I don't want it to be a onetime deal.

Look at the Chicago Bears in 1985. The Bears are a perfect example. They were a really good team, probably should've won about five or six championships. Jim Mc-Mahon told me that the Bears were better in other years but they only won it that one year. I don't want it to be like that in Green Bay. Look at Jim. If he wouldn't have made the *Super Bowl Shuffle* video and been wild, he'd be forgotten. Same thing could happen to me and I don't want that. I want to be dominant. I really do.

The Packers are one of the few teams in the NFL with their own Hall of Fame. I'll walk through it from time to time and look at all the old equipment and all the old names and try to imagine what those guys were thinking back then when they were playing. Then I'll kind of propel myself fifty years into the future and think of some guy going through the Hall of Fame and running across some of my stuff. I want that person to think, "Hmm, that Favre, he wasn't too bad. I wonder if he could play today?" Or I'll dream about some young guy walking up to an old-timer and asking him, "Say, was that Favre guy any good?" And that old-timer will look at him and say, "Hell yeah, you should have seen him play."

It may sound corny but sometimes when I dream about the future and my place in the game, I think about how great it would be to have a street or a school in Green Bay named after me. Favre High School or Favre Boulevard. That would be pretty cool. Although the way I drive they might not want to name a road after me. It might be safer to name a park after me. But I dream about that. It's like when I was a kid and thinking about signing autographs for fans. I used to practice my signature in bed late at night.

But dreaming doesn't get it done. To make my mark in Green Bay, we had to win. If you don't win, people don't notice you; I don't care how good you are. That's just the way it is. The idea of Green Bay as "Titletown U.S.A." meant something to old-time fans but not to the kids. The last time the Packers won a championship Lyndon Johnson was president. Shoot, I wasn't even born yet. But now Titletown means something again, and I'm part of it. Kids know it and so do the old-timers.

There are so many people I run into around the country that tell me they're Packers fans. The country group Little Texas, Darius, the lead singer for Hootie and the Blowfish, comedian David Spade, they've all told me they love the Pack. Chris Farley goes out on the *Tonight Show* throwing cheeseheads into the audience. Charlie Sheen, I talked to him and he tells me, "I watch you guys every week, you're unbelievable."

This past summer I met Gabrielle Reese, the beach volleyball player from Brazil. We were at a Nike convention in Kansas City. Well, she doesn't know me from Adam and I don't know her from Eve, but she came up to me and said, "We were all so happy for you guys. We watched your games on TV and we don't usually watch football but we were just so happy for the Packers."

And I told her that I hear that from a lot of people.

"It's because of your image," she said. "You just seem like such nice guys, you work hard, you enjoy your success with your fans, it's just wonderful."

I thought that was pretty nice. It just goes to show you that people around the country, even if they're not football fans, can appreciate what we've done. They're just so happy for us. I don't think if, say, Pittsburgh would have won it that people would have cared, except for Pittsburgh fans. We have so many people who are not football fans who are now Green Bay Packers fans just because of what we've done over the last couple years. It's pretty amazing.

I can't remember where I heard this but last year someone said: "In other cities, fans throw things at the players. In Green Bay, the players throw themselves at the fans."

The Lambeau Leap, man, that's a big deal for us now. It's cool. People love it and so do the players. It's kind of like being back in grade school and playing at recess. It's just that much fun. Robert Brooks is the best at the leap. He jumps right into the fans' laps. He's got springs. When I try it, I'll have to find a low wall because I don't think I could make it up into the stands the way Robert does. Damn he's good. Robert once told me that he felt like a rock star jumping off a stage and into the arms of his fans. He trusts the fans completely to throw him back.

"It's the best feeling in the world," Robert said. "And I don't think you could do it anywhere but here."

There really is something special between the Packers and our fans. When the team tore up the playing field after the NFC championship game, they packaged the turf in boxes and sold the stuff for ten dollars a box to benefit local charities. About 22,000 boxes of Frozen Tundra were sold in two hours. People went nuts.

Right before the divisional play-off game against San Francisco, Green Bay got hit with a foot of snow. Lambeau Field was buried. They could've held snowmobile races on the field, it was so bad. So what do the Packers do? They ask their fans to shovel them out. Ted Eisenreich, the Packers' buildings supervisor, let everyone know that he needed two hundred people to dig out the field. The Packers paid six dollars an hour. So many people showed up that dozens had to be turned away. Some people even said that they'd work for free. Amazing. You can't get a kid to shovel your driveway for under ten bucks. But in Green Bay, when it comes to the Packers, you'd have people out there shoveling for free just to be in Lambeau Field and just to be part of the team.

Of course, in Green Bay, the fans are part of the team. They own it.

The Packers are the only publicly owned, nonprofit team in football. Hell, in all of professional sports. Something like two thousand stockholders own the Packers. And none of them makes a dime off their investment. Instead, they have a team that they can call their own, forever. Think Cleveland Browns fans wouldn't have liked to have that arrangement before their team skipped off to Baltimore? There are Packers stockholders living in every state in the country and even in three foreign countries. Maybe that makes us the World's Team.

Unlike the rest of the league, where an Al Davis or some other owner threatens to take his team someplace else if he doesn't get what he wants, the Packers will always be in Green Bay. According to the organization's bylaws, if for some strange reason the Packers had to be sold, the money would go to Green Bay's Sullivan-Wallen American Legion Post. Let's see, the Packers are valued at about $170 million or so. Man, those Legionnaires could have one helluva party with that bundle.

People say that there's a college-type atmosphere that surrounds Green Bay and the Packers. But I think the fans treat the Packers more like their high school team.

Green Bay is the smallest city in the league. People here grew up with the Packers. That's all they've ever had. They were born and bred to be Green Bay Packers fans. The team is part of who they are. It's like no other relationship in sports. Look at the Atlanta Falcons, for example. If they win, it's easy to follow them. But what about when the team loses? There's always something else to do in Atlanta. And so many people living in Atlanta have moved there from somewhere else. They're not natives. What do the Falcons mean to them? There's no tie to the team if you just moved there. Your dad didn't take you to a game when you were little. You didn't grow up and go to Jerry Glanville Junior High.

The Packers are different.

The team has been in Green Bay since 1919. Kids go to Lombardi Middle School. People drive down Lombardi Avenue. The stadium is named after Curly Lambeau, the guy who not only started the team but also played and coached it as well. Check out the Yellow Pages. There are forty businesses in town that use the Packers' name. There's everything from Packer City Antique to Packerland Kennel. You know that people love the team when you can find Packerland Chiropractic in the phone book.

Green Bay is Green Bay people, state of Wisconsin people. There are some people who have moved in, but the majority of people were born there and they are going to die there. Team loyalty is incredible. People will come up to me, grown men with families of their own, and tell me stories of following the Packers when they were three years old. Or about their daddy willing them season tickets when he passed away. Some will have tears in their eyes when they talk about the team.

And it's not just the fans that are passionate. Some of the old players are just as emotional. Defensive end Sean Jones has played for the Raiders and the Oilers, but he told me he's never seen anything like what we have here. "What people outside Green Bay don't understand," Sean said, "is that for us to be validated as a great team, we've got to first prove our greatness to the Willie Woods, the Willie Davises, the Bart Starrs, all those great old players. I am convinced that the Ray Nitschkes and those guys probably don't think we could have played with them."

But I don't mind that kind of pressure. We do have a legacy to live up to and that's exciting. We are part of something that is bigger than just the moment.

A few weeks after the Super Bowl I talked with Bart Starr and he told me he was so excited for the Packers that he could still hardly sleep. Now, that's something. Here's Bart Starr, one of the greatest quarterbacks of all time, a Hall of Fame quarterback who won just about all there was to win in the 1960s, and he's as excited as a schoolboy after we won the Super Bowl. That's what this team means to not only the community and the state but also to the old Packers. They want us to do well because they still feel part of the team. That makes me feel proud.

God, Bart Starr, what he did during his career was unbelievable. I wish I could be half as good as he was. That
would mean I would win two or three championships. To
me that would be a helluva career. He was an amazing
quarterback and he's a really nice person. I don't care for
autographs much, but I keep a football autographed by
Bart and myself on a shelf in my home office. Hell, I don't
care about my signature but his means something. I feel
honored to have my name on the same ball as his.

Even when the Packers were bad, Lambeau Field was
sold out for every game. There's a waiting list for season
tickets that has thirty thousand names on it. That's amazing. You know that those fans saw a lot of bad football
during those years. Yet they stuck by their team. You tell
me where else in the NFL, or in any professional sport for
that matter, you would have that. I can't think of any other
place. And that's why I love Green Bay.

Ron Wolf calls Lambeau Field the ultimate place to
play a game. He's right, but I think we need to expand the
stadium another twenty thousand seats. Make Lambeau
hold eighty thousand. Then you'd have some place to
play. Teams don't want to play up in Green Bay now; hell,
with eighty thousand people in the stands, it would be a
nightmare.

Even though there were great players before me in
Green Bay, coming here allowed me to create my own
identity. If I had gone someplace else, it wouldn't have
been the same. If I had gone to Pittsburgh, people would
have called me the next Terry Bradshaw. In San Francisco
I would have been the next Joe Montana or the next Steve
Young. I don't know what I would have been if I had
stayed in Atlanta, probably the next Steve Bartkowski.

Of course, this city and this team have been a perfect
fit for a lot of people. Green Bay has been good for Mike

Holmgren. He had a lot of success as an assistant coach at San Francisco but he established himself as a great head coach in Green Bay. Mike embraced the tradition of the Packers. He brought in all the old players from those Lombardi teams and held their success up as an example. Reggie White came here in the later part of his career and not only enhanced his reputation but earned something he always wanted: a Super Bowl ring. Same for Keith Jackson, Sean Jones, Eugene Robinson, a lot of veteran guys.

Aside from that, Green Bay and I kind of go together. I think I'm fun to watch and that I give 100 percent on the field. I respect my opponent. You won't see me talking shit to the other team. I don't believe in that. And I think that the fans in Green Bay can relate to me. They're hardworking people who like to have fun, just like me. Green Bay is a small-town and I'm a small-town boy. It's easy to get around in. It's comfortable. I enjoy Green Bay. I didn't enjoy Atlanta. It's a great city and all but it's just too big for me. I don't like New York. I don't like L.A. Nothing against them personally; it's just that they're too much for me. I'm more country and small-town. I'm just not at home in a big city.

It's closer knit here. As I said, Robert Brooks lives right next door to me. I go over to his house and we talk football or just hang out. We ride to games together. Robert and I have a much different relationship than other quarterbacks have with their receivers. I doubt Dan Marino rides to games or practices with O. J. McDuffie. I doubt Steve Young and Jerry Rice are in the same car pool. I doubt they all live side by side. In some ways it reminds me of being back in high school, hanging out together and riding to games together.

When I was in high school, though, there weren't many people who would come to the games. I guess everybody in Hancock County came, but there weren't that many folks in the county. When I played college ball at Southern Mississippi, we'd get maybe fifteen thousand people for a big game. Hell, I was out there to show off and there wasn't anybody there to show off in front of. It was upsetting, it really was. So I was thrilled to death when I got to Green Bay and saw that I was going to play in front of more than sixty thousand fans every game.

People here live for football. It's that simple. We'll have four thousand fans show up for a minicamp workout. We had forty-five thousand for our intrasquad scrimmage last year. Lambeau has been sold out since 1960. And the fans let you know they're here. When I run out onto the field, I want the fans to be going crazy and rocking the house. And that's exactly what we get in Green Bay. When I pull up to Lambeau a couple hours before a game, the parking lot is full. People are grilling out and partying, just having a great time. They're out there in sunshine, rain, snow, whatever. The weather doesn't matter. Football matters. I love that. They're pumped. Ready to go.

The first time I had family from back home with me they couldn't believe what was going on in the parking lot. At the house before the game I'm just the Brett my family and friends know, goofing off and having fun. But when I get into the parking lot before the game, it seems like I'm a totally different person. I haven't changed but all these people cheering for me and clapping and hooting and hollering, well it's kind of embarrassing. But at the same time it shows how much our fans really do care.

That gets me in the right frame of mind to play the game. If there were only twenty thousand people out there and they didn't really give a damn, it would be depressing. But Packers fans care. They live and die with the team. I know a lot of players say that about their fans but it's really true here. You ask any former player about Packers fans and they'll tell you the same thing.

We've got fans all over the country, people who used to live in Wisconsin and moved away but still follow the team with a passion. There are others who fell in love with the team during the Lombardi years and stuck by the team. No matter where we play in the league we have fans at the game. In Seattle last fall we had more fans in the Kingdome than the Seahawks did. It was like a home game. Same thing in Detroit. And in Minneapolis. And a lot of places. The type of greeting we get before a game, shoot, a lot of teams would be happy to get it after a big win. That's what's so great about it.

In a lot of ways, the people in Green Bay and in Wisconsin are like the people back home in Kiln. If you just looked at it on the surface, you wouldn't say that. The accents are different. Shoot, the weather is really different. People eat different food. In Wisconsin, people eat brats. Where I'm from we eat crawfish. But that's just surface stuff. The people in both places are all good people. They love to have a good time and they treat their players well. It's almost too nice. I go out to eat in Green Bay and people want to do everything for me. But that makes it great. That's the way Kiln is, too. When I stop and get gas back home, someone comes running out, "Hey, what's going on, Bud, ain't seen you in a long time." Same as in Green Bay. People will see me when I get back for training camp and they'll go, "Hey, how you doing, Brett? Good to have you back. Hope you have a great season." Just like back home, people care.

I've seen players who will come to a community, play football, and when their career is over, they're out of there. It's all business. They don't care where they play. I understand that but it's not for me. I saw that firsthand with

Sterling Sharpe. Sterling was a helluva receiver for us for a long time. There weren't too many any better. But he never got close to the fans or the community.

Sterling was his own man. And I respected that. He chose not to talk to the media and he stood by that decision. He said he was paid to play football and not to talk to reporters. That was fine. Personally I think talking with reporters is part of my job, part of my responsibility. But I had no problem with Sterling's decision. I think he's pretty damn good on ESPN, but I figured he would be. Everyone else seemed surprised but that's only because Sterling never showed that side of himself to the public. But in the locker room he was very animated and a real bright guy

But I didn't think what he pulled on the team in 1994 was real bright. Actually I thought it was bullshit.

Right before our first game of the season against Minnesota, Sterling announced he wasn't going to play unless the Packers renegotiated his contract. I had no idea he was going to hold out. I didn't know anything about it until the team meeting the day before the game. Mike came into our team meeting and talked about what we needed to do against the Vikings. Then he said, "Unfortunately, Sterling is going to hold out." Just like that, matter-of-fact. Mike said that's Sterling's choice and he could do that if he wanted to. He told us that we would be fine without him so let's move on.

A lot of guys were like, shit, we need to pay him, even though they were kind of pissed that he would pull that right before our season opener. I knew that without Sterling it would be much more difficult to win, but I thought, "Screw it, we'll win without him." Sterling walked out on his team. He was our star player, our go-to guy. To do that to our team at that point was really difficult to take. Look, he signed that contract a couple years before and it looked pretty good then. Now it didn't. Well, live with it. I sign a contract, I put my name on a deal, and that's it.

I feel like I should be making more than I am now but I would never walk out on my team. Especially the day before a game. Now, I could do that. I could walk out the day before a game and demand a new contract and, you know what, I could get away with it. I know I could do that. But I'd be hated forever, not only by the players but also by the fans. Having the respect of the fans and my teammates is more important to me than doubling my salary.

Twenty years from now we'll all be gone from here. My career will be over. I'll have enough money in my pocket to last a long time. That's not all that important to me. What the fans think of me, what they remember, and what my ex-teammates think about me, that'll be much more important than what is in my wallet.

That's why when Sterling did that, I couldn't believe it. I came out and said so in the newspapers. I said we'd win without him. I meant it. I wasn't mad at Sterling, just disappointed. Management ended up giving in and Sterling came back the next day for the Vikings game. I threw him a touchdown pass. I went up to him after the score and congratulated him. After we beat Minnesota 16–10 that day I took Sterling aside and told him I meant what I said in the newspapers but that I was happy he was back. Sterling said there was no problem. And that was the end of it. The incident didn't really change things between us. I see Sterling now and we shake hands or hug and have a good time. He's a good person. It's just that we value different things.

The Tuesday after the Vikings game Mike Reinfeldt, the Packers' chief financial officer, called Bus to see if I would be willing to defer $450,000 of my contract so the team could pay Sterling. Bus asked me and I said yeah. I didn't care. I'm pretty easygoing about all that stuff. Scott or somebody will call me about a business deal and say, "Okay, we think this is good." I'll just say do it. I don't go investigate. I don't check out every little detail. So when the Packers asked if I would restructure my contract, I said sure. I didn't ask a lot of questions.

Sterling was still on my team. I like Sterling. I didn't agree with what he did, but I like him. And I thought he was a helluva player. So it wasn't like I disliked him and was thinking, "Screw Sterling." Shoot, we all know people who do things we don't agree with but we still like them.

I told Sterling flat out, "Look, I don't agree with what you did, but I love you to death and I'll still throw to you."

Sterling helped me early in my career. He was a great crutch to lean on. I could always throw to him when we needed something and he always produced. When things went bad, Sterling was always there. He saved my ass a lot. If he was double-covered, all that meant was that maybe I'd try to throw the ball a little harder and squeeze it in there to him. I trusted that he would make the play and he would. So it made things easier when I was a young quarterback. Still, I know that if I hadn't had Sterling those first couple of years, I would've had to find another way to do things. And I would have.

It's funny, but when Sterling set the NFL record for pass receptions with 108 in 1992, I didn't get much credit for getting him the ball. He had an outstanding season and it was an impressive accomplishment but he was never one to spread the credit around. But that's okay, because I know the truth.

It's interesting to see the way Green Bay reaches out to the Packers. A good example is when Reggie White's church, the Inner City Church in Knoxville, Tennessee, burned down. People in the area raised and then donated more than a quarter of a million dollars to rebuild it.

That's Green Bay for you. That's what makes it unique. That's what makes it different than any other city in the league. Our fans embrace the players. If that had happened to any other player, they would have done the same thing. Maybe they wouldn't have raised as much money, maybe they would have raised more, I don't know. But I do know they would do anything they could to help a player. And I don't think the rest of the country really understands that, the relationship Packers fans have with us players. It's unique. You hear a lot of guys around the league talk about how great their fans are, but I know for a fact that Green Bay fans are the best. There's no doubt that no other city in the league would have done what Green Bay did.

Yet there are some people who don't want to believe that. Last year a piece on ESPN's *Outside the Lines* made it seem like Green Bay is a bad place for black players. That's just crap.

First of all, ESPN came in and said they were going to do a story on small-town America and they turned the story into a racial issue. They more or less lied to players. They got guys sitting down to do an on-air interview and they asked them, "What's it like to be a black player here?" Well, what kind of question is that? They could just as well ask me what's it like to be a white quarterback in Green Bay. When I go out to eat, people point and stare. When I'm at a stop sign, people come up to my car and look in. When I'm driving down the road, people recognize me and wave.

Being a black player in Green Bay and having people look at you isn't because of the color of your skin. They look over and see Robert Brooks, a Packer, and that's exciting to people. Reggie White pulls up, you aren't going to mistake him for someone else. People are going to take notice. I've been out with buddies of mine from home and people will come up to me and say, "Hey, Brett." And then they ask my buddies what position they play. That's not racial. People assume if some big guys are hanging around with me that they might be players, too. They may be mistaken but that doesn't make them bad people.

I thought that story was misleading. I thought it was unfair, especially to Green Bay, because I think the people are genuinely friendly. Black guys will say, "Well, you don't see what we go through." And I don't. I'm sure there are some problems. But I thought Keith Jackson and Sean Jones did a helluva job when they said that they were skeptical at first about coming to Green Bay but that their experience here has been great. These are All-Pro players who have played in a lot of NFL cities. They know what they're talking about. So to have them come out and say Green Bay has been a great place for them to play says a lot.

I thought the story was unfortunate but ESPN has been good to me and I like the guys over there. I just thought it was a bad story.

I really can't envision playing someplace other than in Green Bay. I wouldn't know what to think or how to act. I don't know if another city would rally around me like Green Bay has. I don't know if fans someplace else would embrace me, win or lose.

I've been through a lot here with the team and in my own personal life. The fans have always been there for me. That's unusual in professional sports today. Fans can be fickle. They can turn on you. I've seen it happen to other players. But not in Green Bay. You play hard and give it all you've got here and the fans will love you for life.

Leave Green Bay and play for someone else? I don't even like to think about it. That's too hard to imagine. If the Packers want me to play the rest of my career in Green Bay, I'd love to do it. People have asked me about playing for Steve Mariucci in San Francisco. Steve's a close friend. Our wives are close. It was tough on us all when Steve left the Packers to coach at California. We hated to see him go. I could play for Steve, sure, that would be great. But I don't want to leave Green Bay to do it. If Mike ever left and Steve came to Green Bay, that would be ideal. But I wouldn't leave the Packers for Steve. We love to be around each other but Green Bay has been too good for me.

# 10

# INSIDE THE HUDDLE

When I step into the huddle, it's the greatest feeling in the world.

First of all, I get to go in there and tell ten guys what to do and they actually listen. I'd like to think it's because they respect me. I think about that often. In practice, I'll sit there and go damn, there are twenty-two people out here on this field at one time and all eyes are on me. Everyone goes off my cadence. Everyone does the play that I call. It's totally different than the real world. It's not the real world. It's a special feeling. It's a rush of power. That's what makes it great, because when you go back to the locker room and you leave, you can't tell anyone what to do. Then you're just another guy and nobody listens to you. Shoot, that sense of being a leader and having power and all that stuff you don't have otherwise is pretty special. If you don't feel that way, you're in the wrong business.

Getting into that huddle isn't as simple as stepping onto Lambeau Field on a Sunday morning. A ton of hard work and preparation goes into each game. That includes my teammates, the coaching staff, the trainers, the equipment guys. Everybody.

People ask what my week is like. Well, here's a chance to see for yourself. Come along and I'll walk you through it.

## MONDAY

The day after a game I try to get into the locker room by ten o'clock. We don't have to be in until noon, but I like to come in and work out the soreness. I'll stretch out, do some weight lifting, and hop on the treadmill or the Stair-Master to work up a sweat. After that I like to get into the whirlpool to loosen up a bit and relax.

At noon, we'll meet by position to go over the previous game.

By now the coaches have the game film broken down. We'll go in and the quarterbacks coach—it'll be Andy Reid this season—will hand us a sheet that has all eighty plays, or however many we ran in that week's game, listed in order. The coach will have a note written next to every play on the sheet. Good footwork. Poor judgment. Whatever. And he will have a grade for each play. We don't get to see the grade, but that's how the staff grades players at the end of the season. They go over every play from every game and if a player has too many bad grades, he may not be back. Once the sheets are handed out, Coach will roll the film and critique each play. He'll read off the play, like 22 Z IN, and say things like great throw, good read, good judgment. I learn the play doing that. It becomes etched in my mind, so the next time I drop back and it's 22 Z IN, I'll remember it. It's hard to remember every play because we may go ten weeks without calling a certain play, but the repetition is helpful, so we do it over and over again.

When we're finished with the film session, all the players will hop in their cars and drive across the Lambeau Field parking lot to the Hutson Center where Kent Johnston, our strength and conditioning coach, will take us through stretching exercises. Then we'll jog and do wind sprints. It's no big deal. Afterward, we drive back up to the locker room and we're done for the day. Some guys lift weights. Other guys will hang out in the locker room playing dominos or shooting the bull with the media.

If the weather is still nice, I may hustle over to one of the local golf courses to get in a quick nine before dark. If it's late fall or winter, I'll usually head home around four o'clock, take a nap, and get up for supper at six. Most of the time I'll get together with Frankie Winters and Mark Chmura and some of the fellas and we'll watch *Monday Night Football*. It's usually pretty low-key, though, and almost always an early night. Almost.

## TUESDAY

This is my day off.

I always go into the locker room anyway. I'll pick up my check and grab a tape of the upcoming opponent's most recent game. That way I can get a head start on the week. I'll usually watch about an hour's worth of tape, which is broken down so I'm only seeing their defense. It's nonstop. Next play. Next play. Next play.

At this point I'm just trying to get a feel for how their defense plays. If they're in Cover 3 for most of the game, I know it's their predominant pass coverage. I don't pay any attention to what they do in regards to particular down-and-distance situations. That comes later in the week. Right now I'm looking to get a general feel and trying to pick up some keys. The safety cheating is a big one. He may have to cover half of the field, so sooner or later, you know he's got to get over there even if he's creeping toward the line. I'll look for things like that.

If we're playing Dallas that week, I'll try to find a tape of their game against a team such as Philadelphia or Kansas City that runs an offense similar to ours. I think we have the best offensive system in the NFL. It allows me to be precise, but I can also deviate if I have to. It doesn't hurt that I have a great coach in Mike Holmgren. He puts me in situations to be productive, especially if everything's going right. And when things don't go right, I step in and try to make something happen.

To be honest, I'm not sure how to stop Brett Favre and this offense. A couple years ago, teams would play man-to-man coverage and blitz. I love that now, so you can't do that. The latest thing is to try to keep me in containment. Fine. If you don't rush up the middle, I'll just step up in the pocket and beat you that way. The best way to slow me down is to have a rover follow me everywhere and also be able to play good man-to-man coverage, the way Dallas and Kansas City do, behind it. If there's no one to throw to, you're stuck, no matter how good a quarterback you are.

When I throw an interception, the reason most likely is either poor judgment—thinking I can throw the out when a cornerback is too close—or just a bad read because I threw it even though the guy is covered.

I used to let interceptions bother me a lot more than I do now. That, and the fact that I know the offense a lot better now, is why I'm throwing less. I used to try throwing a touchdown on the next play to make up for an interception. It doesn't work that way. Now I'll throw an interception and, more than likely, come back and pick you to death. You don't have to get it all back at once.

I have come to appreciate dinking and dunking and picking defenses apart. In fact, I like that more now than the 70-yard pass because those don't come very often. I'd rather be a surgeon and complete twenty passes than hit one big one for 80 yards. I think about all that stuff while I'm watching tape of the upcoming opponent. No matter how into the tape I get, I still try to be out of the office by midafternoon on my day off.

Especially if it's still golf weather.

## WEDNESDAY

I'm at team headquarters in time for an 8:30 quarterback meeting that's conducted by offensive line coach Tom Lovat. I hate this meeting. It's boring as hell, but I have to admit it's really helpful. Tom will go through the defensive fronts as they relate to pass coverages. For example, Tom will say, "You know they're running man-to-man pass coverage if they're in a 33 front." Or, "You know they're running a particular zone coverage if they're in a 46 front." It helps me begin to relate the two. So when I walk up to the line during the game and see a 33 front, I know they're probably in man coverage. Sure enough, they will be. Tom's excellent at breaking that down. The offensive linemen aren't at this meeting. It's just Tom, the quarterbacks, and the quarterbacks coach. Tom also goes over the opposing defense's blitz package and tendencies.

Now it's nine o'clock, time for our team meeting, which goes by pretty quick. We have a team meeting every day except Monday and Tuesday. Mike will come in for five minutes and say, "Okay, men. New week. Here's what we've got to do." Let's say we're playing Kansas City. He'll come in and tell us we're playing a real good team with excellent special teams. He'll talk a little bit about the previous week. Big win. Good week. Whatever. Then we break down and go to position meetings.

First, we'll get the offense and defense in the same room. We'll go through the scouting report and talk about each opposing player. It's pretty generic. Tom does their defensive linemen. Gil Haskell, who coaches our receivers, will cover their linebackers. Harry Sydney, who coaches our running backs, will talk about their secondary.

Harry will say, "At left corner, Deion Sanders. Six foot one. One hundred and ninety-five pounds. Eighth year. Great player. Covers the field great. We don't want to attack him too much." Then we'll go on to the next player. Gil will say, "Junior Seau. Six foot three. Two hundred and forty-five pounds. Good speed. Covers the field real well. Good side-to-side lateral player. Sometimes a little overaggressive."

It's a good refresher and it lasts only a few minutes.

Then Sherman Lewis, our offensive coordinator, will give a quick summary. Sherm will say, "Good defense. Ranked fifth in the league right now. Good outside pass rushers. We've got our hands full, but if we protect Brett, we'll be all right."

After that, it's time to cover the running game.

Tom will go through twenty, twenty-five run plays. It lasts about thirty minutes. I don't pay attention at all to the run plays unless there's a new running play or a new formation. If there is, I write it down. Most of the runs are the same. When Tom's done going through his sheets on the running game, he takes the offensive linemen into another room. Then either Sherm or Mike will go through the passing attack. On Wednesdays, we cover our passes that week against their base defense. It's about forty-five plays.

When we're finished with meetings, it's time for lunch, which usually lasts from 12:00 to 1:30. Some guys have to go to special teams at 12:15. I'll spend this time getting in a workout, messing around in the weight room, or catching some film upstairs. The media are in the locker room from twelve to one so I hide out. I stay away from the media. I'll go to Kent Johnston's office and use the phone. The last thing I want to do on my hour and a half off is sit around and talk to the media. If I'm in the locker room when they're in there, I'd have to talk the whole time. I think our public relations staff does a good job of scheduling me for one interview down in the auditorium. It makes it easier. I just sit down in the media auditorium and wing it. The media start shooting questions at me and I throw the answers back. It's fun. I like it. I know all the state media. I look around and see Pete Dougherty of the *Green Bay Press-Gazette.* Bob McGinn of the *Milwaukee Journal-Sentinel.* It's pretty casual. I'll walk in and see Bud Lea, who's covered the Packers for the Milwaukee newspapers since before I was born, and it'll be like, "Hey, Bud. What's up?" He'll nod and say something back. I think the state media have been fair to us. If we play good, they write it, and if we don't, they say that, too. I think we have good media. It could be worse. It could be Philly.

After my Wednesday press conference, I head over to practice around 1:30. It usually lasts until 4:00. Then we have a short position meeting and I'll get back at it in the film room. I usually hang around until 6:00 or until my eyes get blurry. Whichever comes first. Then I shower and head home.

## THURSDAY

My day starts with the nine o'clock team meeting. Mike usually comes in and expands upon whatever he said on

Wednesday. After that, Tom will take us through the running plays against their nickel (five defensive backs) defense. Then Mike or Sherman will cover our passes against the nickel. It's a little quicker than on Wednesday. We go over about twenty to twenty-five passes. This is the day everything starts coming together. It's generally our longest and most intense practice of the week.

My position coach is always stressing technique. They want me to do things properly, which isn't always easy. I have the worst footwork in the league, but that's the way I throw the best. I can drop back five steps in a perfect pocket, step up, throw it, and if you ever watch close, you'll notice that as soon as I throw it I'm getting out of there, moving the opposite way. That's not normal, but I've been doing it ever since I was a kid. I think it's because I put so much into the throw, it's like the recoil of a rifle or shotgun.

I'm also the worst at throwing from awkward positions. I'll run left and throw it right or run right and flip it the other direction. You can't teach that and you can't unteach that. Steve Mariucci would have me work on drills when I first started playing for the Packers. Stepping into it. Following through. Throwing it like this instead of that.

Well, I haven't been able to change.

My arm strength is everything on that. There is no way you could run one way and throw the other way without it. You can't do some of the things I do with an average arm. People tell me I play quarterback the way they would like to, kind of sandlot style, but really it's not like that. It's not like I'm on the playground and I go, "Oh, what the hell," and wing it. It's very controlled, even when it looks crazy.

When I flipped a pass to Antonio Freeman for a touchdown against Seattle, people wonder how in the hell I can do that. It even looks awkward, but believe me, I planned to throw it to him the second I started to roll out. I knew where he'd be and it was just a matter of getting the ball to him.

The play I made in the NFC championship game against Carolina was one of my all-time favorite plays. I was chased from the pocket and Kevin Greene was about to smother me. I put the ball in my left hand as I was going down to protect it, but then I saw Dorsey Levens standing there. So before I hit the ground I optioned it to him and he made a great run. It was unbelievable that I could think to do that in that split second. Kevin said, "Wow." And I was like "Wow" myself. How did I do that? I do amaze myself at times. Those plays are fun. It's what keeps you coming back.

Another bad habit I have is throwing off my back foot. You're not supposed to do it that way, but I throw more touchdowns like that. People ask if it drives Mike nuts. I just tell them, "Not anymore." At first, he thought if I would change I would be better, but now he knows that's just the way I am.

Some days after practice, I like to sneak into the hot tub and kick back. That's when I'll cut loose with a song or two. I've always wanted to be a singer. A country singer. Whatever. Just to sing.

Well, there's no better place to practice than in the hot tub. The acoustics are great. It must be the tile walls or something. One day I thought I was the last one out of the locker room, so I was just sitting in there singing. I was belting out the national anthem when John Stephens, one of our running backs, peeks in and says, "I almost started crying it sounded so good." I was like yeah, I'll admit it sounds pretty good in the hot tub. You can get up real high and real loud. Sometimes Kurt Fielding, one of our assistant trainers, will be walking by and stop to give me a thumbs-up.

Actually I got to record a song last year, which turned out to be harder than I ever imagined. I was one of several NFL players who agreed to record a song on an album that would raise money for charity. A guy with the league asked me who I wanted to sing with. I said Tim McGraw. Travis Tritt. Little Texas. Someone like that. None of those were available. He said how about Steve Azar. He's new. He's good. He can sing really well. And he's from Mississippi. Maybe you'll have a connection. Meet him at Pulse Communications in Green Bay next Tuesday. I was excited, but I was nervous, too. Jeff, my little brother, went with me, which made me even more nervous. Well, I walked in and Steve was great. A good-looking country guy who was like, "Hey, man. How ya doin? Your brother used to date my brother's ex-fiancée." We hit it off right away.

He was a perfect teacher.

He handed me the lyrics and I was like, "Shit. I don't know if I can do this," and I'm embarrassed because Jeff is watching me. Steve gave me an overview of the song. We went through the whole process. It took me about an hour before I relaxed. Then I started laying into it and it went pretty well.

I'd be singing, "She likes slow hands, fast cars, long black limousines. . . . She's love eyes and Levi's fitting like a glove. . . ." Steve is snapping his fingers and Jeff is snapping his fingers and I'm getting into it. It was pretty cool. Steve was saying better, better. I must've sung that song a hundred times. I didn't get out of there until seven that night. I doubt I'll ever have a singing career, but for one day it was a blast.

## FRIDAY

Once again, we start with a team meeting at nine o'clock. This can be pretty fun, especially if we're coming off a win. Mike will give out footballs for Offensive Player of the Week, Defensive Player of the Week, Special Teams Player of the Week. Every week the captains get their picture taken before the game. Mike hands those out, too. The players usually clap or cheer and take the ball and flip it around and pass it down.

We joke around a lot, but those awards are cherished.

I always sit in the front left of the meeting room, right by Reggie White, Sean Jones, and Darius Holland. The chairs are pointing every which way. I'll be sitting with my back to the wall and Mike will be looking out at the team. If I played great one week, Darius or LeRoy Butler or someone will say, "You got robbed." I got one game ball during the '96 season. It was after the season-opening victory at Tampa Bay. It was funny because Keith Jackson caught three touchdown passes, so everyone was ragging on me, saying, "Keith got screwed." We have fun with it.

Every week when Mike goes to give out the Defensive Player of the Week award, everyone chants, "Reg-*gee*! Reg-*gee*!" We're pretty sure Mike and Reggie are related. Mike will be like, "Okay, settle down. This week's defensive award goes to . . . Reggie White." And everyone will start laughing. Then Mike will say no, just joking. It goes to Doug Evans or whoever. It's a pretty lively session.

After that team meeting, which lasts about fifteen minutes, we'll watch practice film from the week. Then it's off to individual meetings, where we'll install our red zone runs and passes. It's pretty critical what you do inside the opponent's 20-yard line. That takes about twenty minutes. After that, we go outside for an 11:45 practice. That's usually a quick workout, probably about an hour.

One day in practice I handed off to a running back and for some unknown reason decided to jump into the air and pretend to throw a pass. We call it Johnny High School— things you do to please the coach. Well, Keith McKenzie, a rookie linebacker, shoved his hands into the air when I did that. He said, "You got me," and I said, "Hmm." So I started doing it in games and it worked. Pretty soon players were doing it around the league.

Normally I would just hand off and jog around the end. The more elaborate fakes look goofy, but every now and then I'll be watching game film from the defense's perspective and catch a linebacker jumping. John Madden, the analyst for Fox, was saying here is Favre throwing jump passes, something that hasn't been done since Sammy Baugh. He enjoyed it. Hell, it makes it fun.

On Fridays, I try to get out of the locker room by 1:30. If it's golf weather, I'm out at one of the local clubs. If it's later in the season, I'll go home and kick back. This is when I try to make some time for myself. I'll relax, listen to music, play video games, read, catch up with Bus or other friends on the telephone.

Deanna, Brittany, and I usually go out to eat on Friday night. Most of the time we have people come in from out of town to visit, especially if it's a home game that week. I try to make it an early night on Friday.

## SATURDAY

Every Saturday we have the dreaded review. We meet at nine o'clock and walk through the installation of every single play. God, it's brutal. I've been doing this for five years now. Every Saturday. I'm tired of hearing the first play. Red Right 324 Thunder. And I know Sherm Lewis, our offensive coordinator, is tired of going over it. A lot of

time I'm thinking about something else or dozing off. It
lasts about a half hour. There is a lot of tedium involved
in what we do. A lot of covering all the bases. The team
meeting lasts about an hour. It's a marathon. After that we
meet by position. We're usually in there for only fifteen or
twenty minutes. Every week, Mike scripts the first fifteen
plays of the game. He's been doing it ever since he
coached the quarterbacks at Brigham Young. He uses it as
a guide, but deviates according to the game. He'll ask each
of the quarterbacks plus Sherman, Andy, and Gil to write
down their fifteen suggested plays and he'll take from that.
If there are any plays that make it on all the sheets, he'll
probably use them.

Mike and I don't have a lot of contact during the week.
We may chat in the hallway if we happen to bump into
each other or if he calls me into his office for something
specific, which rarely happens. We're both too busy to
waste time shooting the bull. That may surprise some people, but it's true. Mike's got a lot on his mind when he's
getting ready for a game. He doesn't install a game plan on
a whim. He is a tremendous detail guy and he is secure
enough to delegate. He relies on his assistants a great deal,
which is wise because he's got a terrific staff. I don't know
how other head coaches operate, but I think Mike's pretty
smooth. He is one of the best play callers, if not the best
play caller, in the entire league. He can be conservative,
but he'll wing it, too.

Mike's incredibly bright and he's meticulous in his
game preparation. He puts together this huge card that has
all the plays for that week on it. When people see him
looking at something on the sideline during a game, it's
his card. It covers all the situations. Third-and-long.
Third-and-short. Fourth-and-long. Fourth-and-one. First-
and-ten. Second-and-twenty. Every scenario. He also has

a list of crucial situations. Third-and-one. Game on the line. If it's fourth-and-goal with almost no time left, he knows the absolute play he would run no matter what.

Sometimes getting the play into the game is tougher on Mike than calling it. Typically Mike will ask Sherm what he thinks about a particular play, then he'll decide and give it to the quarterbacks coach on the sideline. Then he hits a button and it patches him into a speaker in my helmet. He tells me the play and I call it in the huddle. When the headset fails or the wireless speaker doesn't work, which has happened once and it was out for a few minutes, the third quarterback will send in the play by hand signals.

We have a walk-through after the position meetings. We'll go out onto Lambeau Field and cover some basic things. We may call some running plays and go through them at three-quarter speed, just to make sure everyone's on the same page.

Even though the walk-through is serious, we usually turn it into joke-around time. We start goofing off and Mike gets a little worried. He'll say, "I know you guys are joking around, but I hope this doesn't mean anything."

Mike says that every week.

Then we're done.

I'll go home, turn on the TV to watch a little college football, and start getting fired up for our game. About 6:30, I pack up an overnight bag and drive over to the team hotel, which is where all the players and coaches stay the night before a home game. I check in by seven o'clock at the back door. Jerry Parins, our security officer, will check my name off the list and give me a key and per diem. I'll head up to the room and Frankie Winters will be up there watching some TV. We'll shoot the bull until eight, when we head downstairs for a team meeting. We'll watch film of practice that week and then analyze the red zone film. What we do inside the opponent's 20-yard line is so key, Mike makes sure it's one of the last things we cover the night before the game. After we cover the red zone, Mike will go over the first fifteen plays with us.

Now's the fun part.

If we won the previous week, Mike will show a highlight film. It's always broken down into the best or funniest or most interesting plays and it's set to some great music.

We critique the Lambeau Leaps during the highlight film. Mike will back up the film and guys will be going, "Oh, yeah. Good one!" It's pretty fun. We'll rate the leaps on a scale of one to ten. Robert Brooks usually scores the highest, although Andre Rison did pretty good for a first-timer. I have yet to jump into the stands. Maybe someday.

When the highlight film is finished, it's time for a snack. We'll have cheeseburgers, french fries, spaghetti, fried chicken, soup, that type of stuff. Curfew is 11:00 P.M., so I'll go back up to the room, hop in bed, and flip on a movie or watch TV.

Sleeping the night before a game is easy. I'm always tired when Saturday night comes. I don't know if it's the stress of the week or the stress of the game or whatever, but I'll be watching TV one minute and the next thing I know, it's time to wake up.

## SUNDAY

I'm not an early riser by nature, but I get up at seven o'clock and us Catholics go down to hear mass. Father John Blaha keeps it short and sweet. He volunteers during the week as an assistant in the Packers' equipment room, so he knows how eager we are to get over to the stadium.

He also has other masses to say at his own parish, so he keeps it brief. Mass usually lasts about twenty to thirty minutes.

Now it's time to eat.

I usually have one of the cooks fry me up a couple eggs to go along with the bacon and biscuits. After I eat I drive home, wake up Deanna, and go into the workout room to watch TV. That's the most relaxed I am the whole week, that little hour right there before I go over to the stadium. Sometimes I'll call home and talk to Mom and Dad to see what's going on back there. I've got to be at the stadium by ten o'clock, so it's usually a quick conversation. I'll jump in my truck, drive to Lambeau Field, walk on in, and start getting dressed. I don't have any butterflies yet, but I am starting to get real excited. Kurt Fielding, one of our assistant trainers, has taped my ankles for five years. When he's finished, I'll go into the locker room and start messing around with the guys.

Pregame warm-up's at eleven.

We go into every game with about 120 plays. It's a lot considering maybe you run only 70 on average and 10 of those are repeated. So I study 120 plays and run maybe half that many. The ratio of plays is 90 percent pass and the rest run. We have probably 1,000 plays in our play-book. If I was quizzed, I could diagram about 900. The plays are all basically the same, just out of different formations. Red Right 22 Z IN. Brown Right 22 Z IN. The 22 Z IN stays the same and you just change the rest.

When people ask what the terminology means, I'll give them an example such as the 80-yard touchdown pass to Antonio Freeman in the Super Bowl. The play was Trips Right Two Jet All Go. The first part of the call is the formation.

Trips Right means three receivers wide to the right and one to the left.

Two Jet, the second part of the call, is the protection. In this case, the Two means the running back slides to the left. If it was Three Jet, he'd slide to the right. It's a six-man protection featuring five linemen and a back.

All Go is four receivers going right up the middle. The idea is to let the quarterback read the best matchup. If they play a soft zone coverage, which is what the New England Patriots did on Freeman's touchdown, you pick your best receiver against their worst defender. When I saw that Antonio was being covered by a safety, I made eye contact right away and he nodded back. Right then I knew it was over. I took the snap, looked the safety away from Antonio's side, and fired the ball.

Touchdown.

If only it were that easy all the time.

I don't have many pet peeves, but the biggest is when we jump offsides. It drives me nuts, and it's usually when we go on two. I could be under center calling out a play like Blue 18, Blue 18, set, hut, hut, and someone will jump offsides between huts. That is why most offenses go on one 90 percent of the time.

People ask what Blue 18 means. All Blue 18 does is prevent the defense from knowing when we audible. If I said down, set, hut, the entire game, and all of a sudden went Blue 67, the defense would figure out something was up. We could use blue or black or green as the "live" color. If it was blue and I said Blue 18, my teammates would immediately know that I'm changing the play at the line of scrimmage.

Now, as much as I get pissed when we jump, I get a kick out of it when the defense jumps. I'll try to draw the linemen offsides by changing the inflection in my voice.

Instead of Blue 18, Blue 18, set, hut, it's Blue 18, Blue 18, set, *hut!* The other way to get them to jump is to move a little bit. The officials are looking up, so I keep my helmet still, but if you look down, my right knee might be doing the Elvis thing.

My only other pet peeve is when guys talk too much in the huddle.

I remember the first time I played in Green Bay, I stepped into the huddle and Ken Ruettgers, our left tackle, is going, "Eighteen. Seventeen. Sixteen . . ." This went on for a while and finally it was driving me nuts, so I turned to Rutt and said, "What is it?" He looked at me and said, "The play clock is running." I'd be like, "Rutt, would you shut up?" Rutt had himself another strange habit. I'd be giving the play in the huddle and he'd be tapping his fingertips along the side of his helmet. Rutt said it helped him remember the play. It aggravated the heck out of me. Now, Rutt's a good guy, an intelligent guy. Probably too intelligent. He was goofy. But you know what? The last couple of years before he retired, when he lined up at left tackle he covered my ass.

All kinds of crazy shit happens during a game.

I'll never forget the game in Green Bay against the Raiders a few years back when it was cold, like thirty-degree-below windchill cold, and I go over to the sidelines during a time-out. Well, Mike had this bunch of snot frozen on that big, thick mustache of his and he's looking at his play card and sniffing. It was a shield of snot. If I would've thumped it, it would've fallen off right there on national TV. Ty and I are about dying laughing and Mike all serious says, "What's so funny?" I said, "Your mustache." He felt it and I could tell he wanted to laugh, but he didn't.

It was cold as hell during the Carolina game last year and Bryan Nehring, one of our equipment assistants, brought me a cup of apple cider. Mike comes over and says, "What is that?" I said, "Bourbon and water. Want some?" I do that shit all the time.

I'll never forget, we had this running play called 96 or 97 Bounce Solid. It was an off-tackle stretch play, the kind of play only a Barry Sanders can make work. Well, we'd run it and get tackled for a loss. Then we'd run it again and get tackled for a loss. We kept on running that damn play. This went on for three or four weeks. Finally we're playing at Dallas and Mike calls 97 Bounce Solid and Edgar loses 4 yards. He turns around and says to no one in particular, "If I ever call that play again, someone should kick me right in the balls." The next week Mike forgot and called 97 Bounce Solid, which proceeded to lose yardage. He immediately turned and looked at Ty Detmer, our backup quarterback, who raised his leg as if to kick him right you-know-where.

Mike just burst out laughing.

When the game ends, I shower, do the interview routine, and head home. A lot of times we'll invite players and friends over for a party. Deanna will call the caterer and handle all the details. She is a wife, mother, and social secretary. We'll all usually go down to the basement, kick on some music, and relax. It's a little more subdued after a loss, but we still hang around and relax. About nine or ten everyone goes home.

Time to get ready for a new week.

# 11

# AROUND THE LEAGUE

**I**n the NFL, all players are not created equal. You have to earn your place in a league filled with incredible athletes and huge egos.

My first real lesson about the NFL pecking order came at the Quarterback Challenge a few years ago in Orlando. The Quarterback Challenge gets the league's best quarterbacks together for a little friendly competition. It tests arm strength, accuracy, and agility. It also tests something else, which I found out innocently enough.

During the competition they have a session where only family and friends of the quarterbacks get together. Mostly you just sit around and bullshit. But some people take the time to get autographs. Deanna and Brittany were with me and Brittany really wanted San Francisco's quarterback Steve Young's autograph. I couldn't have cared less about his autograph. I mean, Steve's a great quarterback but why the hell would I want his autograph? I'm sure he's not dying to have mine. But it was for Brittany, so I went up to Steve and asked.

Steve acted like I was invisible. He didn't even acknowledge me. He kept right on talking to whoever he was talking to. Steve made me stand there like I was some asshole off the street. That pissed me off. Here we are, both in the same profession, both respected and so on, and he pulls that. At the time I thought sure, he's done a little more than me in his career, obviously, but you don't do that kind of shit. I knew I wouldn't have done it to him.

I was thinking in the back of my mind, "I'll get your ass back."

And I did.

We kicked Young's and the 49ers' butts 27–17 in the second round of the 1995 play-offs. San Francisco was the defending Super Bowl champ. The oddsmakers had them as ten-point favorites. So much for those odds. We buried them, and at their place. That was a sweet victory.

That game was one of the best of my career. I felt like I was in total control. I completed 15 of 17 passes in the first half and 21 of 28 overall—good for 299 yards and two touchdowns. After that game I was thinking, "Hey, Steve, sign this." It was a great win not only for the team but for me personally.

I had something to prove to the league and to Steve Young. Just before the play-offs I was named league MVP. We had won the NFC Central Division and I had a great season, throwing for a league-leading thirty-eight touchdowns. Despite all of that, there were still people who doubted me. Both Emmitt Smith and Jerry Rice had super years and a lot of people thought either of those two should have won. On top of that, Steve won the MVP award in 1994 and 1992. So there we were, the league's two most recent MVPs meeting for the first time in the play-offs. It was showdown time.

Okay, I know it wasn't Brett Favre playing Steve Young.

The Packers were playing the 49ers. But to a certain extent, I did feel I had to outplay Steve that day, or at least play well enough for us to win. You have to understand, here's a guy who everyone thinks is the best player in the league. And despite what I had accomplished with the Packers that season, a lot of people still thought Steve was the best. So my way of thinking was, hey, if I'm able to beat the 49ers and play better than Steve Young, then people would have to say: "Brett Favre really is the MVP. He earned it."

After we kicked San Francisco's butt I think all doubts about me were gone.

It's funny the difference that one game made around the league. I saw Young at the Super Bowl that year and it was a totally different encounter than at the Quarterback Challenge a few years earlier. He came up to me and gave me a hug. He's like, "Hey, man, how's it going?" Hmmm, a little respect there now.

As far as I'm concerned, I could win the Most Valuable Player award five times, but if a rookie quarterback came up to talk about something, I'd be more than happy to chat with him. Steve should be thankful that he is successful and maybe he is. All I know is, after that game, he sure changed toward me.

Same thing at this year's Pro Bowl. Hell, I got hugs from guys like the Cowboys' Nate Newton and Erik Williams. Nate and Erik have always been nice guys, but before it was always just, "Hey, Brett, how ya doin'." Real cool. But this year, after we won the Super Bowl and after I won my second MVP award, it was all different. The Cowboys have been our nemesis and in many ways our biggest rivals. They were what we wanted to be: champions. That's why I have a lot of respect for them.

But after our Super Bowl win when I saw those guys,

they came up and hugged me and congratulated me. That was really special. After that, I just said to myself, "Well, it looks like we finally arrived."

Here's another example. After we beat the 49ers 23–20 in overtime on *Monday Night Football,* someone asked Young how he thought I played.

"Well, let's put it this way," Steve said. "I got to play a small part on TV's *Lois & Clark: The New Adventures of Superman.* The way Brett played against us, man, he could play Superman."

When I heard that comment, I thought damn, that's pretty good.

I threw sixty-one passes in that game for nearly 400 yards and got the crap knocked out of me. Afterward Steve came up to me and whispered in my ear, "That's the best performance I've ever seen by a quarterback." I can understand how someone can get caught up in the moment after a game like that and say that. But at that moment in time Steve Young meant it. I appreciate that. A few years ago he wouldn't give me the time of day.

I understand now why Steve had kind of snubbed me at the Quarterback Challenge. He's been through a lot more than I have. So have Dan Marino, John Elway, all those guys. What was I back then? Just some cocky young quarterback ready to take on the world. Young, Marino, Elway, they've earned the respect of the league and the right to be considered among the all-time greats. No question about it. I did well at an early age, but in Steve's eyes I hadn't done enough. And that's the deal. I had to prove myself over time just like they all did.

I think that's just part of the evolution of being a good player. Too many young guys come into the league and think they have the world by the balls. They'll talk shit on the field or treat the media like crap, whatever. When I see it, I think, "Well, boys, you'll learn. Sooner or later you'll learn." A lot of people talk about respect as if they've earned it when they really haven't done anything. A big contract isn't the same thing as respect. If you're a high draft choice, you'll get your money, but that's the last time anything is handed to you. The rest you have to earn, just like everybody else.

I see young quarterbacks in the NFL, not like I'm that much older than them, and it's hard for me to say something real positive even if they play well and may deserve the credit. Like Kerry Collins of the Carolina Panthers. I like Collins. I think he potentially could be very good. He had an okay year, he really did. He got Carolina to the championship game against us. But I didn't really come out and say much to him. I congratulated him after we beat the Panthers and told him he had a good year. Hell, most guys don't even say that.

Respect doesn't come overnight. This league is too damn tough. Look, if someone has a once-in-a-lifetime year, well, maybe that's all it was, once-in-a-lifetime. But if a guy does an outstanding job for a couple years, then maybe you start thinking that he's pretty good. You don't ever want to get ahead of yourself. You never want to heap praise on a player too early. There's a lot of truth to the notion of paying your dues.

There's a difference between respect and fear. I respect a whole bunch of guys but I don't really fear anyone in the league. There's no team that I play against and go, "God, I hate playing these guys." I look at the really good teams and think, "Well, this is going to be tough." And it is tough. I may get knocked down, but I get back up. I may get knocked down a lot, but I'll always get back up again. That never bothers me. I'm not scared to get hit or of anything that happens on the field.

Take a guy like Reggie White, for example. When we played against Reggie when he was at Philadelphia, I got my ass busted all day. We couldn't stop him. If there was anyone I should have been afraid of, it was Reggie, but I wasn't. I did, however, respect the hell out of him. And I was extremely happy the day he became my teammate.

That's the thing, the NFL is filled with great players. You have to respect that fact, but you can't play with fear. It's simple. If you don't think you can beat the other team, then that team sure as hell knows that it's going to beat you.

So who's the best athlete in the league? That's easy. Deion Sanders. He's special. Deion is definitely worthy of all the hype you hear.

Deion's a guy who can play cornerback better than anyone and then go over and play receiver on offense when his team needs him. He can go out and play outfield for the Cincinnati Reds and play almost as well as anyone in baseball. Think about it. He hardly plays baseball and he's just about as good as anyone in the major leagues. And he can play basketball like a son of a gun. He can jam, no problem. Deion's not a great shooter but he can go out and play with the best of them.

Basically, if there's a game going on outside right now and Deion didn't know what sport it was, he could go out and get in it and play, and play well. Not too many guys can do that. Hell, Deion could probably play soccer.

The amazing thing about Deion when he plays football is that no matter how good our guys are—and they're very good—and no matter how good I am, Deion is always better. He's a step ahead of everyone. He's just so fast. I might be having a great game and be throwing the ball perfectly but Deion always seems just a step ahead of everybody. The whole difference with Deion is his quickness.

I don't know if people at home watching Deion on TV can appreciate it. But on the field, playing against him, it's amazing. Robert Brooks can run with the best of them, but there's no comparing his speed to Deion's. If you watch Dallas, no one throws his way. Every once in a while, maybe. But that's about it. There are certain routes you can run against Deion, like crossing routes because he doesn't like to come across the middle and bang around. But if you run out routes and deep routes, forget it, he'll bait you. He'll act like he's 2 yards beat and then—boom!—he just closes so fast.

But you know what, he's only one guy out there. If you can beat the Cowboys by going away from him, that's what you do. There's no ego involved. To me, ego or honor or whatever you want to call it has nothing to do with it. If we have to stay away from throwing Deion's way to beat Dallas, fine, I'll do that.

Here's another great athlete most people don't think of: John Elway. He's probably a better baseball player than he is a football player, and that's saying something. I played golf with John, and wow! If he'd quit football and just played golf, he could be on the PGA Tour. He can flat out play golf as well as anyone. And the funny thing with John is he looks all awkward and pigeon-toed and gimpy, but he can run. I'm like everyone else. I watch him take off and I'm afraid his knees are going to buckle. But he can move. I've seen him play basketball and he's as good as anyone around. You get me out on a basketball court and I'd get killed.

Over the years people have compared me to John because we both have strong arms and we both make things happen on the field. I'm flattered by the comparison. John's one of the greatest quarterbacks to ever play the game. There are some who try to make something out of the fact that he hasn't won a Super Bowl in three tries. To me, that doesn't matter. When all is said and done, and people look back at John's career, they'll remember all the great come-from-behind victories and all the excitement he created; they'll remember his great arm and his ability to move around and make things happen. He's an extraordinary player.

As a matter of fact, I really thought John was going to win MVP in 1996. I certainly didn't expect to repeat. I thought I had a great year, even better than the year before, but John had a great year, too. Besides, he has accomplished so much during his career. The Broncos had a very good team last year, one I thought we might face in the Super Bowl. That's why I thought John would be the sentimental favorite to win MVP. When I won that award, it was extremely satisfying. It's hard to say to yourself, "Damn, you're pretty good." You don't want to say that and I'm not really like that. But that's how I felt. I didn't go around and tell people that, like hey, look at what I've done, look at me now. I never said that and I never would. That's just not me. But when I think about John Elway, Dan Marino, and all these guys who have done unbelievable things and are great quarterbacks, and I think about what I've done the last two seasons, I just go "Wow."

Last year I was hoping that John would have played against us in Green Bay. To me, that game was going to decide the MVP award. When John didn't play because of a hamstring injury and we whipped Denver 41–6, I thought it was really in his favor. That loss was Denver's worst regular-season loss since 1988. We destroyed them. People were saying, see that just shows how valuable John is to their team. Well of course John is valuable to their team, but no way he makes up for a thirty-five-point loss. Last time I checked he wasn't playing defense. I don't think any one player can make up thirty-some points, no matter who it is. It would've been enjoyable to prove that we could beat Denver with John. But more than that, I don't know how many more times I'll get the chance to play against John.

Elway's one of the last links to the great quarterback draft of 1983. Six quarterbacks were taken in the first round that year, including Elway, Dan Marino, and Jim Kelly. Man. Those three are locks for the Hall of Fame. I doubt if you'll ever see a draft like that again. Compare that to the '96 draft where only one quarterback—Jim Druckenmiller—was taken in the first round.

It's probably a cycle and in a few years you might have six or seven quarterbacks taken in the first round again. But I'm not so sure. First off, it's a risky pick taking a quarterback high in the draft unless you're absolutely sure he's the real deal. Even then, what with money and expectations, there's the potential for failure. Probably the biggest reason young quarterbacks struggle is that there's so much pressure on them to play right away. They sign big contracts, multimillion-dollar deals with huge signing bonuses, and owners, management, fans, everybody, expects them to produce. Well, people may expect it, but it just doesn't work that way. Or at least not very often. Defenses are so much more complicated with better, swifter players than in college. Offenses in the pros are much more sophisticated than ever before. When I first came to Green Bay, the offense hit me in the head like a frying pan. My God, my head was swimming. It took me four or five years to really feel comfortable in it. This past year was the first year where I felt like I had full command of the offense.

Joe Montana, who I think is the greatest quarterback of all time, got to sit on the sideline and learn for three years. People forget that. Mark Brunnell, who's doing a good job in Jacksonville, sat on our sideline for two years watching and learning from me. Same with Ty Detmer, who's now in Philadelphia. Both of them were my backups and had time to develop. Something else to remember: Both were taken late in the draft. Mark was a fifth-round pick in 1993 and Ty was a ninth-round pick in 1992. But young quarterbacks who are high draft picks are pushed into starting roles right away. Trent Dilfer, Drew Bledsoe, Rick Mirer, Heath Shuler, all the way down the line young guys are forced into the game. For some, their confidence gets shattered or their team gets fed up with their mistakes. And believe me, there are going to be plenty of mistakes. If there are too many, fans get impatient and turn on them. There were a lot of fans calling for my head when I struggled early, especially in 1993 when I threw twenty-four interceptions.

The quarterback struggles under the weight of all these expectations, and management feels it has to do something with them. But that's not easy, either. Big contracts are hard to move. I was lucky. Atlanta had given up on me in just one season. Fortunately Green Bay saw the potential. So I'm not so sure there aren't a lot of good young quarterbacks out there. There's just way too much being asked of them way too soon.

One thing's for sure: It doesn't take long for a quarterback to find out who can play in this league, especially on the defensive side of the ball. Sometimes I can't even believe how good some guys are. All I do know is, if I wanted to create a defense in a league with no salary cap and on a team with an owner whose wallet is as big as a pickup truck, this is the defense I'd put on the field.

Deion Sanders is my left cornerback. That's a no-brainer. At right corner I'd have Rod Woodson. I haven't played against Rod since he hurt his knee, but when we played against him before, he was so good it was scary. There are a lot of great safeties but I like our own Eugene Robinson. Eugene is the best I've played against. And talk about a leader. He's a natural. Same thing with LeRoy Butler at strong safety. LeRoy has been with the Packers for eight years and he's always been good, but the last couple of years he's been really good. To see what LeRoy did this year was unbelievable. He had six and a half sacks and he returned one of his five interceptions 90 yards for a touchdown. A lot of people don't know that LeRoy was born with ill-shaped bones in his feet. From the ages of six to nine he was forced to wear clunky braces on both legs. Man, you watch him now and he's pretty impressive. I know I wouldn't want to play against him.

At linebackers I'd go with San Diego's Junior Seau, San Francisco's Ken Norton, and Kansas City's Derrick Thomas. Junior Seau, man, he gets it going. He's never hit me, but I've seen him destroy other people so I know I don't want to get hit by him. As for Derrick Thomas, I'll tell you what, I like it better when Thomas drops back to protect against the pass instead of rushing the passer. Man, he's scary. Those three are pretty good.

On the line I'd have Reggie White, Dallas's Charles Haley and Leon Lett, and Minnesota's John Randle. God, now, Randle, holy shit, he may be the only guy I'm scared of. He's psycho. But he's a good player. And a good guy, too. He's so nice that he's mean. Randle will come to the line and say, "Hey, how's your family doing?" I hear him talking to our left guard, Aaron Taylor, and he's saying, "Hey, A.T., how ya doing? Now, you know you can't block me, don't you?" And Aaron will just say, "Yeah whatever, John." We snap the ball and boom! Randle's in the backfield hitting me. He'll look at me and say, "Sorry, Brett, but I told him he couldn't block me." Then he'll start talking to our center, Frank Winters. He'll go, "Now, Frankie, you know you can't block me, don't you?" And Frankie will just go, "Yeah, I know." I'm hearing all this and thinking man, I've got to go back there and try to pass with this guy coming after me. That's not easy. John's a helluva player. Sometimes when we play him in Minnesota on artificial turf, he'll hit me twenty times a game. Sometimes I'll just be standing there watching a play and he'll hit me just to let me know he's there. I'd restructure my contract to get him on my team just so I wouldn't have to get hit by him.

I don't know who I'd have on my All Trash-Talk team but I do know who the captain would be: Charles Haley. Wow, he's nonstop. He'll talk shit the whole game to me, to my teammates, to everybody who'll listen, and even to some who won't.

When I played against him, he'd be talking at the line saying, "I'm going to come in there and bust your ass, Favre." And after he did he'd say, "I'm coming back for more, you better be ready." Or, "If that one didn't hurt, the next one will." That type of talk the whole game. I don't know where he gets the energy. All that talking would tire me out.

But really, that kind of talk never bothered me, even when I was younger. I was too busy trying to remember what I was supposed to do to worry about what other players were saying. And really, after a while it's all just the same. I mean, if you're getting your ass kicked in a game, whether it's in your second or twelfth year, you know you're getting your ass kicked. If some guy's talking crap to you, it's not like he's telling you something you don't already know. Hell, I'm the first guy who knows if he's getting his butt kicked. But some guys talk it when it's not really happening, and that just makes me laugh. It's like, go ahead, keep talking because I'm going to beat you and you're going to know it when we're done with you.

So talk on the field doesn't really bother me or mean too much to me. Some guys do it. Some don't. All that really counts is the final score. That's why we play the game.

Probably the dirtiest player we face is Alonzo Spellman of the Chicago Bears. I don't think Alonzo really tries to be dirty but he'll club you, hit you late, do whatever. And he talks shit the whole game; tells our coaches not to run his way; how he's going to shut us down, silly stuff. Alonzo's a good player but he carries on too much. I've always thought that if you make a great play, fine, pack it up and go back to the huddle. You don't need to talk about it. Everybody knows who made the play. The players on the field know. The fans in the stadium know. The people watching the game at home on TV know. Everybody knows. But that doesn't stop Alonzo. He likes to make sure no one missed the fact that he made a tackle.

Last year at their place I threw a Hail Mary pass to Antonio Freeman right at the end of the first half. I rolled to my right and threw it 50 yards up right over Alonzo. Antonio makes a great catch in the end zone for a touchdown but I can't see anything because Spellman hits me late. It was a great play made better because Spellman was flagged for roughing. I didn't say a word. I let the play speak for itself. Besides, Spellman hit me so hard he drove my helmet down over my eyes. I couldn't see a thing, but I could hear the crowd moan when Antonio scored. Great play by us. Enough said.

Defenses and offenses are natural adversaries. That's just the game. But even though the defense is trying to stop us and we're trying to dominate the defense, we still manage to have fun out there.

Take last year's play-off game against San Francisco in Green Bay. We had the ball in their territory and it was fourth-and-short. We wanted to try to draw them offside, so we called "no play" in the huddle. Basically that means we go up to the line and I call out a bunch of stuff hoping that something we do makes them jump offside so we can pick up the first down on the penalty.

It doesn't work that often but you never know, especially in a play-off game where everyone is wired. I go up to the line and start barking out nonsense, trying to get them to jump. The 49ers linemen are kind of jumping around, nothing too major, but the field is all muddy and they're really slipping around trying to get back. Their middle linebacker, Gary Plummer, is grabbing them by the pants trying to hold them back. He knew what we were doing—hell, he knew it before I even called the play in the huddle. Plummer's been playing in the league forever and he's smart as they get. He's waving his arms, holding onto guys to keep them from jumping offside and I just kind of looked at him and laughed. It was funny. And he laughed back. He knew that I knew that he knew what we were up to.

Here we are in the biggest game of the year for both teams and we're kind of giggling at each other like we're both back on the playground in grade school. See, we *are* just big kids out there.

Like every fan of the game, I have my favorite players, guys I admire. Guys like Elway, Marino, Montana, Troy Aikman, Steve Young, Emmitt Smith, Deion, Reggie, Barry Sanders. Man, Barry Sanders, I think he's unbelievable. I admire good players who seem to be humble. There seem to be a lot of great players that people hate because of their personalities. But I like these guys because they're great players.

When it comes to my favorite place to play on the road, I'd have to say New Orleans. I enjoy going there for obvious reasons. If I were commissioner, I'd designate New Orleans as the permanent site for the Super Bowl. It's an outstanding place to play and you just can't knock Bourbon Street. I also like going to Tampa. We've had pretty good luck down there over the years, which is nice, but more important, we usually go there later in the season when it's cold in Green Bay. The sun feels great after freezing your tail off.

There are a lot of difficult places to play in the league, but Kansas City is probably the toughest. What great fans they have. It's so loud, you just can't hear. There are probably louder places that really get rolling, like in the Metrodome in Minneapolis or the Super Dome when the Saints really had it going. But Kansas City, in a regular-season game, we couldn't hear a lick. You get down near the end zone and you have to go on watching the ball. There's no way of hearing the snap count. Plus the Chiefs are good. So when you combine a loud place to play with a good team, it's tough.

Leading up to last year's Kansas City game, we worked all week in practice with a sound system blaring to try to simulate the Chiefs' crowd. We think it helps us prepare for their noise. But it didn't help us that week. They kicked our ass 27–20 in a game that wasn't as close as the final score might indicate. When you actually get into the environment, it's always much tougher than you thought. At practice everyone kind of knows what's going on, but in a game you can't control what's going to happen

The Metrodome is a tough place to play. We haven't beat the Vikings there since I've been at Green Bay. It's tough, really tough, but it always seems to be more of what we mess up in the games played than the actual place itself.

Dallas is another difficult place for us to play, obviously since we've lost seven straight games to the Cowboys. We've played really good against Dallas and we've played really horrible. Their crowd isn't as loud as Kansas City, it's just a tough place to play because the Cowboys have been so good.

There are reasons for our losing streak against the Cowboys. First of all, they're a pretty damn good team. When they're at their best, there aren't too many teams that can beat them. We sure haven't been able to. That's not something I dwell on, but it's a fact. Until we beat them that's what people will want to talk about. The difficult thing about trying to snap that losing streak is that during that stretch of games, we've had to play them all in Dallas. So it's been kind of a double whammy. We play a great football team and we play it at their place. That's tough. You lose a couple times to them and then it starts to snowball a little bit. That's what has happened to us. And if you start to believe that you can't beat them at their place, that's bad. Plus, during those games we just haven't played very well.

A lot was made about everything Troy Aikman had to put up with in Dallas last year, what with Michael Irvin and Leon Lett getting suspended and the accusations of sexual assualt. I think what helps Troy is that he's such a class guy. He's a great quarterback and person. He's always come up to me after a game and we talk and he's told me that he loves to watch me play. That means something coming from him.

I didn't really get caught up in what was going on in Dallas last season. I don't try to analyze what's going on there with Michael Irvin or other players because who knows exactly what went on? I don't, so I don't spend much time or energy thinking about it. I do know that Michael is a great player and I admire him for that. The times I've been around Michael in the off-season he's been a real nice guy. My personal experience with Michael has been good. What he does in his private life I don't want to get into because it's not my business. Michael's a bit different than me. He's more flashy than I am, but a lot of guys are. It's not too difficult to be flashier than me.

When it comes to coaches, Holmgren is one of the best. He's a really good coach. I admired him when he was in San Francisco working with Joe Montana and Steve Young. He's excellent developing quarterbacks and calling plays. I don't know if Mike gets enough credit around the league or in the media because he's not a real flashy guy and he doesn't try to upstage the team. He's very confident and businesslike. Mike doesn't seem to need the spotlight. Not like Bill Parcells. I respect Parcells as a coach. He's one of the best in the league. But what he did during the week or so leading up to the Super Bowl, grabbing all the media attention, focusing everything on himself instead of his team, that was bush. Mike would never do that.

George Seifert, Bill Walsh, Jim Mora. I always liked Jim, even when I was in college. Don Shula, Tom Landry. All of them are real professional. They've all done something that other coaches haven't been able to do. Jim Mora hasn't won the Super Bowl like those other coaches but he did an amazing job with the New Orleans Saints. Before he got there they were nothing. I know because I watched them play all the time as a kid. They were terrible. They didn't even have a winning season. But he built them into something pretty good; at least at one time they were damn good. When I look at those coaches, I think of success, winning. They're all different in their own little

ways but I think I could play for all of them and have success.

All of these coaches have there own philosophies, their
own way of doing things. I think I could have played for
all of them and been successful. I'd manage in almost any
offense because I can adapt. That's something I do best. I
adapt to the elements. I've always been able to play pretty
well in cold weather. I read where I'm 19–0 in home
games when the temperature at kickoff is thirty-five degrees or colder. I think there are a couple of reasons for
that. One, I have really big hands, which helps me grip the
football when it gets cold and hard. The other is we really
have a tremendous home-field advantage, especially in
cold-weather games, so I'm going to win more of those
games than I'll lose. I adapt to new players. Last year we
lost Robert Brooks, our leading receiver, after the seventh
game of the season. We lost our second-leading receiver,
Antonio Freeman, for a month. We lost tight end Mark
Chmura for three games. We got Andre Rison at the end of
the season and added Don Beebe at the beginning of the
season. And despite all these changes and new faces and
injuries, we still won the Super Bowl and I still threw
thirty-nine touchdowns.

The funny thing is, I really don't think that I fit that
well into the mold of a West Coast offense quarterback. I
think you could take some quarterbacks in the league and
put them in the West Coast offense and they should function better in it than I would. But I think that I have
adapted to it well. I think I've taken it to a different level.
I won't say *up* to a different level but *off* to a different
level. That offense is designed to step back, read, and
throw. To me it's kind of drop back, read, throw, sometimes run.

We don't throw deep posts or deep corners or deep ins
and all the stuff where my arm strength can really be uti-

lized. We throw a lot of 10-yard hooks that every quarterback out there better be able to complete. I think I throw
the 20-yard comeback or the deep crosses and those type
of patterns as well as anyone, but we don't throw them
that much. So this offense really doesn't give me a chance
to set myself apart from other quarterbacks in that sense.
But the slants, the outs, my arm strength makes a difference because the ball gets there just a little bit quicker
than maybe a ball thrown by some other quarterback. And
in this league, a little advantage is all you need.

When it comes to putting a team together to win it all,
Ron Wolf is the best at what he does. And I don't say that
just because he's with the Packers but because I've had a
chance to see what he does and how he handles himself.
I'll go up to his office in Lambeau Field and we'll talk
about stuff and I'm always impressed. Ron's real keen.
He's sharp. And obviously he knows football. You look at
him and you wonder how this guy knows so much about
football. He didn't play. Heck, you'd think a guy who
played football would know more than Ron. But that's not
the case.

Ron doesn't say a whole lot. He just doesn't talk much.
He waits for you to say something and then he says what
he has to say. I know him pretty well, so I think I have a
little insight into the man. He doesn't really understand
my personality, though. We'll be talking and I'll say some
country thing, like "You don't want to get in a pissing
match with a skunk," or I'll tell him that some guy "dog-
cussed the hell out of you" and he'll just look at me and
say, "Well, I don't know what the hell that means but it
sounds kind of funny." He has no clue about some of the
things I'm talking about. He just kind of laughs at me and
I laugh at him.

I have a lot of respect for Ron and for what he's done
in Green Bay. He came to a team that hadn't won anything

for a very long time and he built a winner. That's not easy
to do. And I think he respects me and what I've accomplished. When I've had problems, he's always stuck by
me. He knows I'm a good person, he knows I'm a good
player.

Ron doesn't put up with much. If you hold out and he
doesn't want to put up with all your crap, he'll just let you
go. That's kind of what happened with Tony Bennett.
Tony was our best linebacker but Ron didn't want to put
up with his contract demands so he just let him go and
he ended up in Indianapolis. Hell, we were all surprised.
That's the last thing any of us players thought would happen. But Ron had just had enough of it. He knows talent
and he's shrewd. He'll do whatever it'll take to win. And
guys on our team know that. He won't put up with a whole
lot but he will take care of his players, the guys who can
lead him to a Super Bowl. Like a couple of years ago he
got us a 747 to go down to Dallas for a game. Some people
would say so what, but that was a big deal. Guys on the
team were just in awe that he would do that. That's just
one example. A while back I told him we needed a workout room in the gym area, someplace to put our aerobic
stuff and treadmills. The next day they were working on
it to get it done. If there is something that can help his
team win, Ron will do it.

Ron stays out of the coaching things. He really stays
behind the scenes. He lets Mike run the show. So guys
don't know a lot about Ron other than seeing him walk
around practice looking real mean. He watches everything. Just when you think he's not paying attention, that's
when he is. There's not much he misses. And you can see
that in the players he's brought in.

All I know about Ron is that I'm sure glad he brought
me to Green Bay. For that, I'll always think he's one of the
best.

# 12

# FAME: THE PRICE
# YOU PAY

Some people don't get it. They look at my life and go, man, he's got it made. They think the attention, the excitement, the fame—all that stuff that goes with being Brett Favre—is great. It is, but not all the time. I get tired of it. I've had enough ego strokes to last me until I'm ninety.

I don't have the same kind of freedom that other people take for granted. I miss that. I miss being able to come and go as I please. I miss just hanging out with the guys.

My agent, Bus Cook, owns 135 acres outside of Hattiesburg. It's nice out there. Lots of trees, open space, a pond. Bus and his wife, Jeanine, are building a home out there. I don't live too far from Bus in the off-season. That works out nice for all of us. One day Bus and I took Brittany and his daughter Madison camping on his land. We pitched a tent, got a big fire going, toasted some marshmallows, just relaxed.

Later that night Bus and I were sitting in his pickup truck. Had us a couple of beers. Country music on the radio. I was looking at the stars and I said to Bus, "Damn,

I could do this forever. I could really sit here forever. I wish tonight would never end. That you could do this for a hundred hours straight, not get tired, not get drunk. Just sit like what we're doing."

Man, if the world could have seen us then. We were having a great time. No cares, no worries. Just the kids, the stars, and Bus messing around with the fire.

I miss that during the season. Every day is work. It's serious. And that's the problem. I'm really not a guy who likes to be serious, *ever*. I love going out to the country club. Play some golf. Sit back in the card room afterward. Shoot the shit. Have a good time. I can't go out to the Green Bay Country Club and cut up because everyone looks at me as this immortal hero. They're good guys, but they'll be sitting there talking about fooball and sucking up to me. I need to get away from that.

Honestly, there are times that I think about cutting my career short just so I can have more free time. That's important to me. To be able to hang out, relax. Shoot, Deanna says it's the most important thing to me. But being in the position I'm in, it's hard to appreciate your friends unless you're away from them for a bunch. Back in high school, I couldn't have cared less about hanging out with the guys. Now being able to go back in the woods with four or five guys and drink beer and not have a soul bother you is a luxury.

I like to go out with buddies and have a beer. If there are people in the bar, they'll come up and interrupt us. It'll happen. But I still go out with the guys because I like to do it. I appreciate the time with guys who knew me before I was a pro quarterback. I'm just Brett to them and they give me shit just like they give everyone else shit. I know Deanna gets mad. It's hard for her to understand.

But if you could be in my body for a day, you would want to get away, too.

We took a trip to Tennessee after the season. Me, Bus, and another golfing buddy, Leon Perry. We just jumped in my truck, got some beer, and took off. We stopped in Birmingham, played golf, drove up to Tennessee, played golf. We had the best time. Other people would never do that. Well, there was a time I wouldn't have done that, either. But now I just don't get away that often. The football season has gotten so damn long. To me just taking off, that's fun. It's an escape from all the serious shit I have to do.

I love playing football. I enjoy the hell out of it. But for nine months I have no social life. After the game I'll have guys come over and I look forward to that. It's not so much the partying, it's the sitting around and sharing stories, laughing, being myself.

I really can't go anywhere without being recognized. That started when I was in Green Bay my second year. In Atlanta, no one knew who I was and nobody gave a shit when they found out. If you're playing well, people recognize you. That's what I wanted. When I was just getting started and I'd be out with Troy Aikman, Steve Young, or some other big name, people would run past me, brush me aside to get to them. Now it happens the other way to me. It's kind of embarrassing.

Imagine going out and every five minutes someone is coming up to you wanting to talk or wanting you to sign something. It's nonstop. Deanna and I can't go out to dinner and have a private conversation to talk over things we need to discuss as a family. We'll be eating and look up and there's ten people standing around the table staring. It's kind of frustrating because people don't understand we're just out for one hour to have dinner. It's not time for autographs. And if you don't sign, people think I'm an asshole or that Deanna's a bitch. That's not it at all. There's a time and place for autographs. People need to respect the fact that we're just like them and we need some private time.

The Prime Quarter in Green Bay used to be our favorite place to eat. But Deanna and I can't go there now without hordes of people coming around asking for autographs. One time we were at the salad bar and I'm holding a plate and a fork. People were lining up to have me sign something. I have no hands free, I'm getting a salad, and people are asking for an autograph. Can they wait until I sit down, or until I'm finished eating? And if I sign one autograph, a whole line forms and there goes dinner.

Just one time I'd like to go into a restaurant and walk over to every table and say, "Excuse me, would you mind signing something for me?" I'd love to go up to someone just as he's stuffing a cheese stick in his mouth and ask him a question. If people didn't know me, they'd tell me to get the hell away from them.

There are some things we go out to do. Like a movie. No one can bother us there. We sort of sneak in and out when it's dark. We love Green Bay, the area and the people. I'm glad we have the fans. I don't want this to sound negative, but most fans feel like we owe them autographs. We probably do to a certain extent but I think they owe us respect, too, and a little bit of privacy when we're out to dinner. It can be frustrating. People always think that they're the only one, that one autograph is no big deal. And one autograph isn't a big deal—it's the other ten or twenty or fifty that are following right behind that one.

Sometimes I wish I could go back to high school football and just get away from all the media and fan attention. When I was a quarterback in high school, nobody ever asked me for my autograph. Shoot, I was hoping they would. Just one would have been cool. But now, man, let me just eat in peace.

It's different. I never thought it would be this way. I enjoy the game and still want like ten more years of it, but the privacy part of it is gone. The fame can get to you. If you ask any athlete, they'll tell you that lack of privacy is the toughest part of professional sports.

The whole autograph thing I don't get. I had an autograph session in Boston this past summer. It was two hours long and they paid me $75,000. Amazing. It's kind of a pain in the ass to do them. Try signing two thousand pieces of paper in two hours and see how much your hand cramps. Yeah, I can hear people now. What's Favre complaining about? He's got it made. I'm not complaining. It just seems kind of silly. But you've got to take advantage while the money and attention are there. Ten years from now people won't want my autograph. Fame is fleeting. One minute you're in the limelight and the next minute it's Brett who? I'm not naïve about that.

A lot of athletes are shocked that people forget about them. Not me. I don't remember Austin Carr, but Bus talks about him like he was unbelievable. Joe Namath, I've been at parties when he's there and a lot of older people go up to him and drool. Other people are like, hmm, Joe Namath, yeah, I've heard of him. Unless you're part of that generation and watched him or played with him, you don't care. That's just the way this deal works.

I know I'll walk into a place someday and some old fart will come over with his boy and say, "Son, you don't know who this is, but this s.o.b. was the best quarterback I've ever seen."

The kid will look at me and go, "Oh really? Who is he?"

Then the old man will say something like, "Brett Favre, meet my son."

And the name won't mean a thing to the kid.

But I'll be thrilled to be recognized. I'll be going, "Hey, what's your name, son? Let me sign something for you."

When you're going through your career, you think it's going to be this way forever. But there comes a time when the next generation takes over. Hell, five years from now Brittany will forget who Dan Marino is. She might recognize the name but that's about it. She'll like Drew Bledsoe or Rick Mirer or Peyton Manning or someone younger and cuter.

I have an appreciation for all that I've accomplished and all that I might be able to accomplish in football. The success, the fame, the attention, I know it won't last. I try to enjoy the moment as best I can. The fans have been great to me. Hell, I get more mail than Santa Claus. Right now I'm hot.

Parents in Wisconsin are starting to name their kids after me. In 1994, Brett was the seventy-first most popular name for boys that year. In 1995, when we reached the NFC championship game, the name moved up to forty-third place. Not bad. But I'm hoping for a spot in the top ten if I put together a couple more good seasons.

The name game aside, I also have an appreciation for my nonfootball life.

It's not like I don't have a life without football. There are a lot of guys who don't know what to do with themselves once it's all over. I know what I'll do. I'll hang out. Play golf. Relax. Just enjoy life.

The funny thing about success is that it changes people's perception of you without you ever changing.

In my mind, people who think I'm some hick from Mississippi, I've got them all beat. All those idiots who think

I'm a little country hick, I just let 'em keep on believing because I'll just keep on beating them. On the field, off the field, I love being around people who underestimate me.

Now that I'm performing well, everyone thinks I'm unbelievable. A couple of years ago they just thought I was a dumb redneck. I spoke at a Miller Lite function after the Super Bowl and I had everyone rolling. It was a little question-and-answer deal. I love that shit. I could've been there all day. It was a lot of fun.

A few years ago I did the same routine and everyone thought I was like Huck Finn's dumb cousin. Now I'm awesome. Go figure. There are still times when I have to be careful. Like when I was on *David Letterman.*

Letterman can make you look like an ass if he wants to. He can be sarcastic as hell. That's why I decided not to say much on his show. I'm not normally a quiet guy but I didn't want to go on *Letterman* and look like an idiot. I didn't want to open myself up to his sarcasm. If I had him down home on the golf course, I could talk his ears off, and if he gave me any shit, I could give it right back—and then some. But I'm sitting there in his chair on his show. I've seen what he can do to people. I had just won the Super Bowl, I was an MVP quarterback, but he could make me look like a fool if I let him. So I decided to make my answers short and sweet and get out of there. I just didn't want to get out there and make an ass out of myself.

That was my plan. So what happens? Before I go on, Letterman's people asked me if I would pick up a baseball with my toes.

I did that for John Madden. That's one of my claims to fame, long toes. We were on his bus last season and I picked up a ball with my toes. He just about died. So Madden talked about it on TV during one of our games. He was laughing and making it sound real funny, which I guess it is.

So now I have Letterman's people asking me if I would do it on the show. I told them hell no. Like picking up a baseball with my toes on national television wouldn't make me look like too much of a hillbilly.

If I want to make a fool out of myself, I don't need Letterman's help to do it. Believe me, I've had enough practice.

I joke around a lot but there are things that I take seriously. I'm very loyal. I learned that from my dad. I watched the way he worked with his high school teams all those years. I know he would have done anything for his players. And I'd do anything for my team. I'd do anything for my teammates. I'd do anything for Deanna and Brittany. My family. For Frankie and Chewy. Scott. Bus. All my friends. People don't have to worry. If I'm your friend, you don't have a worry.

That sense of loyalty got me in a jam with some fans after we won the Super Bowl. After the game there was a welcome-home party for the team in Lambeau Field. Some fans were upset because I couldn't make it back for the celebration. The thing is, I couldn't make it back. A friend had chartered a private plane to take my family, Bus and his family, and my friend's family to Hawaii.

Five days before the Super Bowl I'm told that Green Bay is planning a postgame celebration, win or lose. I told Ron Wolf and I told Mike Holmgren that I couldn't make it. First off, I have to go to Hawaii. I can't be late. I can't postpone the trip that my friend had planned three weeks before the Super Bowl. That would have cost him $35,000. I just couldn't do that. Both Ron and Mike said that was totally understandable because it was set up long before the postgame celebration. If Ron or Mike had been upset about it and told me that I had to come back, then more than likely I would have.

I'm sorry I couldn't make it back for the celebration but I don't regret it. I'll be back in Green Bay playing and giving it my all. Fans have to understand. There's going to be plenty of time to enjoy our victory. We have until the next Super Bowl, and hopefully, we'll be in that one, too.

It's a difficult balancing act between professional and private life. I've tried to be fair with both. I've tried to be there for the fans, for my teammates, and for my family.

I've done a lot of things for people. I've tried to help my parents out, but I can never repay them for what they've done for me. I got Mom and Dad a car and a truck, built a pool house and a deck around it, added onto the kitchen. I had the driveway blacktopped. That was pretty expensive. The road is a half mile long. But I enjoy doing that stuff. It's fun.

I gave my grandfather a truck. Paw Paw is seventy-nine. He's always giving me money. When we were kids, we always used to kid him about his wallet being so thick. Even today, he'll shake my hand and he'll stick a twenty in my palm. "Paw Paw, I don't need this," I'll tell him. But he won't take it back.

So I went out and bought him a new truck. I wasn't there to give it to him but my sister, Brandi, had a party for him and they took pictures of him with the truck. He started crying. I was like, God, I can't imagine my grandfather crying. He's full-blooded Choctaw Indian. Real tough. Can't hear a lick. He'll have one Red Dog, that's his beer of choice, then he goes to bed at 6:30 every evening.

But I got him his truck and he cries. Unbelievable.

When I talk to him, I'll ask him, "Paw Paw, how's your truck?" And he'll say, "It's doing good. I don't want to drive it too much because I don't want to ruin it."

I'll say, "Paw Paw, drive the damn truck."

Helping others is important to me. That's something I learned from my parents, too. That's why we started our charity work. You get to a point where you earn so much money that you either have to give some of it away or go out and earn it for somebody else. Deanna and I started the Brett Favre Fourward Foundation in 1996 to help youth-oriented charities. In our first year we raised about $200,000 for the Special Olympics, cystic fibrosis, and the Boys and Girls Club. My annual celebrity golf tournament is a major part of the fund-raising efforts. We also donate $150 for every touchdown pass I throw. Last season there were like ten companies that matched that amount.

One of the toughest things in pro sports is choosing the right agent. Some people are surprised when I talk about Bus as my friend. But that's what he's become, one of my best friends. I asked Bus to be my agent a long time ago.

Bus has been an attorney in Hattiesburg for something like twenty years. We met there when I was in college. After my senior year I asked him if he would be my agent. Bus was a personal injury attorney. He had never been an agent before. Of course, I hadn't been a pro quarterback before, either. So I figured we were made for each other. It's worked out that we are.

Bus is a pretty good athlete and one helluva golfer. I've lost enough money to him on the golf course to know. Bus played basketball at American University. He likes to brag that he was a defensive specialist. One game he held Pete Maravich to forty-four points. In the first half. So in his own small way, Bus helped another athlete on his way to the Hall of Fame.

I have never, ever dreamed of getting rid of him. Other agents might be able to get me more money. Maybe. But I'd have to do this or do that. Stuff I don't want to do.

Besides, Bus is probably my best friend. I love the fact that we can joke around and give each other shit.

One day Bus, Leon, Sparky Walker, and I were out on the golf course and Bus starts in on me.

"You know," Bus said, "if I had an athlete who was worth a shit, maybe we could get a new contract."

I doubt Leigh Steinberg is saying that about Steve Young. But that's what they're missing out on and we're not. I turned to Sparky and Leon and said, "Fellas, either of you know a good agent?"

"I do," Leon said.

"Who?" I asked.

"James Bond," Leon said. "I hear he's a good one."

Funny guy, that Leon. But to be honest, I wouldn't trade Bus for anyone, even James Bond. We're close. Real close. If I knew today that Leigh Steinberg could get me $5 million more than Bus could get me, I'd still say, sorry, Leigh. Hell, $10 million, $100 million, it wouldn't matter. There's no way I'd get rid of Bus.

We trust each other, and that's rare in professional sports. The only reason we signed a contract is that the NFL says you have to. We do business deals on a handshake or by giving our word. Like the day I bought four hundred acres down the coast in Mississippi. I told Bus and Leon, "You guys want part of this acreage?" They said sure. I said, "Okay, you're in." We've done several deals like that. I'll get my money if we make it. I ain't into signing contracts. A handshake's good enough for me. I know trust is a rare commodity today, but I can't understand how people can screw someone else. I really can't.

When I was in college, agents were flocking around me. It was funny. Bus may have been worried because all these agents were wining and dining me, flying me places and giving me shit, but he didn't have to. It was a joke.

When I went to the East-West Shrine game my senior year, Steinberg took me out. Me and Browning Nagle were hanging out the whole week, having fun, partying. So Leigh called me up and said he wanted to take me out to eat, that he wanted to talk to me about signing with him. Typical me. I said, "Do you mind if Browning comes along?"

"Well, I'd really like to talk to you alone," Steinberg said.

"We're kind of hanging this week," I said.

Steinberg said all right.

Steinberg picks us up in a tiny, two-seater Mercedes. It was an older one, pretty cool. I think he still wanted to talk to me alone so that's why he brought the small car. But I thought, what the hell, and hopped back in the hatchback and let Browning sit in the front. I'm all scrunched up in back, but it was a blast.

Leigh talked to me the whole night, but I wasn't interested. So he ends up signing Browning.

A year later, I'm talking to Browning, who was drafted by the Jets right after I was picked by the Falcons. I ask him, "How's it going with Leigh?" Browning said, "Shit, I can't get in touch with him." I go, "Really? I talk to Bus every day."

Ralph Cindrich was another agent after me at the East-West game. He's a good guy. Ralph had two of his guys take Browning and me out to play golf during the week. We got kicked off the twelfth hole. We were playing on a golf course out by the 49ers' complex and there was this big office building with shiny reflector windows. The building is just off the fairway. We're teeing off on No. 10 and I sent my shot right at the office building. Whack! It smacked into the window and left a little dent. Browning thinks it's pretty funny so he does it. We just shelled the building with about five or six balls.

Cindrich's boys didn't know what to think. They paid for the round and bought us some golf shoes. Now they didn't know what the hell to do with us. We played two more holes and this guy comes out. We figure it's trouble. We were right.

"We've had complaints that you fellows have been hitting a building," he said.

"You're crazy," I said. "We wouldn't do that."

Shoot, there are beer cans all over the cart. He knew we were partying.

"The people in the office building identified you," he said. "Two big guys. White shirt. Red shirt."

"Look, we didn't do it," I said. "But if you want, we'll leave right now."

"Well, that's what we're asking you to do," he said.

"If we have to go, you can take your shoes back," I said.

So Browning and I take the shoes off that Cindrich had bought us and walked off the course barefoot.

A year ago I got a package from Steinberg explaining everything he could do for me. I showed it to Bus and told him it looked mighty good. He told me, "Damn, it does look good. Maybe you should go." Bus knows he doesn't have to worry. He knows I'll stick with him to the end.

I think guys are screwing up by not going with someone they're comfortable with. They get all caught up in the money. That's just not that big a deal. The money will come if you deserve it. How you get along with people matters more. Look at Bus and me. We're a perfect match. We're both country and we're both a little crazy.

Bus has this big tractor with a bucket in front that he plays around with on his land. One night we were out there burning a brush pile, listening to some country

music, and having a few beers. Bus pulled up in the tractor and I hopped into the bucket. He hoisted my ass about
ten feet in the air. I'm singing and dancing a bit, just goof-
in' off, when Bus starts driving. It's pitch-black, the stars
are out, and I'm hanging on for dear life. Bus hauls me
about a quarter mile across a field to the edge of this pond.
He hangs the bucket over the water and I start to wonder,
"Is this s.o.b. crazy enough to dump me in?"

Bus dangled me there for a while and then drove back
to the fire. He got out and left me in that damn bucket
while he got another beer. Somehow I can't picture Leigh
Steinberg leaving Steve Young up there in that bucket. Bus
told me the next day that if he would have had one more
beer in him, he would have dumped me in that pond.

I can't see any other player and his agent doing that.
That's one reason I hate introducing Bus as my agent. It
doesn't sound right. He's not my agent. He's my friend. I
ought to just say this is my best buddy, Bus. I don't know
how he feels, because he's my friend first and agent second. He's done great with me, if not better. We're going to
be the highest-paid player in the league real soon. If not,
we won't sign. It's that simple.

You could be my agent. We'd go in and say, it ain't no
secret here. This is what we need. And we'd get it. I told
Bus, you don't tighten up, I'm going to fire your ass and
hire Leon. Hell, Leon likes that idea.

But I don't worry about the money. It'll come. Bus gets
on me all the time about that. He'll call and say, "Look,
I've talked to Reinfeldt. Here's the deal, okay, seven years
with a $10-million signing bonus. I'm trying to get him up
to twelve. Mike Reinfeldt is the Packers' chief financial
officer.

I'm like, really? Twelve, huh? Hey, can we play golf
today?

And Bus would say, "Do you know what we're talking about here? Fifty million dollars!"

"Well, I know. I'd just really like to go play golf."

It drives Bus crazy. I listen, but I have no concept of it. It's important because I think I deserve the big contract. I've proved myself. In two years, I may be able to say someone else should be the highest paid. Right now I should be.

It'll all work out. I ain't hurtin right now. As they say at the country club, I'm holding pretty good.

# 13

# THE FUTURE

It's impossible for anyone to know what the future holds, but I've got a pretty clear idea of how I'd like to see things unfold for me over the next fifteen, twenty years.

Naturally I'd like to see the Green Bay Packers repeat as Super Bowl champions. I'm confident we can do it again, but I'm also well aware of how hard it is. It is so damn hard it's unbelievable. I know that now because I've been through it once.

Hell, the 1996 season wasn't exactly easy. Even though we played superbly, it still wasn't a guarantee that we'd win Super Bowl XXXI. What if we played Dallas in the play-offs? I feel good about our chances, but until we beat the Cowboys it's not a slam dunk. What if we played San Francisco and it was a clear day and Steve Young's healthy? It might've been a different story. I try to be realistic about that.

It's difficult to repeat because there are too many great players and too many great coaches for it to be easy. Anybody can beat you. I know that's a cliché, but it's true. And you don't have that many games. It's not like the NBA or Major League Baseball or the NHL where it's like, if you lose a game, so what? You know you're going to get forty or fifty or sixty more chances. In the NFL, you can't afford to lose more than four or five games if you want the home-field advantage in the play-offs, which is everything. Eleven victories doesn't guarantee anything. Every game has to count. Every team you play can beat you. They really can.

Now with that said, I'm also very confident that if most of our guys come back—and we already re-signed Gilbert Brown, our terrific nose tackle—I think we can do it again. In fact, I think we can be even better than we were last season. It helps to have the confidence that you've done it once. That is such an important factor it's beyond description. It means everything in a game where the talent is so evenly matched.

Personally I will continue to set my goals high as long as I'm in the NFL. The thought of winning a third straight Most Valuable Player award gives me chill bumps. Nobody in the history of the league has ever won the MVP award three times, let alone three times straight. I know it's a lofty goal, maybe even impossible, but it's what I'd like to accomplish. It's what helps motivate me to get up each morning in the off-season and work out for a couple hours before I go play golf. Nothing comes easy and no one is going to hand anything to you. Life's not that way. You've got to earn it.

I can't tell you how exciting it was for me to win back-to-back MVPs. The voting concluded on the Monday before our regular-season finale against Minnesota and I swear I was in Jeff Blumb's office twice a day all week. Jeff is the Packers' public relations assistant and I pestered the hell out of him trying to find out the results of the balloting. Every day he would say, "I haven't heard yet, but you'll be the first to know."

I'll never forget it was Friday night and I'd gone out to eat dinner with some friends. I got home and it was about 11:30. I checked the caller ID on my telephone and it said Jeff Blumb had telephoned. Right away my heart started pounding. I had this little conversation in my head while I was dialing: Well, he wouldn't call me if it was bad news; he'd just wait until tomorrow to tell me in person.

Well, Jeff's wife answered on the third ring. They were already in bed and I apologized for calling so late. Jeff got on the phone and he sounded like he was in a fog. When he told me I'd won the MVP award, I probably sounded the same way.

I was stunned. I was like, "No shit . . . No shit." That went on for a bit while it was sinking in. Finally I told Jeff, "Sorry to bother you this late, but if I'd have known what it was about, I'd have called at three in the morning."

I felt that winning the MVP award twice, especially after all I'd been through in the off-season, really validated me as a pretty good quarterback. Now people say, "That Favre's not too bad." If I had won the award once and came back with a so-so season, then there might've been doubt in some people's minds. People could say, "Hell, anyone can get hot for one season and win the award." Now I want to win it three times, something that has never been done before. I really want to win it.

And I'm going to give it a run.

The great thing about my teammates is they seemed truly happy for me. I never want my teammates to think I'm all full of myself. I feel bad for the guys that only one player can win the MVP and usually, if your team wins, it's the quarterback who gets recognized. That's why it's great that my teammates bask in it with me. They take pride in knowing that I'm their MVP. Without them I don't win the award. It's that simple.

I've got to tell you there is one individual record I'd love to break: Dan Marino's single-season touchdown record of forty-eight. I rank that right up there with Joe Di-Maggio's 56-game hitting streak, Hank Aaron's 744 career home runs, and Nolan Ryan's strikeout record. What Marino did in 1984 was awesome, but I do think it's reachable. When I got to twenty touchdown passes in five games, I thought I was going to break it. I really did. Then when Robert Brooks got hurt and Chewy got hurt, I said no way. Then when Antonio Freeman got hurt, I really said no way. If I'd have had those guys, there's no doubt in my mind I'd have broken it. As it was I only ended up nine away.

I don't know if that record will fall, though. It's a hard record. If I throw at least thirty touchdown passes in '97, that would be four straight seasons. I already have the NFL record with three straight, so it's possible. Forty touchdown passes in a season is my goal. If I could do that, it would be ideal. Down the road, I'd like to make a run at Marino's career record. He's got something like 360 right now and he's still playing. I keep up with that shit. I've got 147 touchdown passes right now, so if I throw twenty-five a year for the next ten years, I've got a shot at it, depending how many more Dan throws before he's finished.

I think it's crazy that I broke Bart Starr's career touchdown record in five seasons. That's pretty amazing. Pretty productive, too. I'm proud of that. When I get inside the red zone, I feel like there is no way the defense is going to stop me. My first couple of seasons when I was throwing eighteen or nineteen touchdown passes, I thought that was pretty good. Now I get that many in half a season. That's a tribute to our offense and the way Mike calls the plays. When we get around the goal line, we throw it. When we have to run, we run and we get them, but Mike's not afraid to put it up down there.

It's fun to talk about things like breaking Marino's record, but I don't want anyone to think I'm getting ahead of myself. I know a lot of things have to happen in order for something like that to come together. I'd like to think I've got a pretty decent sense of my place in history among NFL quarterbacks and right now it's not on top.

To me, Joe Montana is the greatest quarterback of all time. I watch him on film and I am amazed. Now, I've watched a lot of quarterbacks: Terry Bradshaw. Roger Staubach. Archie Manning. I haven't seen a lot of the older quarterbacks such as Joe Namath and Johnny Unitas because I wasn't around in that era, so it's hard to compare, but to me, Joe Montana is the best. What Joe did in winning so many Super Bowls with San Francisco is no different than what Terry Bradshaw did in Pittsburgh, but Joe was so picture-perfect. I know this offense and I know how difficult it is to master, but Joe handled it like a surgeon. He was so precise it was scary.

I look at Joe Montana and what he accomplished and how he accomplished it and that's what I want. I want someone to write a book someday and say, "Damn, that Brett Favre was the greatest quarterback of all time. He could do it all."

That's what I'm striving to be.

Whether people think I can do it or not doesn't really matter. In my mind, I think I can be the best ever. That's my goal, to be the best. I don't know if that will ever happen, but I think it's important to set high goals. I always have. A kid from Kiln, Mississippi, has to set some big goals if he wants to make something of himself. You've got to be able to dream. Then you have to want to work hard to make those dreams come true because nothing comes easy in life. There are a lot of people out there who don't want to see you succeed. Shoot, some people thought I'd never play college football, let alone make it in the pros. But I always knew that I would. That's why I still dream and work hard.

My goal is to be the best of all time and up to now I've had pretty good luck in reaching that goal.

Physically I think I have better skills than Joe Montana. I'm bigger, stronger, faster. I have a stronger arm. But that doesn't make you the best. That's something you have to earn. Physically Joe wasn't all that impressive but people were scared of him. They were afraid of what he could do, which is beat you.

I want other teams to be scared of me.

After this year, I think I proved I could make it happen anywhere on the field. At least I believe that in my mind and I would hope other teams believe that, too. Teams will find ways to stop me occasionally. That's just the way things go. If you were perfect, you'd be in another league, but that's what I strive to do, to go into every season with new goals.

I'll never forget something I heard when I was playing in the Senior Bowl. I was talking with Coach Marty Schottenheimer, whose Kansas City Chiefs had just lost to the Miami Dolphins in the play-offs. I said, "Well, Coach, you almost made it to the Super Bowl. It was close. I thought you had 'em." Coach Schottenheimer looked at me and said, "That damn Marino is something else. You just never know when that son of a bitch will beat you. The guy is unbelievable."

That's what I want some NFL coach to say about me someday. Whether it's Carolina or Detroit or Chicago, somebody saying, "Damn, if we could only get rid of

Favre, we could make it to the Super Bowl." That's the kind of career I want. I want people to think that as long as I'm playing it's going to be tough to beat the Packers.

Now along the way I have to have some luck.

Health plays a huge factor in all of this. I wonder if down the road I may experience some health problems because of the painkiller abuse. I hope nothing ever comes of it but who knows? The doctors tell me there isn't anything to worry about because I didn't do it for a long, long period of time. Some guys get up to sixty pills a night before they stop or die. I was up to fifteen. When I tell people I was taking fifteen pills a night, they're like, my God, but imagine what the stomachs are like of the guys who are taking sixty a night. It can't be too good.

My left hip occasionally bothers me, but at least it hasn't gotten any worse in the past five years. The range of motion is pretty good, although it's not like my good hip. The top of the ball inside the socket is smooshed down on top, so instead of being round it's flat. When my hip rotates in there, the little ridges of bone spurs catch the nerve at times. That happened the other day. I got out of the golf cart and went to walk to my ball and I almost fell down. It felt like a knife was poking me in the hip. So I'll shake it and move it around and it'll be okay. I remember one time I was bending over on one leg to put a tee into the ground and I dropped like someone stabbed me.

It makes me aware of how tenuous an NFL career can be. When I'm forty years old, I don't want to be all crippled up. When you're twenty-seven, you take things for granted, but I try to think about what it'll be like in twenty years. Hell, I'll still be fairly young and I'll want to be able to run around and play with my kids. Deanna tells me I can play as long as I want, but that she doesn't want to see me all beat up so I can't walk straight. She wants me to be normal when I finish playing, which is fair enough.

Deanna and I want to have more children. We love Brittany to death and we'd like for her to have some little brothers and sisters. I think it'd be great to be like Archie Manning someday and have a son like Peyton to go watch play football. In the meantime, Brittany keeps us plenty busy.

For eight years old, she's scary smart. When people come up to us in a restaurant and ask for my autograph, she'll grab me and say, "Sorry, but my daddy doesn't like to be bothered when we're eating." It's funny because when it comes from this little girl, people seem to be a lot more understanding about the whole deal.

I love the fact that she's Daddy's little girl. Bus and I took our daughters fishing the other day and I happened to catch a quarter-pound bass. The lure was bigger than the fish. Brittany didn't care. She just kept saying, "My daddy can fish really good." Now, I'm no fisherman. I can't even put the lure on. Bus knows he can fish circles around me, but Brittany doesn't care. She'll say, "My daddy is the best." It makes me feel good, but it's kind of embarrassing. I know the truth and she probably does, too, but she's still proud of me. I think that's how it should be for kids. Their daddy and mama should be the greatest thing to them. I used to say my daddy can hit a baseball farther than anyone. I'd tell the other kids, "I saw him hit one a mile once." They'd say, "No, he didn't." I'd give it right back to them and say, "Yes, he did. I saw it." That was in the first grade.

I can already tell that Brittany's a competitive little girl. I think she gets that from both Deanna and myself. Deanna's a great athlete in her own right and she'd never quit until she won. I'm the same way, so I guess it's no surprise that Brittany's like that, too.

I get a kick out of doing things with Brittany, probably because like me, she's up for anything. It doesn't matter what we're doing, so long as we're together. That's why I doubt I'd ever pursue a career in TV when football is over. I think I could do the TV analyst thing, but I doubt I'd want to. It's too time-consuming, which is the reason I'd retire from football in the first place.

I think I've got eight good years left in me. If I sign a seven-year contract extension with the Packers, that'll make me thirty-four and I'd be done, but who knows? Maybe I could do like all these cats are doing now and sign a three-year deal then for like $7 million and hit the big payday at the end. There's a lot of good that can be done in the world with the kind of money we pro athletes make. I'd like to think I'm pretty generous. At least that's what my friends say. I like to help people out. It's not because I have to; it's because I want to. Shoot, as long as I've got enough money in my pocket to get me some gas, pay my bets out at the golf course, and buy food or a few rounds for the guys, I'm happy. I think I'm pretty loyal, too. I tell people that if you're my friend, you don't have a worry in the world. I think that's the way it should be. I mean, if I was making absolutely no money, I'd love it if a good friend who hit it big spent some of it on me. I wouldn't ask for it, but it would be nice.

It's why I started the Brett Favre Fourward Foundation. I want to give back something to people who are less fortunate, especially the kids. When I go to the Children's Hospital of Milwaukee or I speak to kids with some horrible disease, I think, "That could just as easily be Brittany and I'd want someone to help her if they could." There really and truly is a responsibility that goes along with being an

NFL player. Now, I don't think that necessarily includes being a role model. I think parents have the responsibility to be the role models for their children. Too many times I've seen parents put it off on pro athletes when really, to my way of thinking, it should start at home. On the other hand, I'm not naïve enough to think kids don't watch NFL stars closely. If all the big-leaguers smoked or drank, a lot of kids would smoke and drink, too. That's why parents are so important. They've got to instill those values at home.

When I was growing up, I was lucky to have great parents who were always there for me. I know I've made some mistakes along the way. Who doesn't? But whatever I've accomplished I owe it to them. I really enjoyed playing football for my dad. It was a great experience. At an early age, it taught me to respect my coaches, who were the authority. That's why I could see myself getting into coaching someday. I'd be comfortable with that, especially at the high school level. That's where you can make a pretty big impact and kids that age are a lot of fun to be around. When I was student teaching in college, I worked with mentally retarded students and it was great. I'd go in there and give them as many hugs and as much attention as I could. I learned that from Mom, who taught special education for twenty years. She used to say that was every bit as important, if not more so, as just sticking to the lesson plan.

If she had a student who loved football, she'd tell him to bring in the scores from Sunday's NFL games. Then she'd sit with him and teach him to add and subtract using the scores. It made learning fun for the student. That's what I'd try to do.

In the meantime, I want to make a lasting mark on professional football. I want to see the Green Bay Packers return to glory like they had in the sixties. I'd love to see us go on a five-year run where we're regarded as the NFL's best team. I want people to think that as long as the Packers have number 4 at quarterback, they're going to make a run for the Super Bowl year in and year out.

I want my team to be remembered like the old Packers. When you think of the Packers, you think of Fuzzy and Bart and Ray. Jim Taylor and Paul Hornung. Vince Lombardi. How many other Super Bowl teams are there that you can name so many guys off of. The Raiders? Philadelphia? Ron Jaworski? We have a popular group of guys who like to have fun. And I think everyone on our team, and that includes our fans, had fun.

We enjoyed it and it was fun watching us.

That's how I want people to remember this team and its quarterback.

# 14

## THE 1997 SEASON IN REVIEW

I was baffled.

I looked up at the scoreboard and couldn't believe it was 17–7. The Broncos had just gotten to me with a blitz, I fumbled, and they kicked a field goal to take the ten-point lead. When I came off the field, I looked at Frankie Winters and he looked back at me and we both said, "Oh, shit." Right then, I knew we were in trouble.

It was still early in the second quarter, so we had a lot of time left to make up the points, but I had a feeling we couldn't stop them. Everyone knows it's never good when you jump on a team early and they come right back, which is exactly what the Broncos did to us.

One minute we were dominating them. The next minute we were down by ten. It was like a bad dream that goes on an on all night.

Our 7–0 lead was gone. So were any thoughts of blowing out the Broncos. We were in a fight for our lives and we knew it. We didn't think it would be easy, but nobody could've expected what happened, especially with how the game started.

The first time we touched the ball we marched right down the field. The Broncos' defense was on its heels, so we kept feeding Dorsey Levens the ball. When Denver blitzed their safety, Steve Atwater, I drilled Antonio Freeman on a quick slant for thirteen yards.

Then, on first down from their twenty-two, Free lined up in the slot right and ran a "go" route, which is one of our favorite plays. The guys up front gave me plenty of time to throw and I lobbed it toward the back of the end zone. Free hauled it in and we were jumping up and down and yelling and acting like we'd just won the game.

You've got to admit, we made it look pretty easy. And I couldn't help but think, "Well, here we go."

No one said it over on our sideline, but in the back of our minds everyone was thinking that this might be one of those 52–17 deals like Dallas and Buffalo a few years back. Who could blame us? It wasn't like we thought it would be easy going into the game. Far from it.

All week long I kept telling anyone who wanted to listen—the media, the fans, my teammates—that Super Bowl XXXII wasn't going to be like the previous thirteen. I kept saying this wasn't going to be the same old story: NFC KICKS AFC AGAIN.

I knew how bad John Elway wanted to win this game. When we beat New England in Super Bowl XXXI, I told myself, "I never want to lose one of these. It would hurt too much." Heck, Elway had already lost three Super Bowls, so there was no doubt in my mind he would do everything in his power to beat us. Except no one wanted to write that stuff. I guess it's not that sexy or interesting or whatever to write about how Brett Favre believes the Broncos are for real. I remember being at one of the press conferences and thinking to myself, "All of these reporters just think I'm just saying all the right things so I don't piss off the Broncos."

Then the game starts and we're up by a touchdown and suddenly it crossed my mind that maybe they were right and I was wrong. Maybe we were going to kick butt today. Everyone knows it wouldn't be the first time a Super Bowl went that way. Maybe I was just being a worrywart, which is pretty typical because I never think it's going to be easy against anyone, especially not against John Elway and Terrell Davis and Denver's defense.

Especially not in the Super Bowl.

I've had a million people ask me what happened to the Packers.

Well, like always, it's never just one thing.

My greatest concern going into the game was Denver's blitz package, which is excellent. I knew they were going to be tough and I knew they were going to blitz us a lot. The game went exactly like I thought it would, though I didn't think we'd be behind. I figured they'd blitz us and get to me on some plays, but that we'd come right back and hit some big ones, too. That's pretty much what happened.

People say, "Well, if you knew they were going to blitz, why didn't you handle it?" If only it were that simple. The problem wasn't knowing whether they were going to blitz. It was knowing what blitz they were going to come with. They could come with a million different blitzes, which is about what they did. I give them all the credit in the world.

We had two turnovers that led to ten points—both turnovers were caused by blitzes—and we lost 31–24. It doesn't take a genius to see what the difference was in the game. Both of those blitzes were ones they hadn't used.

Neither one showed up on any of the film we studied, and believe me, we studied a lot of film.

They were new for the Super Bowl and they got us with them. The fact that we got behind didn't help.

This isn't the easiest thing to admit, but sometimes when we get behind I get a little anxious. I try to do everything at once. I mean, it's like I'm trying to score three touchdowns in one possession. You can't do that. It's like golf. You want to play all eighteen holes at once. What happens is you forget a hole along the way and get a double-bogey. Afterward, you go, "How did that happen? That's the easiest hole on the course?"

Hey, I'm still learning and trying to get better all the time. I just have to keep reminding myself that I've got to treat every possession individually. You can't start looking to the fourth quarter when you've just started the first.

I didn't watch the film from Super Bowl XXXII until our post-draft minicamp in April. Man, I could've killed myself. I thought I played pretty good and the numbers were okay. I was something like 25 of 42 for 256 yards and three touchdowns. Not bad.

Then I saw four plays—all in the fourth quarter—that I really wish I had back.

I was watching the film and I just couldn't understand how I missed them. The first was a pass to Free up the left sideline. The Broncos were in a zone, Free found the seam between the corner and safety, and our line gave me time. So what do I do? I fire it about four feet over Free's head. The worst part is that the way he runs after the catch; that might've been six if I had hit him and he made the safety miss.

The second came two plays later.

On third-and-eight at about the Broncos' forty, I had Robert Brooks wide open on a post route, but I got some pressure just as I released. I thought I led him perfectly, but the ball hung up in the air a bit and Atwater just had time to get a fingernail on it. There's no doubt Robert would've scored a touchdown on that play.

The third misfire came on our next possession.

I was rolling to my left and I started to run for the first down, but then I spotted Free coming open across the middle. I turned and threw back to him, but it was just a hair behind. He reached back and got a hand on it, but he couldn't bring it in. That one really hurt, especially because it's a play I feel like I can make with my eyes closed.

Amazingly, we still had one more chance to tie the game.

On our last possession, we moved from our thirty-yard line to Denver's thirty-five, which put us in pretty good position to do some damage. I dumped a four-yard completion to Dorsey, but on second down Free dropped what would've been a tough catch over the middle. He usually brings that one in, but that's how our day was going. On third-and-six, Robert just got crushed by Atwater right when the ball arrived.

That brought up fourth down and I was starting to have my doubts. It was like, "Hell, if it's come down to this, what makes you think it's going to be any different this time?" I didn't give up. Believe me, I wanted it worse than anything, but they had played well in those situations all day long and I didn't think it would be any different now.

We needed eight yards, so we ran a play called All Hook.

Derrick Mayes, who lined up wide left, ran a squareout. Free, who was slot left, and Robert, who was wide right, each ran hooks. That left Chewy one-on-one with linebacker John Mobley. When I came up to the line, I could see that they were going to blitz, which means I had to pick a side. You don't have time to look all over the field.

On the film, I saw that Mayes got open, but I decided to go with Chewy one-on-one. Heck, he's one of the best tight ends in the game. It's like basketball. You'll take Michael Jordan or whoever is your best player one-on-one every time. That's what I did.

Except this time Mobley covered it.

Sort of.

When you look close at the replay, you can see that Mobley was mugging Chewy eight yards downfield. You can only touch a receiver within five yards, so it was interference, but there was no way the referees were going to call it in that situation. If they would've called a penalty and given us a first down, the Broncos would've killed them. They couldn't have shown their faces.

Well, I went ahead and threw the ball, but Mobley knocked it away.

When the ball hit the ground, it wasn't a total shock.

That's how things pretty much went for us the whole day.

I also think the NFC Championship Game took something out of us. We had two weeks to get ready for the Super Bowl, but that was a pretty emotional and physically draining win at San Francisco. When we ran off the field, it felt like we'd already won the Super Bowl.

I remember telling Frankie, "This win is bigger than the feeling when we beat New England in the Super Bowl, even though the circumstances weren't nearly as big." There were so many connections between us and the 49ers. Mike is from there. He used to coach there. Steve Mariucci, the 49ers' head coach, and I are best friends. Plus, Mooch used to work for Mike in Green Bay. And on top of that, Steve Young and I are good friends.

Plus, we knew we had to win to get back to the Super Bowl, which we wanted badly. It's the first time I can remember going into a game not knowing if we were going to win. I always think we're going to win, no matter who we're playing. I never think it's going to be easy, but I always feel like we'll pull it out. This time it was different. I had no clue.

I truly didn't know how it would turn out until the game was in hand.

Besides, I had a little extra motivation going into the San Francisco game. That week Mooch told the media that the difference between me and Young is that I make more big plays, but I'm also more prone to throwing interceptions because of the risks I take. That bugged me.

I agree that I take some risks, but when it comes right down to it, I always felt like I played really well in big games, and I wouldn't trade that for anything. I love Mooch to death and I always will, but I really wanted to beat him bad that day.

The two dumbest reasons I've heard why we lost to Denver is that:

1. We were out partying too much in San Diego and we were overconfident. Neither one is true. If you look at how much time we spent going out to dinner and so on compared with what Denver did, I'm sure there wasn't much of a difference, if any. We knew what was at stake, especially since we'd been through it the year before in New Orleans. We knew what it meant to win the Super Bowl, so I don't buy that for a minute.

2. That we were distracted by the rumors that Mike might be leaving for Seattle to become the head coach/general manager. Give me a break. We're all professionals here. To think that the typical Super Bowl rumors would bother us is ridiculous.

Mike would never have talked about Seattle if he wasn't asked about it first.

Besides, I figured a couple of years ago that Mike wouldn't be here forever. It's no secret he's a West Coast guy. His heart is in Green Bay, but his roots are somewhere else. He is certainly talented enough to be a coach and a general manager. I think the fans in Green Bay should understand that and I think they do understand it. Players move, so why not coaches?

If Mike takes a job somewhere else and leads that team to the Super Bowl, sort of like Bill Parcells did with the Giants and then the Patriots, that would definitely put him in an elite group. He's a great coach now, but that would establish him as one of the greatest coaches of all time. I'm sure that's important to him. It would be important to me.

If that's what Mike wants, I'm behind him 100 percent.

I feel like I'm old enough now to the point where I can handle myself if he leaves. There was a time when I needed to be led. Now I can do the leading.

That isn't to say I wouldn't miss him. Heck, we've got a great relationship. I don't hesitate to talk to him about anything. I'm not reluctant to go to him no matter what's up. I used to be scared to go to him, even if I knew I was right about something, but it's not like that now.

It's funny. We talk about other things more than we do football. That's important. We have a pretty good understanding of each other. The bottom line is we both want to win more than anything else. We'll always have that in common.

I also know he's the coach. He calls the shots. I'm paid to execute the plays the way he wants me to execute them. That will always be the case. I'll never feel like I'm bigger or better than him. That's what makes our relationship special. We can always be friends and talk on a certain

level, but when it comes right down to it, he's the coach.
He calls the shots.

That's how it is supposed to be between a player and
a coach and too many players tend to lose sight of that
nowadays. For me it's pretty much the opposite.

It seems like the more I accomplish, the more I appreciate it.

The Most Valuable Player awards are like that. It's not
every day a player wins a MVP, much less three straight.
Think about all the terrific players who've never won one.
Reggie White, as great a player as he is, he's never won
one. For me to have won in only my fourth season in the
league is pretty good. When I think about it, I still have to
pinch myself.

Each of the MVPs represents something different.

The first one was like: "Okay, you've arrived. You're
established." It meant a lot to me to know that my peers
realize, "Hey, this guy can play." Now there won't be any
more doubts, where before there were.

The second MVP was like: "I told you so." To me, it
represents my ability to overcome. I came back clean and
healthy from my Vicodin addiction. I've often thought
about the transformation from one year to the next. It's
huge. I can remember people saying, "God, you're not taking pain pills anymore. Your mind should be clear. How
much better are you going to be?"

I said, "Not much."

What I did during my first MVP season amazes me. I
never slept. Then, the night before a game, I wouldn't take
any pills and I'd sleep for twelve hours. When I woke up
on Sunday morning, I'd ache all over. I felt weird because
I didn't take anything. I was uncomfortable playing the
game. My joints ached. It was like I needed to take the

pills to get me through, but I wouldn't take them. After the game, I'd be like, thank God for getting me through this.

The third MVP represents consistency.

The last three seasons have been very similar. We went to two Super Bowls and we had a chance to go in the other. Heck, we were leading Dallas with ten minutes to play. The statistics are almost identical, too. If no one knew I was on pain pills, there's no way they could pick out which season I was hooked.

Selfishly, it was gratifying to win the third MVP because so many people thought it couldn't be done. I remember reading somewhere that ESPN's Joe Theismann said he didn't think I'd do it. It was halfway through the season and he said I'd only had one very good game. It was frustrating that people didn't realize how well I was playing.

The focus is on the numbers, but the only number that matters is the number of wins. We went 13–3 during the regular season and finished 15–4 overall. There's only one team in the entire league that wouldn't trade us.

I think our fans, the media, and the people associated with the Packers get spoiled a bit, kind of like how it was in San Francisco and Dallas. If the 49ers won, but Jerry Rice didn't catch fifteen passes, everyone acted like he was having an off-day. That's crazy.

The third MVP always will be special because I got to share it with Barry Sanders. People have asked me if I was upset I didn't win it outright. Heck, no. I love watching Barry run with the football, unless it's against our defense. He's one of the all-time great running backs, maybe the greatest. To have our names linked in NFL history is awesome.

Actually, the third one was a surprise.

I talked to *Sports Illustrated*'s Peter King a week before

the voting and he said he thought Barry was going to win it. He knew I'd made a strong surge and we were winning, but he felt like it would be Barry. Then he told me he voted for the Steelers' Carnell Lake. He went through his reasoning and it all sounded pretty legitimate. When he got done, I said, "That's fine." Then I said, "If you think that's who NFL general managers would start their team with, okay."

I didn't mind, although if I'd have lost to Barry by one vote, I'd have killed Peter. Now the question is whether I can win a fourth straight MVP. It won't be easy because the expectations have gotten so high, but I do think it's possible. I mean, I've got to believe that forty touchdowns and a division title would clinch it. I still haven't hit forty touchdown passes in a year, but that's not out of the question. I have to be healthy and I have to play well, of course, but I don't see why I can't maintain the level of play I've established.

The competition should be fierce this year.

Barry Sanders is always a threat to do something unbelievable. He had a terrible start last season and he still rushed for over two thousand yards. The Cowboys' Emmitt Smith, if he catches fire, you never know. Emmitt's capable of scoring twenty touchdowns in a season.

Then there's Steve Young. Man, I love watching him on film. Same with Barry. And when Jerry Rice is healthy, he has the potential to be really something. You've got to go with the guys you know who've done it before. They're all capable. So am I. The thing that's working against me is that the sportswriters are looking for something different now, which is okay.

I'm looking for something different, too.

Despite all the things I've accomplished, I'd like to do more. I'd love to throw six touchdown passes in a game.

And as soon as I did it, I'd want to go for seven. I would love to throw for 500 yards in a game, too, but only if we won. In this offense, it's been proven that the more you have to throw, more than likely you'll lose. I've had two 400-yard games and we've lost both of them.

I would like to throw a touchdown pass left-handed. I've always liked to do things, good or bad, that make people say, "What in the hell was that?" Or "Was that awesome?" Just like throwing it off my knees. Yeah, I'd like to have that pass back against Detroit. I didn't want Reggie Brown to intercept it and return it for a touchdown. But I just knew I could complete it. I still do. That's the way I play the game. I think that's why people like to watch me play.

Some guys don't like to watch themselves on film, just like some singers don't like to hear themselves on the radio and some writers never read their own stuff. Me? I like to see myself on film. It's still fun to me. I like to say, "God, that was just awful." I can laugh at myself, but I can also pat myself on the back.

I don't know if there's any one thing that can stop me. The one person who can stop me is myself. In that way, I'm kind of like Mark McGwire in baseball. He'll strike out every once in a while, but he'll get you in the long run. I approach the game the same way. You may stop me, but not forever. So I don't feel like there's anything I can't do.

Heck, I know I can't outrun guys, but I know I can get us out of any situation. I really feel that way and I think the team feels that way, too. That's one thing that has enabled the Packers to be better. We have a trust in each other that we didn't have five or six years ago.

My teammates expect me to make MVP-type plays. So when I do, it's fun, but it isn't like I'm thinking, "I'm the greatest." Hey, that's what I'm supposed to do.

The touchdown pass to Dorsey at Tampa Bay, the play when I tossed it underhand, now that was what I would call an MVP-type play. The two spin moves against Buffalo in the last game of the season—pumping to one side, stopping and twirling in midair—those are MVP-type plays, too. The Monday night opener against Chicago when I started to throw to Free because I expected him to be open, but then just as I released, I latched onto the ball and pulled it back in because he wasn't—that was a tough play. I turned and hit Robert for a touchdown when maybe another quarterback would've thrown it into coverage and been intercepted.

Those are the kinds of plays that make the difference between an MVP and an also-ran. It's like what Antonio Freeman said when he heard I'd signed my new contract. He said he appreciates the way I can turn bad plays into good ones. That's what a quarterback is supposed to do. That's why I think I'm deserving of my new contract. People see it and say, "Geez, he's making $47.5 million over seven years. He's the highest-paid player in the league. He's got it made."

Well, I know I'm making good money. Great money. I can't complain. The reason I think players renegotiate is that they feel like they're a better player than another guy at their position who is making more money. We all do it. I feel like I'm the best player in the league. I definitely feel I've proven it. The Packers must agree, because they made me the highest-paid player in the league. I look forward to playing in Green Bay through 2003.

Green Bay has been great to me. There's no better place to play football.

The downside of it is it is a small town and we do live in a fishbowl. That's the truth. It doesn't mean the people are bad people. But if you were in New York City, people couldn't care less. There are millions of people there and you can get lost. You can go do whatever you want and no one cares. But here it's different.

For the most part last season, people have been better than they have in the past. I think it's because my private life has been out in the open. People are saying, "Give the guy some space. We know he's going to be around. It's nothing to see him driving down the road now. He lives here. This is his home. This is where he works. Respect that." And people have done that. That says a lot about the people of Green Bay.

If I was just a fan and I saw this guy making millions of dollars playing a sport that every kid would love to play—there are millions of people who don't get the chance we get—it's like what do you expect? For them to feel sorry for you? I would feel that way. I've got fame, fortune, all that stuff. It's what I asked for. I'm not complaining. If I did, I'm sure people would be like, "Yeah, right. We're supposed to feel sorry for you?" I can't blame them. Too many times, players do complain. But it's what you ask for.

Let me tell you, though, there are times when this so-called celebrity status stinks. The bullshit that went on the day of our Monday night game at Minnesota was unbelievable. Some jerk on a Minneapolis radio station faked a stunt in which I was supposedly staying in some woman's hotel room in town. The story was complete garbage and the disc jockey has been fired, but it caused a lot of aggravation.

When our public relations staff told me what was going on, I thought, "This figures." Then my dad came into my hotel room and said, "You better call Deanna, because she's pretty upset." Hell, I couldn't blame her. She didn't think it was true, but it still hurt to have the rumors.

When I got to the Metrodome that night, I saw a couple of signs that read: WHO'S THE BIMBO? And WHERE'S YOUR WIFE? Crap like that. All it did was just fire me up even more. Better still, it fired up my teammates. About half the team came up to me and said, "Don't worry. We're going to do some serious ass-kicking tonight."

Even the Vikings' Brad Johnson came up to me and apologized for the stunt and the signs. I was like, "Hey, don't worry about it. You had nothing to do with it."

I'll tell you what. That bullshit backfired. I was so fired up, I knew we weren't going to lose, even though we hadn't won in the Metrodome since Mike became the head coach.

Well, we ended up going out and kicking some ass. We won 27–11. When I won that game and got on that plane and came home, that was one of the best feelings I had all year. The thing is most people treat you with respect and kindness. It's always just a couple of jerks who ruin it for everyone else. If we would've lost, there would've been people who'd have said, "Good. That's what we wanted. That's why we did it." Well, that didn't happen.

It try to not let that stuff stick with me.

There are way more important things to worry about.

This off-season has been pretty hectic. Shoot, they're all hectic now. I'm opening a steakhouse in Green Bay that will be similar to the Brett Favre Steakhouse in Milwaukee. It's funny. When I was a kid, I hated it when I'd have to stop playing outside because we were going out to eat in a restaurant. Now I'm going to own two of them.

Actually, it's pretty exciting. The food's going to be great. I know I'm going to be over there a lot. Probably almost every night. We'll have red beans and rice, blackened steak, shrimp, and catfish. It'll be nice. My teammates will be there a lot, too. It'll be a whole lot easier than having them go down to Milwaukee to hang out. It'll be located on Lombardi Avenue and Advance Street, which one of the developers is trying to get changed to Brett Favre Pass. That would be pretty neat if it happens. I don't know if I deserve to have a street named after me, but if it helps customers find the restaurant, it can't hurt.

Things are finally getting back to normal for my family. Thank God.

My older brother Scott was involved in a car accident that killed one of our best friends, Mark Haverty, in 1996. He received one year of house arrest for driving under the influence and then was jailed for violating terms of the house arrest. It turned out the supervising officer of the Mississippi Department of Corrections gave Scott privileges he shouldn't have had, which included being able to go fishing on Memorial Day. When he was stopped at a holiday roadblock near his home, he was arrested and ordered to prison for fifteen years.

My parents just about went crazy over that. After a lot of worry and a lot of headaches, it turned out Scott didn't do anything wrong, which we knew all along. The judge returned him to house arrest, which he has served.

My younger brother Jeff managed my restaurant in Milwaukee last year. Now he has decided to return to Mississippi and work down there. He wants to be closer to home, I guess. My little sister Brandi made it as a walk-on with the South Alabama women's varsity basketball team. She always was a great athlete when she worked at it.

Mom and Dad keep busy these days, as usual. The number of people who stop by to see where the NFL's three-time MVP grew up has slowed down which gives them more time to do what they want instead of talking football. Right now, the biggest thing in the off-season, for me, is trying to spend more time with Brittany and De-anna. We're trying to have a baby.

I'd really like to have a little boy. Sort of like Archie Manning and Peyton some day. Deanna and I are trying, but it's been a struggle to get pregnant. It's been two years now, so I'm getting a little worried. It's like, "How did I ever take something like that for granted?"

Brittany's an only child right now and I want her to have some brothers and sisters. It was always fun for me growing up to have brothers to mess around with and a sister to watch grow up. It gives you something to do all the time. We always had our own team, no matter what was going on. A lot of times Brittany sits in the house by herself and that can't be fun.

That's why I try to spend as much time with her as I can. We'll go hit some golf balls, go out and eat dinner, go catch a kids' movie. Or maybe we'll play some racquetball or basketball at the house. One of our favorite things is for me to read to her at night. It's funny. When I'm away from her, I can't wait to get home to see her. People tell you all the time, "If you don't watch out, they'll grow up right in front of you and you'll never notice." Well, it's true.

She's nine years old and she's developed her own little personality. She's pretty cool. When she was still a baby, Deanna and I would take her with us to the Quarterback Challenge down in Orlando. Now I'm fired up because she's big enough to go on the rides with me. We have a great time together.

The Vicodin addiction is in the past. I have no desire to go back to that. I haven't been hurt bad enough where I've said, "Sorry, I've got to take something." In the past, I'd think I was hurt and it was just my mind playing tricks on me. It wasn't the pain in my knees or my joints. It was the pain in my head telling me I needed to take the pills. That craving isn't there anymore.

Now when I'm sore, I just take a lot of Motrin and get in the hot tub. When I wake on a Monday morning after a game, I'll get in the hot tub, get in a good workout, and go home and kick it in on the couch.

I'm sure the competition this season is going to be as fierce as last season. It seems like everyone is gunning for us. I suppose San Francisco and my good friend Mooch will be right there again trying to knock us off. The New York Giants are on the rise and Carolina ought to be better, too. You can never count out Dallas, especially now that they've got a new coach. And, right in our own division, it won't be easy.

Tampa Bay is a tough, hard-nosed team with a great coach in Tony Dungy. They're just like we used to be with Dallas. We'd be close, but we couldn't get over the hump. They've got a great defense and Trent Dilfer keeps getting better every season. I think it's just a matter of them finally doing it and beating us. That could happen. I just hope it isn't any time soon.

The Vikings will be a handful, too. They always are. The defense will always be good as long as John Randle is there and Brad Johnson and those receivers make that offense scary. If Robert Smith can stay healthy, you've got to figure they'll be in the hunt, too.

Then there's Detroit.

Any time you've got Barry Sanders in your backfield, you can't be counted out.

Over in the AFC, Denver will be good again, especially if John Elway comes back. Kansas City is getting to the point where either they'll get in the Super Bowl or fall out of contention and not be heard from.

The thing is I think we'll be right there at the end.

We've got everyone back on offense and Fritz Shurmur, our defensive coordinator, always seems to find a way to put it together on his side of the ball.

Each season is special for me, probably because with each year that passes it becomes more and more clear to me that it won't last forever.

If I can play my six years out, that might be it for me. I'd be thirty-four by then. I don't know how Dan Marino and John Elway do it each year, but I know why they do it. They want the Super Bowl ring. Well, I've won one and I'm sure we'll win one or two more. To me, that would be enough. I don't have to throw for 400 touchdowns. I don't have to have all the records. I won't play for that. I want to leave the game as healthy as possible. I don't want to just play for the money or for the hell of it and jeopardize my body.

I want to be able to come out and throw the ball with my kids and not have surgery everytime I do it. That's important to me. I want to be able to have fun with Deanna like a normal person when all of this is finally over. I would miss football, but I think I could walk away from the game and enjoy that, too.

I also don't think I'd want to play for another team. If I played for a couple more years and for some reason I started to struggle and they wanted to trade me, I'd probably just go ahead and give it up. Green Bay's been too good to me to think about playing anywhere else.

# APPENDIX 1

## BRETT FAVRE

### PROFESSIONAL STATISTICS

| Year | Team | G/S | Att. | Comp. | Yds. | Pct. | TD | Int. | LG | Rating |
|------|------|-----|------|-------|------|------|----|------|-----|--------|
| 1991 | Atlanta | 2/0 | 5 | 0 | 0 | 0.0 | 0 | 2 | 0 | 0.0 |
| 1992 | Green Bay | 15/13 | 471 | 302 | 3,227 | 64.1 | 18 | 13 | 76t | 85.3 |
| 1993 | Green Bay | 16/16 | 522 | 318 | 3,303 | 60.9 | 19 | 24 | 66t | 72.2 |
| 1994 | Green Bay | 16/16 | 582 | 363 | 3,882 | 62.4 | 33 | 14 | 49 | 90.7 |
| 1995 | Green Bay | 16/16 | 570 | 359 | *4,413 | 63.0 | *38 | 13 | *99t | 99.5 |
| 1996 | Green Bay | 16/16 | 543 | 325 | 3,899 | 59.9 | *39 | 13 | 80t | 95.8 |
| **Totals** | | 81/77 | 2,693 | 1,667 | 18,724 | 61.9 | 147 | 79 | 99t | 88.6 |
| **Play-offs** | | 10/10 | 317 | 194 | 2,430 | 61.2 | 18 | 7 | 81t | 94.7 |

*Led NFL

All stats include Atlanta #s.

# APPENDIX 2

## BRETT FAVRE'S
### YEAR-BY-YEAR, GAME-BY-GAME STATISTICS

#### 1992 GAME-BY-GAME PASSING

| Date | Opponent | Att. | Comp. | Yds. | Pct. | TD | Int. | LG | Sack | W/L |
|------|----------|------|-------|------|------|----|------|-----|------|-----|
| Sept. 6 | Minnesota | | | | -did not play- | | | | | |
| Sept. 13 | at Tampa Bay | 14 | 8 | 73 | 57.1 | 0 | 1 | 20 | 4 | — |
| Sept. 20 | Cincinnati | 39 | 22 | 289 | 56.4 | 2 | 0 | 42 | 5 | — |
| Sept. 27 | Pittsburgh | 19 | 14 | 210 | 73.7 | 2 | 0 | 76t | 2 | W |
| Oct. 4 | at Atlanta | 43 | 33 | 276 | 76.7 | 1 | 1 | 24 | 2 | L |
| Oct. 18 | at Cleveland | 33 | 20 | 223 | 60.6 | 0 | 0 | 21 | 2 | L |
| Oct. 25 | Chicago | 37 | 20 | 214 | 54.1 | 1 | 1 | 45 | 4 | L |
| Nov. 1 | at Detroit | 37 | 22 | 212 | 59.5 | 2 | 0 | 30t | 2 | W |
| Nov. 8 | at N.Y. Giants | 44 | 27 | 279 | 61.4 | 0 | 3 | 43 | 1 | L |
| Nov. 15 | Philadelphia | 33 | 23 | 275 | 69.7 | 2 | 2 | 34 | 2 | W |
| Nov. 22 | at Chicago | 24 | 16 | 209 | 66.7 | 1 | 0 | 49t | 1 | W |
| Nov. 29 | Tampa Bay | 41 | 26 | 223 | 63.4 | 1 | 0 | 27 | 1 | W |
| Dec. 6 | Detroit | 19 | 15 | 214 | 78.9 | 3 | 0 | 65t | 1 | W |
| Dec. 13 | at Houston | 30 | 19 | 155 | 63.3 | 1 | 1 | 21 | 3 | W |
| Dec. 20 | L.A. Rams | 23 | 14 | 188 | 60.9 | 2 | 1 | 43 | 3 | W |
| Dec. 27 | at Minnesota | 35 | 23 | 187 | 65.7 | 0 | 3 | 29 | 1 | L |

## 1993 GAME-BY-GAME PASSING

| Date | Opponent | Att. | Comp. | Yds. | Pct. | TD | Int. | LG | Sack | W/L |
|---|---|---|---|---|---|---|---|---|---|---|
| Sept. 5 | L.A. Rams | 29 | 19 | 264 | 65.5 | 2 | 1 | 50t | 3 | W |
| Sept. 12 | Philadelphia | 24 | 12 | 111 | 50.0 | 2 | 2 | 28 | 1 | L |
| Sept. 26 | at Minnesota | 31 | 20 | 150 | 64.5 | 0 | 2 | 16 | 0 | L |
| Oct. 3 | at Dallas | 37 | 21 | 174 | 56.8 | 0 | 0 | 20 | 1 | L |
| Oct. 10 | Denver | 32 | 20 | 235 | 62.5 | 1 | 3 | 66t | 0 | W |
| Oct. 24 | at Tampa Bay | 35 | 20 | 268 | 57.1 | 4 | 1 | 51 | 2 | W |
| Oct. 31 | Chicago | 24 | 15 | 136 | 62.5 | 1 | 1 | 21t | 2 | W |
| Nov. 8 | at Kansas City | 34 | 20 | 213 | 58.8 | 1 | 3 | 35t | 4 | L |
| Nov. 14 | at New Orleans | 32 | 18 | 150 | 56.3 | 1 | 0 | 54 | 6 | W |
| Nov. 21 | Detroit | 33 | 24 | 259 | 72.7 | 0 | 2 | 36 | 1 | W |
| Nov. 28 | Tampa Bay | 36 | 23 | 159 | 63.9 | 1 | 0 | 28 | 2 | W |
| Dec. 5 | at Chicago | 54 | 36 | 402 | 66.7 | 2 | 3 | 34 | 1 | L |
| Dec. 12 | at San Diego | 23 | 13 | 146 | 56.5 | 0 | 1 | 25 | 2 | W |
| Dec. 19 | Minnesota | 33 | 20 | 256 | 60.6 | 2 | 1 | 42 | 1 | L |
| Dec. 26 | L.A. Raiders | 28 | 14 | 190 | 50.0 | 1 | 0 | 26 | 2 | W |
| Jan. 2 | at Detroit | 37 | 23 | 190 | 62.2 | 1 | 4 | 39t | 2 | L |
| *Jan. 8 | at Detroit | 26 | 15 | 204 | 57.7 | 3 | 1 | 40t | 0 | W |
| *Jan. 16 | at Dallas | 45 | 28 | 331 | 62.2 | 2 | 2 | 48 | 2 | L |

## 1994 GAME-BY-GAME PASSING

| Date | Opponent | Att. | Comp. | Yds. | Pct. | TD | Int. | LG | Sack | W/L |
|---|---|---|---|---|---|---|---|---|---|---|
| Sept. 4 | Minnesota | 36 | 22 | 185 | 61.1 | 1 | 0 | 24 | 3 | W |
| Sept. 11 | Miami | 51 | 31 | 362 | 60.8 | 2 | 1 | 35 | 4 | L |
| Sept. 18 | at Philadelphia | 45 | 24 | 280 | 53.3 | 1 | 2 | 48 | 6 | L |
| Sept. 25 | Tampa Bay | 39 | 30 | 306 | 76.9 | 3 | 0 | 36 | 0 | W |
| Oct. 2 | at New England | 47 | 25 | 294 | 53.2 | 1 | 2 | 38 | 4 | L |
| Oct. 9 | L.A. Rams | 41 | 25 | 222 | 61.0 | 1 | 1 | 26 | 2 | W |
| Oct. 20 | at Minnesota | 10 | 6 | 32 | 60.0 | 0 | 1 | 7 | 1 | L |
| Oct. 31 | at Chicago | 15 | 6 | 82 | 40.0 | 1 | 0 | 22 | 0 | W |
| Nov. 6 | Detroit | 36 | 24 | 237 | 66.7 | 3 | 1 | 28t | 1 | W |
| Nov. 13 | N.Y. Jets | 28 | 20 | 183 | 71.4 | 2 | 0 | 17t | 1 | W |
| Nov. 20 | at Buffalo | 40 | 22 | 214 | 55.0 | 3 | 1 | 29t | 1 | L |
| Nov. 24 | at Dallas | 40 | 27 | 257 | 67.5 | 4 | 0 | 36t | 2 | L |
| Dec. 4 | at Detroit | 43 | 29 | 366 | 67.4 | 3 | 2 | 47t | 1 | L |
| Dec. 11 | Chicago | 31 | 19 | 250 | 61.3 | 3 | 1 | 35 | 2 | W |
| Dec. 18 | Atlanta | 44 | 29 | 321 | 65.9 | 2 | 1 | 40 | 2 | W |
| Dec. 24 | at Tampa Bay | 36 | 24 | 291 | 66.7 | 3 | 1 | 49 | 1 | W |
| *Dec. 31 | Detroit | 38 | 23 | 262 | 60.5 | 0 | 0 | 33 | 1 | W |
| *Jan. 8 | at Dallas | 35 | 18 | 211 | 51.4 | 0 | 1 | 59 | 1 | L |

## 1995 GAME-BY-GAME PASSING

| Date | Opponent | Att. | Comp. | Yds. | Pct. | TD | Int. | LG | Sack | W/L |
|---|---|---|---|---|---|---|---|---|---|---|
| Sept. 3 | St. Louis | 51 | 29 | 299 | 56.9 | 2 | 3 | 29 | 4 | L |
| Sept. 11 | at Chicago | 37 | 21 | 312 | 56.8 | 3 | 1 | 99t | 2 | W |
| Sept. 17 | N.Y. Giants | 25 | 14 | 141 | 56.0 | 2 | 0 | 19t | 4 | W |
| Sept. 24 | at Jacksonville | 30 | 20 | 202 | 66.7 | 2 | 1 | 29t | 2 | W |
| Oct. 8 | at Dallas | 41 | 21 | 295 | 51.2 | 1 | 1 | 30 | 0 | L |
| Oct. 15 | Detroit | 34 | 23 | 342 | 67.7 | 2 | 0 | 35 | 2 | W |

| Date | Opponent | Att. | Comp. | Yds. | Pct. | TD | Int. | LG | Sack | W/L |
|------|----------|------|-------|------|------|-----|------|-----|------|-----|
| Oct. 22 | Minnesota | 43 | 22 | 295 | 51.2 | 4 | 0 | 32 | 3 | W |
| Oct. 29 | at Detroit | 43 | 26 | 304 | 60.5 | 1 | 3 | 77t | 1 | L |
| Nov. 5 | at Minnesota | 30 | 17 | 177 | 56.7 | 0 | 2 | 21 | 4 | L |
| Nov. 12 | Chicago | 33 | 25 | 336 | 75.8 | 5 | 0 | 44t | 3 | W |
| Nov. 19 | at Cleveland | 28 | 23 | 210 | 82.1 | 3 | 0 | 27 | 2 | W |
| Nov. 26 | Tampa Bay | 24 | 16 | 267 | 66.7 | 3 | 0 | 54t | 1 | W |
| Dec. 3 | Cincinnati | 43 | 31 | 339 | 72.1 | 3 | 1 | 29 | 1 | W |
| Dec. 10 | at Tampa Bay | 46 | 27 | 285 | 58.7 | 1 | 1 | 35 | 0 | L |
| Dec. 16 | at New Orleans | 30 | 21 | 308 | 70.0 | 4 | 0 | 40t | 2 | W |
| Dec. 24 | Pittsburgh | 32 | 23 | 301 | 71.9 | 2 | 0 | 28 | 2 | W |
| *Dec. 31 | Atlanta | 35 | 24 | 199 | 68.6 | 3 | 0 | 20 | 1 | W |
| *Jan. 6 | at San Francisco | 28 | 21 | 299 | 75.0 | 2 | 0 | 53 | 1 | W |
| *Jan. 14 | at Dallas | 39 | 21 | 307 | 53.9 | 3 | 2 | 73t | 4 | L |

## 1996 GAME-BY-GAME PASSING

| Date | Opponent | Att. | Comp. | Yds. | Pct. | TD | Int. | LG | Sack | W/L |
|------|----------|------|-------|------|------|-----|------|-----|------|-----|
| Sept. 1 | at Tampa Bay | 27 | 20 | 247 | 74.1 | 4 | 0 | 51t | 1 | W |
| Sept. 9 | Philadelphia | 31 | 17 | 261 | 54.8 | 3 | 0 | 38 | 1 | W |
| Sept. 15 | San Diego | 33 | 22 | 231 | 66.7 | 3 | 1 | 32 | 2 | W |
| Sept. 22 | at Minnesota | 27 | 14 | 198 | 51.9 | 2 | 1 | 80t | 7 | L |
| Sept. 29 | at Seattle | 34 | 20 | 209 | 58.8 | 4 | 0 | 28 | 2 | W |
| Oct. 6 | at Chicago | 27 | 18 | 246 | 66.7 | 4 | 1 | 50t | 1 | W |
| Oct. 14 | San Francisco | 61 | 28 | 395 | 45.9 | 1 | 2 | 59t | 2 | W |
| Oct. 27 | Tampa Bay | 31 | 19 | 178 | 61.3 | 0 | 1 | 26 | 2 | W |
| Nov. 3 | Detroit | 35 | 24 | 281 | 68.6 | 4 | 1 | 65t | 4 | W |
| Nov. 10 | at Kansas City | 49 | 27 | 314 | 55.1 | 2 | 1 | 49 | 4 | L |
| Nov. 18 | at Dallas | 37 | 21 | 194 | 56.8 | 1 | 0 | 25 | 4 | L |
| Nov. 24 | at St. Louis | 38 | 25 | 192 | 65.8 | 2 | 2 | 14 | 1 | W |
| Dec. 1 | Chicago | 27 | 19 | 231 | 70.4 | 1 | 0 | 41 | 2 | W |
| Dec. 8 | Denver | 38 | 20 | 280 | 52.6 | 4 | 2 | 51t | 1 | W |
| Dec. 15 | at Detroit | 25 | 16 | 240 | 64.0 | 1 | 1 | 40 | 3 | W |
| Dec. 22 | Minnesota | 23 | 15 | 202 | 65.2 | 3 | 0 | 37 | 2 | W |
| *Jan. 4 | San Francisco | 15 | 11 | 79 | 73.3 | 1 | 0 | 18 | 1 | W |
| *Jan. 12 | Carolina | 29 | 19 | 292 | 65.5 | 2 | 1 | 66 | 1 | W |
| †Jan. 26 | New England | 27 | 14 | 246 | 51.9 | 2 | 0 | 81t | 5 | W |

*Play-off game        †Super Bowl XXXI

# APPENDIX 3

## REGULAR SEASON

## WHO HAS CAUGHT BRETT FAVRE'S PASSES
## (REGULAR SEASON)

| Comp. | Yds. | TD | Brett Favre to |
|---|---|---|---|
| 300 | 3,696 | 41 | Sterling Sharpe |
| 236 | 1,881 | 10 | Edgar Bennett |
| 205 | 2,690 | 22 | Robert Brooks |
| 95 | 1,210 | 6 | Mark Chmura |
| 95 | 1,182 | 6 | Jackie Harris |
| 79 | 665 | 9 | Dorsey Levens |
| 64 | 1,039 | 10 | Antonio Freeman |
| 57 | 730 | 8 | Anthony Morgan |
| 57 | 618 | 2 | Ed West |
| 53 | 647 | 11 | Keith Jackson |
| 45 | 357 | 1 | Harry Sydney |
| 39 | 699 | 4 | Don Beebe |
| 38 | 461 | 3 | Mark Ingram |
| 35 | 299 | 1 | Reggie Cobb |
| 33 | 224 | 0 | Vince Workman |
| 32 | 331 | 3 | Mark Clayton |
| 30 | 261 | 1 | Darrell Thompson |
| 30 | 224 | 1 | William Henderson |
| 24 | 227 | 2 | Terry Mickens |
| 22 | 281 | 0 | Ron Lewis |
| 13 | 135 | 1 | Andre Rison |
| 13 | 109 | 0 | Sanjay Beach |
| 13 | 95 | 0 | Desmond Howard |
| 12 | 162 | 0 | LeShon Johnson |
| 7 | 117 | 2 | Charles Jordan |
| 7 | 79 | 0 | Reggie Johnson |
| 6 | 60 | 0 | Buford McGee |
| 6 | 46 | 2 | Derrick Mayes |
| 5 | 31 | 0 | John Stephens |
| 5 | 31 | 0 | Jeff Wilner |
| 4 | 48 | 0 | Jeff Thomason |
| 2 | 63 | 1 | Kitrick Taylor |
| 2 | 18 | 0 | Marcus Wilson |
| 2 | 11 | 0 | Corey Harris |
| 1 | -7 | 0 | Brett Favre |
| **1,667** | **18,724** | **147** | |

**Owns 12 Packers Regular-Season Records Outright (these records do not include the 5 attempts and 2 interceptions Favre threw in Atlanta):**
Highest passer rating career (89.1)
Most passes attempted game (61 vs. 49ers 10-14-96)
Most passes completed season (363, 1994)

Most passes completed game (36 vs. Bears 12-5-93)

Highest completion percentage, career (62.02% [1,667 completions in 2,688 attempts])

Highest completion percentage, season (64.12%, 1992 [302 completions in 471 attempts])

Most games 300 or more yards passing, season (7, 1995)

Longest pass completion (99 yeards to Robert Brooks vs. Bears 9-11-95)

Most touchdown passes, season (39, 1996)

Lowest percentage, passes had intercepted, career (2.86 [77 in 2,688 attempts])

Most games, 4 or more touchdown passes, season (5, 1996)

Most games, 4 or more touchdown passes, career (10)

**Shares 2 Other Records:**

Most games, 200 or more yards passing, season (14, 1995; shares with Lynn Dickey, who had 14 in 1983)

Most touchdown passes, game (5 vs. Bears 11-12-95; shares with Cecil Isbell, Don Horn, and Lynn Dickey twice)

## MOST PROLIFIC QUARTERBACK-RECEIVER COMBINATIONS IN PACKERS REGULAR-SEASON HISTORY

| Tandem | No. | Yds. | TD |
|---|---|---|---|
| Starr to Dowler | 336 | 5,145 | 28 |
| Dickey to Lofton | 325 | 6,337 | 32 |
| **Favre to Sharpe** | **300** | **3,696** | **41** |
| Dickey to Coffman | 243 | 3,132 | 35 |
| **Favre to E. Bennett** | **236** | **1,881** | **10** |
| Starr to McGee | 229 | 4,037 | 25 |
| Dickey to Ellis | 208 | 1,943 | 9 |
| **Favre to Brooks** | **205** | **2,690** | **22** |

Brett Favre is 50-27 as a *starter* during the regular season: at Lambeau Field, 26-3 (.897); at Milwaukee, 7-2 (.778); away, 17-22 (.436):

## BREAKDOWN BY OPPONENT

| Team | Record | Pct. | Team | Record | Pct. |
|---|---|---|---|---|---|
| Broncos | 2-0 | 1.000 | Rams | 4-1 | .800 |
| Chargers | 2-0 | 1.000 | Lions | 7-3 | .700 |
| Saints | 2-0 | 1.000 | Eagles | 2-2 | .500 |
| Steelers | 2-0 | 1.000 | Browns | 1-1 | .500 |
| Bengals | 1-0 | 1.000 | Falcons | 1-1 | .500 |
| 49ers | 1-0 | 1.000 | Giants | 1-1 | .500 |
| Jaguars | 1-0 | 1.000 | Vikings | 3-6 | .333 |
| Jets | 1-0 | 1.000 | Bills | 0-1 | .000 |
| Oilers | 1-0 | 1.000 | Dolphins | 0-1 | .000 |
| Raiders | 1-0 | 1.000 | Patroits | 0-1 | .000 |
| Seahawks | 1-0 | 1.000 | Chiefs | 0-2 | .000 |

| Team | Record | Pct. | Team | Record | Pct. |
|------|--------|------|------|--------|------|
| Buccaneers | 8-1 | .889 | Cowboys | 0-4 | .000 |
| Bears | 8-2 | .800 | | | |
| | | | **Totals** | **50-27** | **.649** |

Favre's regular-season record (*does not include* two games with Atlanta, *does include* two games with Packers as nonstarter) when he:

| | | | | | |
|------|------|------|------|------|------|
| Throws 5 TD passes | 1-0 | 1.000 | | | |
| Throws 4 TD passes | 8-1 | .889 | Passes for 400+ yards | 0-1 | .000 |
| Throws 3 TD passes | 12-2 | .857 | Passes for 300–400 yards | 9-4 | .692 |
| Throws 2 TD passes | 13-7 | .650 | Passes for 200–300 yards | 29-13 | .690 |
| Throws 1 TD pass | 14-10 | .583 | Passes for 100–200 yards | 12-8 | .600 |
| Throws 0 TD passes | 3-8 | .273 | Passes for < 100 yards | 1-2 | .333 |
| Totals | 51-28 | .646 | Totals | 51-28 | .646 |

## POSTSEASON

| Year | Team | G/S | Att. | Comp. | Yds. | Pct. | TD | Int. | Rating |
|------|------|-----|------|-------|------|------|-----|------|--------|
| 1993 | Green Bay | 2/2 | 71 | 43 | 535 | 60.6 | 5 | 3 | 89.8 |
| 1994 | Green Bay | 2/2 | 73 | 41 | 473 | 56.2 | 0 | 1 | 70.2 |
| 1995 | Green Bay | 3/3 | 102 | 66 | 805 | 64.7 | 8 | 2 | 106.9 |
| 1996 | Green Bay | 3/3 | 71 | 44 | 617 | 62.0 | 5 | 1 | 107.5 |
| **Totals** | | **10/10** | **317** | **194** | **2,430** | **61.2** | **18** | **7** | **94.7** |

## WHO HAS CAUGHT BRETT FAVRE'S PASSES (POSTSEASON)

| Comp. | Yds. | TD | Brett Favre to |
|-------|------|-----|----------------|
| 34 | 523 | 4 | Robert Brooks |
| 31 | 170 | 0 | Edgar Bennett |
| 17 | 267 | 2 | Keith Jackson |
| 17 | 203 | 2 | Dorsey Levens |
| 16 | 166 | 2 | Mark Chmura |
| 14 | 151 | 0 | Anthony Morgan |
| 13 | 217 | 2 | Antonio Freeman |
| 11 | 229 | 4 | Sterling Sharpe |
| 7 | 143 | 2 | Andre Rison |
| 7 | 81 | 0 | Ed West |
| 6 | 86 | 0 | Darrell Thompson |
| 5 | 22 | 0 | Mark Ingram |
| 4 | 22 | 0 | William Henderson |
| 3 | 55 | 0 | Terry Mickens |
| 2 | 31 | 0 | Don Beebe |

| Comp. | Yds. | TD | Brett Favre to |
|-------|------|-----|----------------|
| 2 | 30 | 0 | Reggie Cobb |
| 2 | 9 | 0 | Darryl Ingram |
| 1 | 9 | 0 | Mark Clayton |
| 1 | 9 | 0 | Reggie Johnson |
| 1 | 7 | 0 | Ron Lewis |
| 194 | 2,430 | 18 | |

**Holds 12 Postseason Packers Records:**

Most passes attempted career (317) • Most passes attempted game (45 vs. Cowboys 1-16-94) • Most passes completed career (194) • Most passes completed game (28 vs. Cowboys 1-16-94) • Highest completion percentage, career (61.2 [194-317]) • Highest completion percentage, game (min. 20 att.) (75.0 vs. 49ers 1-6-96 [21-28]) • Most yards gained career (2,430) • Longest pass completion (81 yards to Antonio Freeman 1-26-97) • Most consecutive completions (11 vs. 49ers 1-6-96) • Most attempts, no interceptions, game (38 vs. Lions 12-31-94) • Most passes had intercepted, career (7) • Most consecutive passes, none intercepted (86, 1994–95)

**Shares 1 Other Record:**

Most consecutive games, touchdown passes (6; shares with Bart Starr 1965–67)

## MOST PROLIFIC QUARTERBACK-RECEIVER COMBINATIONS IN PACKERS POSTSEASON HISTORY

| Tandem | No. | Yds. | TD |
|--------|-----|------|-----|
| **Favre to Brooks** | 34 | 523 | 4 |
| **Favre to E. Bennett** | 31 | 170 | 0 |
| Starr to Dale | 24 | 443 | 3 |
| Starr to Dowler | 24 | 369 | 5 |
| **Favre to K. Jackson** | 17 | 267 | 2 |
| **Favre to Levens** | 17 | 203 | 2 |
| Starr to J. Taylor | 17 | 108 | 0 |
| **Favre to Chmura** | 16 | 166 | 2 |
| **Favre to A. Morgan** | 14 | 151 | 0 |
| **Favre to A. Freeman** | 13 | 217 | 2 |

# APPENDIX 4

## FAVRE VERSUS THE NFL AS A PACKER— REGULAR SEASON
### (Does not include his 5 attempts with Atlanta)

| Team | G | Att. | Comp. | Yds. | TD | Int. | Rating |
|---|---|---|---|---|---|---|---|
| Bears | 10 | 309 | 195 | 2,418 | 22 | 8 | 100.2 |
| Buccaneers | 10 | 329 | 213 | 2,297 | 20 | 5 | 99.1 |
| Lions | 10 | 342 | 226 | 2,645 | 20 | 14 | 91.8 |
| Cowboys | 4 | 155 | 90 | 920 | 6 | 1 | 85.4 |
| Eagles | 4 | 133 | 76 | 927 | 8 | 6 | 80.0 |
| Rams | 5 | 182 | 112 | 1,165 | 9 | 8 | 78.2 |
| Vikings | 9 | 268 | 159 | 1,682 | 12 | 10 | 77.1 |
| Steelers | 2 | 51 | 37 | 511 | 4 | 0 | 130.4 |
| Saints | 2 | 62 | 39 | 458 | 5 | 0 | 112.2 |
| Browns | 2 | 61 | 43 | 433 | 3 | 0 | 106.8 |
| Bengals | 2 | 82 | 53 | 628 | 5 | 1 | 103.1 |
| Falcons | 2 | 87 | 62 | 597 | 3 | 2 | 92.0 |
| Chargers | 2 | 56 | 35 | 377 | 3 | 2 | 85.2 |
| Broncos | 2 | 70 | 40 | 515 | 5 | 5 | 74.4 |
| Giants | 2 | 69 | 41 | 420 | 2 | 3 | 68.5 |
| Chiefs | 2 | 83 | 47 | 527 | 3 | 4 | 67.7 |
| Seahawks | 1 | 34 | 20 | 209 | 4 | 0 | 115.9 |
| Jets | 1 | 28 | 20 | 183 | 2 | 0 | 112.6 |
| Jaguars | 1 | 30 | 20 | 202 | 2 | 1 | 94.0 |
| Dolphins | 1 | 51 | 31 | 362 | 2 | 1 | 87.2 |
| Bills | 1 | 40 | 22 | 214 | 3 | 1 | 84.8 |
| Raiders | 1 | 28 | 14 | 190 | 1 | 0 | 83.9 |
| Oilers | 1 | 30 | 19 | 155 | 1 | 1 | 73.6 |
| Patriots | 1 | 47 | 25 | 294 | 1 | 2 | 61.8 |
| 49ers | 1 | 61 | 28 | 395 | 1 | 2 | 59.1 |
| **Totals** | **79** | **2,688** | **1,667** | **18,724** | **147** | **77** | **89.1** |

## FAVRE VERSUS THE NFL AS A PACKER—POSTSEASON

| Team | G | Att. | Comp. | Yds. | TD | Int. | Rating |
|---|---|---|---|---|---|---|---|
| 49ers | 2 | 43 | 32 | 378 | 3 | 0 | 124.0 |
| Falcons | 1 | 35 | 24 | 199 | 3 | 0 | 111.5 |
| Patriots | 1 | 27 | 14 | 246 | 2 | 0 | 107.9 |
| Panthers | 1 | 29 | 19 | 292 | 2 | 1 | 107.3 |
| Lions | 2 | 64 | 38 | 466 | 3 | 1 | 91.0 |
| Cowboys | 3 | 119 | 67 | 849 | 5 | 5 | 75.2 |
| **Totals** | **10** | **317** | **194** | **2,430** | **18** | **7** | **94.7** |

# APPENDIX 5

## TOP-RATED PASSERS IN NFL HISTORY

|  | Years | Att. | Comp. | Yds. | TD | Int. | Rating |
|---|---|---|---|---|---|---|---|
| Steve Young | 12 | 3,192 | 2,059 | 25,479 | 174 | 85 | 96.2 |
| Joe Montana | 15 | 5,391 | 3,409 | 40,551 | 273 | 139 | 92.3 |
| **Brett Favre** | **6** | **2,693** | **1,667** | **18,724** | **147** | **79** | **88.6** |
| Dan Marino | 14 | 6,904 | 4,134 | 51,636 | 369 | 209 | 88.3 |
| Jim Kelly | 11 | 4,779 | 2,874 | 35,467 | 237 | 175 | 84.4 |
| Roger Staubach | 11 | 2,958 | 1,685 | 22,700 | 153 | 109 | 83.4 |
| Troy Aikman | 8 | 3,178 | 2,000 | 22,733 | 110 | 98 | 83.0 |
| Sonny Jurgensen | 18 | 4,262 | 2,433 | 32,224 | 255 | 189 | 82.6 |
| Len Dawson | 19 | 3,741 | 2,136 | 28,711 | 239 | 183 | 82.6 |
| Jeff Hostetler | 11 | 2,194 | 1,278 | 15,531 | 89 | 61 | 82.1 |

## CAREER PCT. INT. (Min. 1,975 att.)

| | | | |
|---|---|---|---|
| 1 | Joe Montana | 139-5,391 | 2.578 |
| 2 | Bernie Kosar | 87-3,365 | 2.585 |
| 3 | Steve Young | 85-3,192 | 2.66 |
| 4 | Ken O'Brien | 98-3,602 | 2.72 |
| 5 | Neil Lomax | 90-3,153 | 2.85 |
| 6 | Jeff George | 78-2,712 | 2.88 |
| 7 | Jim Harbaugh | 78-2,680 | 2.91 |
| **8** | **Brett Favre** | **79-2,693** | **2.93** |
| 9 | Dan Marino | 209-6,904 | 3.03 |
| 10 | R. Cunningham | 105-3,362 | 3.12 |

## CAREER PCT. COMP. (Min. 1,975 att.)

| | | | |
|---|---|---|---|
| 1 | Steve Young | 2,059-3,192 | 64.51 |
| 2 | Joe Montana | 3,409-5,391 | 63.24 |
| 3 | Troy Aikman | 2,000-3,178 | 62.93 |
| **4** | **Brett Favre** | **1,667-2,693** | **61.90** |
| 5 | Jim Kelly | 2,874-4,779 | 60.14 |

|  | Att. | Comp. | Yds. | TD |
|---|---|---|---|---|
| Favre | 2,693 | 1,667 | 18,724 | 147 |
|  | 65th | 54th | 66th | 55th |